HALLS, HOUSES & HOVELS

THE PACKES

IN

GREAT GLEN

LEICESTERSHIRE

Heather MacDermid

Dedicated to the memory of my parents
1898-1982
Born into poverty, experiencing two world wars and years of unemployment, they lived to appreciate the security of the Welfare State.

He loved big, rambling houses.
She secretly longed for a 'neat little bungalow'.

Cover: S James

First published 2005

ISBN 1-904-207367

Further copies available from
hmacd@airpost.net
Gamekeepers Lodge, London Road, Great Glen
Tel. 0116 259 2932

Printed in China through Colorcraft Ltd., Hong Kong

ACKNOWLEDGEMENTS

I should like to thank:
Great Glen Village Design Statement group, whose work taught me to identify, describe and defend those features of the village which need and deserve protection.
The staff of Leics Record Office for their unfailing courtesy and help.
Martin Ayres, a fellow student there, who introduced me to useful documents in the early stages of my work.
Members of the U3A history group for their response to the proposed study.
All those residents of Great Glen who have encouraged me, shared memories, lent pictures and given me tours of their houses.

Special thanks are due to all those contributors mentioned in the text: Sheila Allen, Walter Allen, Edna Aston, Sheila Ball, Mrs Chapman, Bill and Valerie Chapman, Thomas Clarke, Lilian Haines (Lilian Gash), Fraser Gilbert, Joe Goddard, Stan Gibson, Gladys Moody, Ray Pickard, Fred Stocks, Melvyn Copley, Richard Hull, Eric Orbell and above all to Margaret Packe for her enthusiastic collaboration throughout the whole project and to her cousin, the late William Packe, who provided valuable information and material I could not have found elsewhere.

Judy Phythian-Adams has played a major part in collecting material and in editing. Her enthusiasm has supported me at all stages and her skill in eliciting interesting information from knowledgeable villagers and 'oldest inhabitants' has been of inestimable value. Her skill in proof reading has saved me from many errors.

My debt to Stan James of Oadby for his support as my computer guru is beyond measure. Without his help the project could not have come to fruition.

I hope the book will be read with pleasure or dipped into for information and that readers will go on to explore further for themselves, filling in the many blanks I have left.

heather macdermid

Photographs taken by Stan James and the author
Other photographs courtesy of The Leicester Mercury, The Record Office, Fraser Gilbert, Walter Allen, Stan Gibson, Sheila Ball, Lilian Haines (Mrs Gash), Joe Goddard, Margaret Packe, William Packe, Simon Packe-Drury-Lowe, Lesley Selway, Richard Hull, Nigel Hurst, Melvyn Copley, Jane Myatt and Edna Aston.

CONTENTS

CHAPTER 3 PACKES IN THE VILLAGE

CHAPTER 4 THE CHURCH

CHAPTER 5 THE SCHOOL

CHAPTER 6 THE SALE OF PACKE HOUSES

ABBREVIATIONS and TECHNICAL TERMS

Ag Lab: agricultural labourers, farm workers
FWK: Framework Knitting, Framework Knitters
Great Glen, Glenn, Glen Magna: alternative forms
Leics: Leicestershire
Leic: Leicester
LRO: The Record Office for Leics, Leic and Rutland
Messuage/tenement: dwelling house (not flats, as in modern usage)
GER: Gross Estimated Rental (1878)
GAV: Gross Annual rental (1910)
RV: Rateable Value in pounds, shillings and pence
Pounds, shillings, pence: 12 pence = 1 shilling; 20 shillings = 1 pound
Acres, Perches, Rods: measurements of land

Hovel : The word is used in the Packe documents in its technical sense of **an open shed, an outhouse used as a shelter for cattle, a receptacle for grain or for tools.**[1] It does *not* indicate a poor dwelling place, in our more usual sense of the word. Very few hovels remain in Glen, relics of its agricultural past. The hovels referred to in this study have long since disappeared.

The few that do still exist appear as substantial garages

or delightful garden sheds.

[1] OED Oxford English Dictionary

INTRODUCTION

This study began, as so many local history books do, with a desire to know about my own house, when it was built, who lived in it and what life was like for those people. It so happens that my house was a part of an estate bought by the Packe family and this led me on to look at their history, their halls and the part they played in the village of Great Glen. The search to find the date for my house led me through many documents relating to the Packe family, as lords of the manor and owners of much of the property in the village. These documents are stored in the Leicestershire Record Office,[1] a treasure trove of documents to be explored. Visits to it become addictive! I started by looking up 'Great Glen' in the *Parishes* catalogue, found the references for *Packe,* and was hooked!

My first and favourite breakthrough was in a sale document of houses sold in 1919 by Col E C Packe with a map of numbered plots for sale. My house was not included but the map was so fascinating it inspired me to walk round the village to look at the properties that were for sale at that time, to take photographs and to find out as much as possible about each of them. This involved talking to 'oldest inhabitants' and other residents of the village, and proceeding to research all available documents. I vowed to be single minded in my study and ruthlessly determined to exclude anything not strictly related to the Packes and their properties but, even so, the task has taken me far further afield than I intended.

I was very privileged to have been put in touch with members of the Packe family. Margaret Packe, the daughter of the last Lord of the Manor, born in Stretton Hall and brought up in Glen Hall, has been particularly generous in her collaboration and contributions, including the loan of original diaries and pictures and introductions to other members of her family. The result has become an 'Upstairs Downstairs' view of Great Glen in the time of the Packes, looking at their lands and buildings and their roles as Lords of the Manor in relation to the homes of their tenants and other residents of the village.

It is amazing that despite the huge expansion of Great Glen, so much is still visible to remind us of the Packes and their time here. We are lucky to be able to see remaining so many of the fields and buildings depicted in our records and to be able to hear from the people who have lived in these houses in the past or who live in them today. We can reflect upon the decline in wealth and power of the squirearchy and the rising prosperity of people who might once have been their tenants.

---

[1] The Record Office for Leicestershire, Leicester and Rutland, Long Street, Wigston Magna, Leics . Footnotes refer to documents kept here.

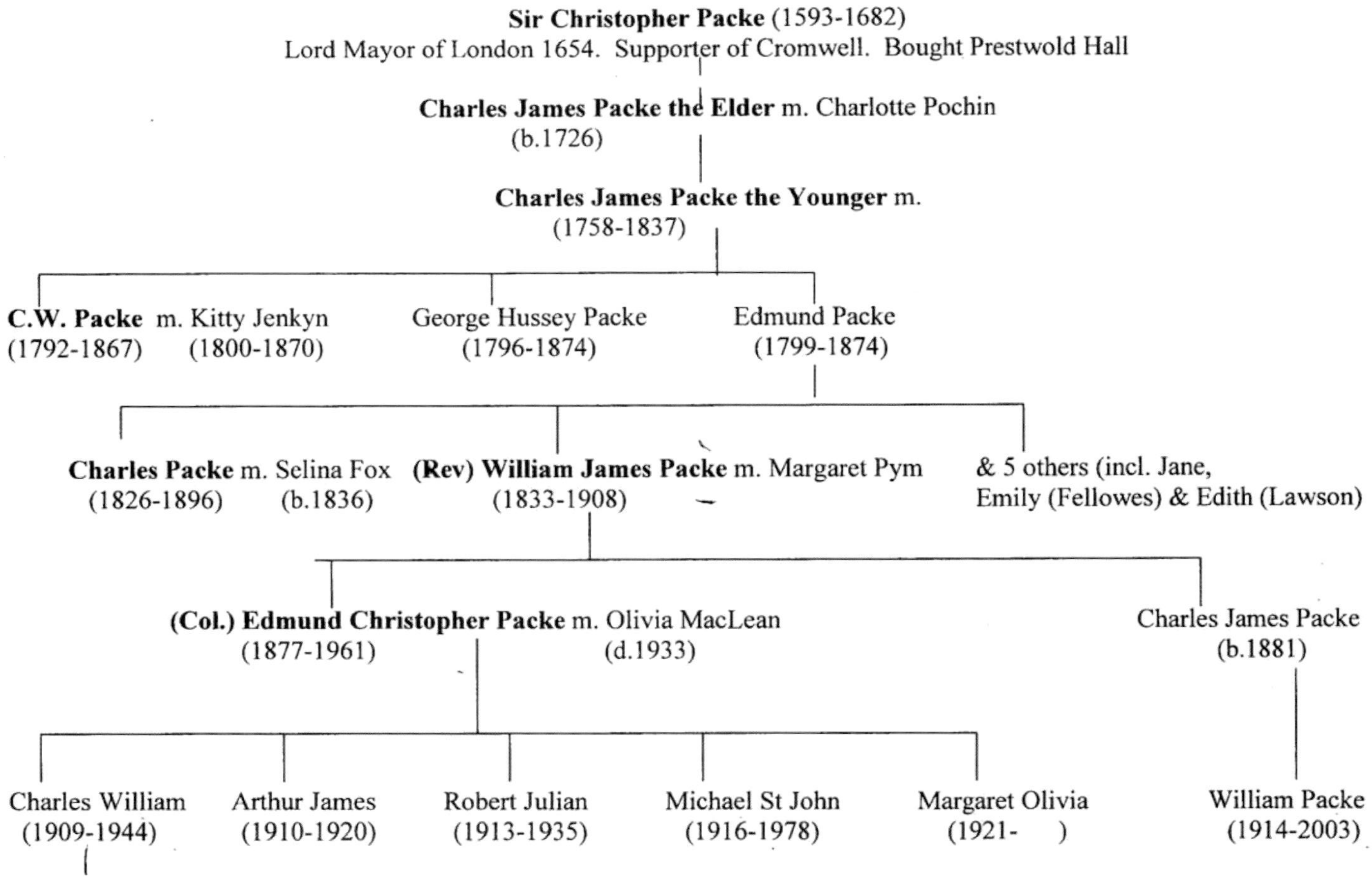
Sir Christopher Packe (1593-1682)
Lord Mayor of London 1654. Supporter of Cromwell. Bought Prestwold Hall
Charles James Packe the Elder m. Charlotte Pochin
(b.1726)
Charles James Packe the Younger m.
(1758-1837)
C.W. Packe m. Kitty Jenkyn
(1792-1867) (1800-1870)
George Hussey Packe
(1796-1874)
Edmund Packe
(1799-1874)
Charles Packe m. Selina Fox
(1826-1896) (b.1836)
(Rev) William James Packe m. Margaret Pym
(1833-1908)
& 5 others (incl. Jane,
Emily (Fellowes) & Edith (Lawson)
(Col.) Edmund Christopher Packe m. Olivia MacLean
(1877-1961) (d.1933)
Charles James Packe
(b.1881)
Charles William
(1909-1944)
Arthur James
(1910-1920)
Robert Julian
(1913-1935)
Michael St John
(1916-1978)
Margaret Olivia
(1921-)
William Packe
(1914-2003)

But before we hasten to the display of dignity and the splendour of particular possession let us remark that the great have a mixture of bitters and moments of tribulation, in common with the humblest of their nature.

Throsby, *Excursions 1790*

CHAPTER 1 CHARLES WILLIAM PACKE (CWP) 1792-1867

The Packe connection with Great Glen begins with CW Packe, MP for South Leicestershire, who bought Glen Hall in 1837 and, some ten years later, Stretton Hall. With the acquisition of Stretton Hall and its surrounding land he became Lord of the Manor.

Charles William Packe lived through the reigns of George III, George IV, William IV and Queen Victoria. He was born at Carlby in Lincolnshire on 3rd Sept 1792, the eldest of five sons of Charles James Packe the Younger. His ancestors had acquired Prestwold Hall and its estate when Christopher Packe bought it from Sir Henry Skipworth[1] in 1649. He lived through, and played an important part in, the troubled times of the Civil War. Son of a woollen draper in Kettering, he became rich when he moved to the big city, was elected alderman of Cripplegate and, like Dick Whittington, became Lord Mayor of London. He was in Parliament during the Civil War and was a firm supporter of Oliver Cromwell. In 1657 he presented a celebrated petition to him in Parliament desiring him to become King.[2] Cromwell did not in fact agree to claim the throne, but took the title of Protector. Sir Christopher was knighted by Cromwell in 1658.

When Charles II returned to the throne, in 1660, all was not lost for Sir Christopher, because the king generously pardoned those who 'engaged by God's assistance to remain His Majesty's loyal and obedient servants'. As a former republican, he was nevertheless excluded from certain high offices and found it expedient to retire to his estate at Prestwold, near Loughborough, with its manor house in nearby Cotes. He died in 1682 and was buried in Prestwold church with a monument which gives his age (in Latin) as 84. Generations of Packes followed, taking on various important local roles. Charles James Packe the Elder became High Sheriff for Leicestershire in 1765 in the reign of George III and was one of the earliest and chief benefactors and governors of the Leicester Infirmary, founded by Dr Watts and opened in 1771. Charles James Packe the Younger, CWP's father, was born and died at Prestwold.

CWP was born into a long tradition of power, wealth and public service. He was educated at Eton, Oriel College, Oxford and Lincolns Inn and married Kitty Jenkyn on Nov 13 1821. She was a rich heiress but CWP does not seem to have

---

1. Sir Henry Skipworth was a Royalist who had supported Charles I against Cromwell. When Charles was executed in 1649 Skipworth was then out of favour.
2. The Humble Address and Remonstrance (later called the Humble Petition and Advice) calling for the Return of the Monarchy and the House of Lords, was presented to Parlt by Sir Christopher Packe, a man of much standing and gravitas, well over 60, former Lord Mayor of London and still an alderman and member of many influential committees. Cromwell was invited to accept the title and office of King. The house voted 123 to 62 in favour of offering the invitation. Antonia Fraser (1973) *Cromwell Our Chief of Men*

appreciated the benefit of their combined wealth. He complains that he married: *with the full consent and approbation of his father from whom he received £1000 a year but this allowance not being paid in advance and having no money from his wife till her rents were paid the following summer, he began his married life with literally not a sixpence.*[1]

In 1822 the newly married couple rented Lowesby Hall on a three year lease, paying £300 yearly plus £76 10s a year for the use and enjoyment of the land *with coach houses, Stables, Outbuildings, Yards, Gardens, Pleasure Ground and Shrubberies.* His rental agreement includes furniture, glass, china, household goods and effects and a pledge to keep the Mansion and the grounds in good repair and neat order.[2]

In 1828 they left England and made their Grand Tour of Europe[3] for the next two years. Their route took them from Brussels, through Wiesbaden, Frankfurt, Heidelburg, Zurich, Augsburg, Munich, Dresden, Berlin, St Petersburg and Moscow, Pisa, Rome, Naples and Paris.[4] Presumably still counting every penny, he kept a Private Expenses notebook to record all his purchases in each of these places. This gives us the cost of his haircuts, theatre visits, flute lessons, French lessons, items of clothing and gifts for his wife but nothing about his reactions to the glories of the cities. Unfortunately it does not tell us whether he frequented first class hotels or travelled first class in the railways or systematically preferred driving to walking or if he paid in advance for all these expences. But he does give us a reasonable idea of his tastes and habits.

He records the price of his entertainments. In July 1828 he goes to the theatre *for rope dancing and pantomime* in Coblenz (1s 3½d) and in August to the *opera fest* (2s 1½d) and the *Camera Obscura* in Heidleberg (4½d). In Munich, where he makes a long stay, he has a month's subscription to the Musee (5s 0d) and buys a catalogue for pictures at the Royal Gallery (3s 2d). In 1829 he goes to a Military

---

1 CWP Family Narrative DE 5047/200

2 DE 5047/14 DE 5047 rental agreement: *CWP doth hereby agree not to fell lop tap or plash any of the trees...or alter any of the fences or cut or plash any of the hedges But to cause all the fruit trees and ornamental shrubs to be properly pruned and dressed and to preserve the same from spoil or damage And not to make any alterations And to keep 3 labourers constantly at work in the gardens... in addition to a skilful gardener. Signed Sir Fredk Gustavus Fowke and CWP. Map drawn by Thos Miles, surveyor.*

3 The Grand Tour, 18th century custom where wealthy young men travelled across Europe as part of their cultural education.

4 For his grand tour he was possibly just too early to have the benefit of the guidebooks of Baedeker, whose printing and bookselling firm, begun at Koblenz in 1827 published guidebooks treasured by generations of travellers for their wealth of reliable and useful information. Baedeker's *Guide to the Rhine* from *Mainz to Cologne* was published in 1828. We have no evidence that CWP used it.

Concert in Berlin *in aid of sufferers in the north of Russia by floods* (3s 2½ d) and in June he goes to the Opera (12s 6d) at St Petersberg.

He buys generous presents for his wife: *a yellow China crape shawl (£3 11s 8d)* in 1829, an etching *(5s 4d),* an iron basket and a ring and a box to pack them in, from Berlin and *5 Coloured Views (£1 8s 9d)* from St Petersberg and from Moscow a *Crimson and gold bordered handkerchief .* As a present for Christmas 1829, he buys her *a Diamond clasp to Pearl necklace (£31 16s)* and in January *a mosaic paper-weight in the shape of a lizard (£1 7s 3½d).* In Rome in April she gets *a malachite and gold brooch (£1 2s 9d)* and a cross and chain bracelet and earrings in Naples *(£11 11s)*

For himself he buys: *a single blade pocket knife (3s 4d),* and collectors' items of coins and *a leather hat case and padlock (8s 6½d)* in Brussels, *new short boots* at Frankfurt *(19s 4d)* and a *pair of gloves* at the fair at Zurich *(1s 10d)* and *doeskin gloves* at Munich *(2s 5d).* He has his boots mended in Coblenz for five pence. He spends a great deal on clothes: *White silk stockings, dress military spurs, dress sword belt, evening hat, yards of silver lace and blue cloth cloak lined with scarlet and silver facing and blue military trowsers* [sic] *to match (£6 12s 0d)* in Dec 1828 and in April 1829 he pays *Mr Hilbert for great coat wadded and trimmed with sable fur Plus black coat and cashmere waistcoat (£8 17s 4½d).* We get the impression of quite a dandy!

He studies music, playing the flute and the piano, and pays for *Flute concertos in one volume* (9s 10½d) and *Mr Bohm for 34 lessons on flute (£4 2s 2d)* in Munich. He pays *M Richelle £5 18s 3d* for French lessons three times a week for four months in Munich and pays *Mons Fabri £2 9s 0d for 21 lessons in French* when he is in Pisa, for two months. Even more intriguingly, in December he pays for a writing master for lessons to teach the maid to write (£10 7s 0d), *Two copies to teach the maid at Pisa to write (!s 10½d)* with an additional *Copy Book 10½d* for a notebook for her to write in. This seems a surprisingly generous amount! And when he leaves, he tips the housemaids *11d for housekeeping* in Pisa.

He has his hair cut each month at these various cities (1s 4d in Zurich, 1s 3d with M Rossi and 1s 2½d to Kitty's hairdresser for haircutting in January 1829 in Munich, 1s 1d in Dresden and a very expensive cut in St Petersburg for 3s 7d and in Naples one for 2s 2d in May 1830). When he returned from foreign parts in October 1830 he was welcomed at Prestwold, where his parents were still living, and gave the Prestwold bell-ringers £1 5s *for ringing on my return.* In November he paid Mr Trufitt 1s 6d and in December he paid Mr Derbyshire 1s 0d for haircutting. (He does not comment on the relative merits of the cuts nor on the quality of Mr Derbyshire's bargain price.)

A page of CWP's Private Expences 1829

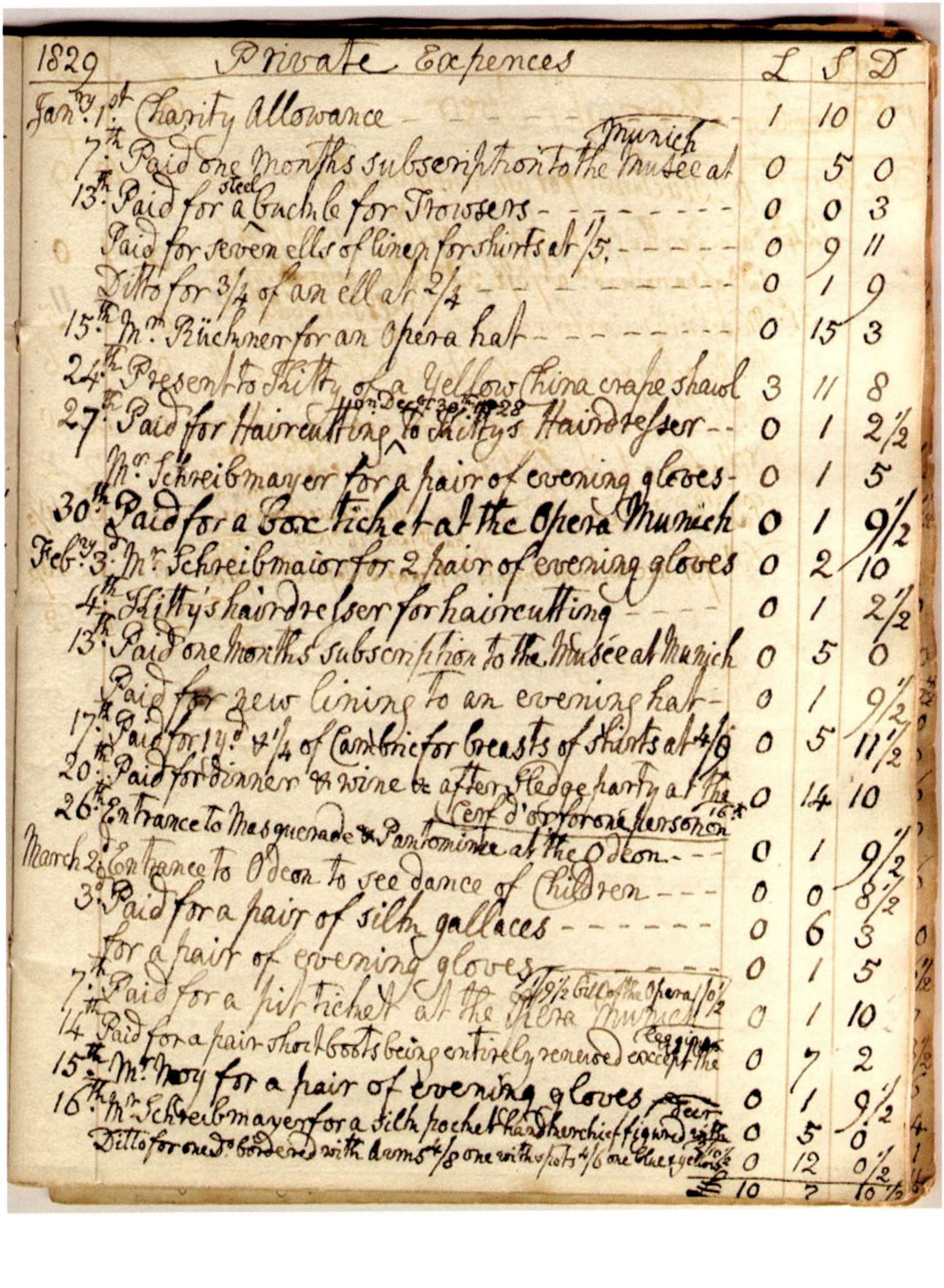

1829 Private Expences	L	S	D
Jany. 1st Charity Allowance	1	10	0
7th Paid one Months subscription to the Musée at Munich	0	5	0
13th Paid for a steel Buckle for Trowsers	0	0	3
Paid for seven ells of linen for shirts at 1/5	0	9	11
Ditto for 3/4 of an ell at 2/4	0	1	9
15th Mr. Büchner for an Opera hat	0	15	3
24th Present to Kitty of a Yellow China crape shawl	3	11	8
27th Paid for Haircutting to Kitty's Hairdresser from Decr 30th 1828	0	1	2½
Mr. Schreibmayer for a pair of evening gloves	0	1	5
30th Paid for a Box ticket at the Opera Munich	0	1	9½
Feby. 3 Mr. Schreibmaier for 2 pair of evening gloves	0	2	10
4th Kitty's hairdresser for haircutting	0	1	2½
13th Paid one Months subscription to the Musée at Munich	0	5	0
Paid for new lining to an evening hat	0	1	9½
17th Paid for 1 yd. & 1/4 of Cambric for breasts of shirts at 4/9	0	5	11½
20th Paid for dinner & wine &c after Sledge party at the Cerf d'or for one person 16/-	0	14	10
26th Entrance to Masquerade & Pantomime at the Odeon	0	1	9½
March 2d Entrance to Odeon to see dance of Children	0	0	8½
3d Paid for a pair of silk gallaces	0	6	3
for a pair of evening gloves	0	1	5
7th Paid for a pit ticket at the Opera Munich 1/9½ Bill of the Opera 1/0½	0	1	10
14th Paid for a pair short boots being entirely renewed except the leggings	0	7	2
15th Mr. Mory for a pair of evening gloves	0	1	9½
16th Mr. Schreibmayer for a silk pocket handkerchief figured with deer	0	5	0
Ditto for one do. bordered with arms 5/8 one with spots 4/6 one blue & yellow 2/10½	0	12	0½
	10	7	10½

CWP continued to keep account books in Prestwold from 1838 to 1856 but unfortunately the family has preserved only a summary of these, listing just the art treasures. We learn from them that he paid Mr Pickersgill £147 in 1844 for the

portrait of himself, and in 1846 £100 to Mr Westmacott for the marble bust of himself.[1]

Before he inherited his Prestwold estate, he began negotiations for the purchase of Glen Hall (in 1835) and in Feb 1836 he became MP for South Leicestershire. He entered parliament at a time of great change. Reform Bills had been passed in 1832 permitting a widening of the franchise with votes for men above a certain income. In 1834 the Poor Law Reform amendment had ruled that no able-bodied men should receive assistance unless they entered a workhouse. Slavery (upon which much of the upper classes wealth was founded) was abolished and in the same year a spectacular fire had destroyed the House of Commons chamber and much of the Palace of Westminster. It was not rebuilt until 1851, so CWP had to wait some time to enter as an MP into the full glory of Barry's building as we see it today! His own home rebuilding did not take quite so long!

He took out a mortgage for Glen Hall in March 1837, when his father died and then proceeded to spend a great deal of money on the Prestwold estate, which he

[1] Found in Prestwold Hall, courtesy of Margaret Packe and Edward Packe Drury Lowe.

inherited.[1] He refurbished Prestwold Hall, commissioning the fashionable architect William Burn.[2] (He went on to spend vast sums on the building of a new mansion, Branksome Towers[3] in Dorset in 1854, using the same architect.)

CWP had certainly overspent and later complained[4] that his monetary problems had arisen because of a restriction imposed in his father's will *as to the cutting down of timber limited to £200 a year* at Prestwold. This meant the loss of a big part of the possible income accruing from an estate and CWP went cap in hand for help from his younger brother George Hussey Packe, who had inherited a much bigger estate in Lincoln from his great aunt Pochin. George Hussey's name appears on various mortgage documents taken out by CWP and it is probable that he attempted to keep some control over his brother's financial dealings. CWP resented George's interference and the brothers quarrelled. Kitty Packe Reading of course supported her husband's view of the matter. In letters to their nephew she writes: *Your uncle Hussey's envious and jealous interference put an end to everything by occupying your uncle* [CWP] *Charles's means of doing good and destroying all his pleasures in doing so.* CWP himself tells us[5] that he *determined to quit Prestwold for ever* and shut up the mansion in 1858 because he *could not afford to keep up two country houses.*

---

[1] CWP's initials can be seen on houses in Prestwold and the neighbouring villages of Hoton and Burton on the Wold with the date 1834. Later houses there bear the initials of his brother, George Hussey Packe, who succeeded to the estate. The Packe Arms inn at Hoton has CJP for Christopher James Packe and the date 1851.

[2] William Burn had designed the nearby stately home of Harlaxton (c.1830) and who later did parts of Burghley House and Stoke Rochford (1839).

[3] CWP and Kitty had spent holidays at nearby Brighton and chose this as their favourite main residence. They also had their house in London and lands in Jersey.

[4] In his *Family Narrative* DE 5047 /200 written from Branksome Tower in Oct 1860 and professionally printed. There are 5 copies in LRO!

[5] ibid

It was evidently hard for CWP to abandon Prestwold. As a childless couple, both CWP and Kitty seem to have been inordinately fond of their various nephews and nieces. As Kitty put it, he *had a truly paternal feeling for all his nephews and nieces*[1] and he had been happy to entertain his relatives in his home. Before the quarrel of the two brothers, CWP had purchased Glen Hall (1837) and Stretton Hall (1846). Edith Lawson[2] remembered an event in her childhood when she came to Glen Hall at Christmas in 1848 *when the Husseys were so rude to all of us; who were children then.* The ill feeling between the two branches of the family had evidently gone on for some time.

The decision to leave Prestwold caused CWP much distress. Kitty wrote in her letters to her nephew Charles after her husband's death that *he never could contemplate the subject of his imposed exodus from Prestwold with anything like coolness.* It must have been in extreme anger that he left, removing the expensive William Burns marble floors and fireplaces. (Kitty Packe Reading acknowledges that he may indeed have gone beyond his legal rights in doing this!) His quarrel with his brother rankled for many years and in his will he ignored George Hussey in favour of his younger brother Edmund's family. The lengthy court case that followed continued for many years after CWP's death, when his widow Kitty took up the cudgels. The saga of the quarrel is referred to in a letter written in 1922 by his niece, Edith Lawson, as *the Husseyana*![3]

In 1846, with the purchase of Stretton Hall, CWP became Lord of the Manor of Great Glen and Stretton. Although not permanently resident here he did involve himself in local affairs and this took money. The National School was built in the village in 1846 *at the cost of Mr Packe.*[4] He bought land and built houses and his initials can be seen on Bott Stone house (1851) as well as the schoolteachers' houses (1846) in Main Street. For details of his involvement in Great Glen affairs, we have multifarious mortgages and deeds of sale and purchase of lands, and, after he closed Prestwold, we have his account books of 1862-70.[5] His signature appears in the village parish meetings records in August 1864[6] but in other meetings JS Marriott signs as representative for him.[7] He took his Leicestershire responsibilities

---

[1] DE 5047 123 KPR letters

[2] Edith Lawson, daughter of Edmund Packe and aunt to ECP, writing to him in 1922

[3] It is interesting to note that George Hussey Packe 1796-1874, four years younger than CWP, fought in the battle of Waterloo in May/July 1815 and was a Lt/Col of the Leics Militia. He inherited Caythorpe, a much larger estate than Prestwold, through a Hussey grandparent and became an MP (as a Liberal) for South Lincs from 1859 to 1868. Both brothers were in Parliament at the same time, members of different parties.

[4] White's Directory.

[5] See chapter 3.

[6] Where decisions were made about the Small Tenements Ratings Act.

[7] DE 1667/16 Vestry Minute Book, March 1863 and 1864

seriously, was a Colonel in the Leics. Yeomanry and chairman of Leics. Quarter sessions and was proud of having his portrait displayed in the city.

Later, he made many bids to be given a peerage. His claims, written to Lord Derby, are based on his political loyalty over a long period of time: *I have been upward of thirty years in the House of Commons and with the single exception of Col Lowther, I believe I am the oldest English County member who has been a consistent supporter of the Conservative Party. I have through life been devoted to public business and my portrait has been placed in the County Hall, Leicester.*[1] He also pleads for a little respite from the hurly burly of the House of Commons! *Since I have been in Parliament I have taken the deepest interest in Political Questions and I have not been indolent in my duty in the House of Commons, but I am obliged to confess that although my zeal to the conservative party has by no means diminished, the work of the house has become more difficult for me as I advance in life. If I could be included in the House of Lords…it would enable my interest in Politics to be continued in a quieter sphere.*

In another letter, dated April 7th 1859, CWP puts forward his ancestral claims through two branches of the family. His first claim is through Sir Christopher Packe who was knighted for his support for Cromwell when he presented the petition to him to take the crown after the execution of Charles I. More tactfully, he also makes the claim through the female side of his family, which supported Charles II: *It is a singular fact that in my person are united both the heir in the Male Line to the mover in the House of Commons 'that the offer of king should be made to Cromwell' for which he was raised to the Upper House: and the heir in the female line to the Defender and Protector of Charles II in the Island of Jersey during the Commonwealth. For this act of devotion to the King, a Royal Grant was made to him at the Restoration of all the Waste Lands belonging to the Crown in that island.* He naturally preferred to stress the loyalty to the king rather than the republican episode: *Loyalty to my sovereign animates me to an appreciation of the honour which derives from my ancestors affording an asylum to a former King of England.*

But playing for both sides is perhaps not a good tactic and by May 13th 1859 he was trying the sympathy ploy for his failing health: *My health is now not up to the hard work required there* (as an MP). He points out that he is only requesting a Life Peerage, not a Hereditary one, as he has no children: *Having no family I can assure you I have no personal ambition to be raised to that honour.* His claims to a peerage did not bear fruit and he died without his knighthood, at Richmond Terrace, London, on Oct 27th 1867, aged 75. He was buried in his private mausoleum at Branksome.

---

[1] Letter to Lord Derby Sept 6th 1866

His will leaves possessions to his wife, Kitty Jenkyn Packe Reading during her life and after her death *to my nephew Charles Packe, the elder son of my brother Edmund Packe* [ignoring George Hussey Packe's family] *and successively to my nephew the Rev Wm James, his younger brother.* The succession did in fact follow this pattern. The Rev William James inherited the estate after his elder brother Charles and it was his son, E C Packe, who followed him. Col EC Packe was thus, the son of CWP's younger brother's younger son. ECP wrote in 1922 a *Life of CW Packe,* where he described his great-uncle as *Generous, of considerable wealth* but with a certain *megolomania…a shrewd businessman, strict accountant, of a jealous disposition and given to litigation.* (Perhaps a relative can be allowed a little plain speaking but it seems a bit harsh!) The obituary in the *Leics Chronicle,* Sat Nov 2nd 1867, similarly tempers its admiration with a critical eye (the politics of the writer being very different from that of his subject).

DECEASE OF C W PACKE ESQ

On Sunday evening (27th October 1867) Charles Wm Packe Esq MP for the southern division of this county, died at his residence in London aged 75 years. Occupying a prominent position in this county as he did, we cannot record Mr Packe's decease without presenting to our readers a brief sketch of his public life and career. Having been before the public as a politician, a magistrate and a county gentleman for 50 years it must needs be said he has played a part in the affairs of this district which is worthy of mention in an obituary notice. Mr Packe was the representative of a family long seated in this county. [Here the writer gives a brief summary of his family, including the Cromwell-for-King saga.] *His parliamentary career began in 1836 when he was elected a member…*[He] *retained his seat from that time to his death. He took his stand from the first Tory principles:'I am deeply attached to Conservative principles' and he had a professed horror of wild visionary things. Household Suffrage* [1] *must have seemed to him synonymous with anarchy. He was essentially a narrow, unprogressive reactionary spirit.*

But enough of Mr Packe as a politician. We must do justice to him as a magistrate. He was eminently useful and assiduous in the prosecution of the county business, a friend of Leicester Infirmary, with sterling business qualities. His consistency (mistaken as we think he was in politics) rendered him always respectable. None could distrust his word and everybody trusted in his integrity. Firm and undeviating in his friendships, he ensured confidence, prompt in his engagements he secured the implicit trust of his magistrates colleagues, shrewd and sagacious, he withheld his followers from practical blunders and in many respects he exemplified some of the best qualities of an English country gentleman.

---

[1] Votes for all householders

KITTY PACKE READING (KPR)

Photo of a painting by Beechey, courtesy of Wm Packe 2003.

Kitty Jenkyn Packe-Reading (nee Hort) 1800-1870
Wife of Charles William Packe M.P.
From painting by Sir William Beechey... R.A.

Kitty Packe Reading was the only daughter of Thomas and Ann Hort and the sole heir of Jenkyn Reading, her godfather, whose name and arms she assumed lin 1818. After her marriage in 1821 to CWP she becomes known as Mrs Packe Reading. The couple were childless and she outlived her husband by just over two years.

In 1822 the young couple made their home in Lowesby Hall.[1] One of Kitty's earliest duties as a wife would have been to entertain, returning hospitality offered to her and CWP after their marriage. We are fortunate that, as a conscientious young wife, she kept a record of who these people were, what they ate, what they talked about and what she thought of them.

Her dinner party book[2] is in an ordinary little notebook with the menu and her judgement as to the meal's appearance on one page and, on the opposite side, the seating arrangement and her comments on the people and their conversation. The host and hostess sit at each end of the table, with guests seated alternately male and female beside them. She refers to CWP as *Mr Charles Packe* and herself as *Mrs Charles Packe.* (Mr and Mrs Packe are his parents.) Some of these parties are held at Lowesby Hall, where she and CWP sat at the table ends, presiding over their guests; some take place in neighbouring great houses where the hosts preside. She entertains on two consecutive days at Lowesby in August 1822 having a dozen people to meals and three days later goes to Prestwold Hall to be entertained by her parents in law for five consecutive days. A week later she is at Launde Abbey with the Simpsons for two meals and then goes on to the Halfords at Wistow Hall for two meals. All in the month of Aug 1822! In September and October she entertains at Lowesby. In 1823 she has only one entry, for a meal at Lowesby in July, and in 1824 one entry for a visit to Connington Castle. In 1825 she again entertains at Lowesby Hall (in March) and in April goes to Col Cheney at Gaddesby, with sixteen people at table. The book ends with a visit to Lord and Lady Howe at Gopsall Hall in 1826.

She does not seem to have enjoyed herself often at these lavish banquets! As a hostess she was nervous. At *the first dinner at which I presided...I was frightened out of my wits and had hardly power to speak but Charles* (CWP) *talked a great deal and my two neighbours talked across me and there was plenty of noise. We waited an immense time between courses, but Charles was very agreeable...I was so vexed.* She often praises her husband for his contributions to the conversation

[1] Lowesby Hall, between Hungarton and Tilton on the Hill.
[2] Bill of Fare notebook, kindly lent to me by Margaret Packe

when he is host: *Charles told a good anecdote of the late Charles Pochin.* On another occasion they had: *A very stupid dinner. I thought the party not large enough and nobody agreeable except Charles, who certainly did his best to keep up the conversation.* She is happier when there is lots of conversation and judges the success of her meals by the amount of talk. She often condemns guests who do not join in the conversation: *Miss Heathcote seldom uttered which was rather a wet blanket but upon the whole I was better pleased than expected.* On the next day Miss Heathcote is absent and *our party was infinitely more agreeable for having Mr and Mrs Hartopp who both talked.*

She likes her dinners to be pretty and is pleased when the meal looks good, regardless of taste: *The dinner went off remarkably well. Every dish looked pretty. As to the taste I am quite indifferent.* She was, however, obviously gratified when her mother in law, on her first visit to them, *whispered in my ear the welcome intelligence that I had a very good cook.* When visiting others, *handsome* is her favourite accolade. Her comments often refer to the *handsome dinner.* At Prestwold: *The first course looked very well but [I] did not admire the damson tart as a remove.* The following day she praises the *very pretty looking dinner* and the next one is *a very handsome dinner. The Breast of Mutton rolled I must remember as a very pretty dish.* At Wistow the soufflé in a round silver dish looked very handsome. Gopsall Park has very impressive features but Kitty is critical of the mix of gold and silver. *Gold Plates in the Centre, wine coolers and appurtenances – most superb. I did not admire the mixture of gold and silver on the table.*

The comments on the conversation are very revealing. A sequence of formal meals with the same people must have been a strain. After two consecutive days at Prestwold Hall, she remarks: *Yesterday there was a good deal of conversation at dinner but the second day of the same party is a sad trial for the intellects of country squires.* Even Charles fails to shine at his parent's table: *at home he was the life of the party; here he never uttered!!* Sometimes she gives us interesting snippets of what was said, as on the occasion her neighbours annoyed her by speaking of bunions and gout. She seems to have been amused by Mr Hartopp's contribution: *I hope you will allow that* [a bunion] *is not quite so genteel a Complaint as Gout!!* Occasionally she does seem to have enjoyed the conversation: *This dinner was particularly amusing. Mr Shakerly told of a house of Mr Rothschild's in Paris where the walls are marble which in summer are iced and in winter heated. Sir Robert immediately after said he knew a house in which there were 64 staircases and 400 fireplaces! Mr Thorpe the banker…very eloquent on all money subjects.*

She seems to have relaxed and enjoyed the company of the Pares brothers, bankers who provided mortgages for CWP on several occasions. When they come to a meal in Lowesby Hall in Sept 1822 she writes: *This was much the pleasantest dinner we have had. I feel (I do not know why) so much better acquainted with the*

Pares party than most of our neighbours. A very pretty looking dinner. I do not remember anything particular that was said but the conversation was very agreeable and amusing.

She is usually critical of the quality of the dinner-table talk: *The conversation* [at Prestwold Hall] *was not very brilliant. X made us laugh a good deal with a puzzling account of his banker giving him five per cent for his money. Y is intolerably vulgar when he does speak and it is therefore fortunate that he is usually silent.* In general, her comments are usually condemnatory, the men having *nothing to talk about but horses and hunting* and the women being *vulgar and loud.* The conversation often bored her.

Her comments on individuals are often very derogatory. At Wistow Hall she comments that her host, Sir Henry Halford,[1] sitting next to her, had said *nothing worth hearing!* It is difficult to believe this about the man who was admired for his courtly charm and good manners and who had inspired a sentimental passion in the princess Augusta when he was one of the doctors for George III. He had been with the king throughout his bouts of madness. In 1810 he was the courtier chosen to convey all sorts of tidings, good and bad to the sick king and in 1813 he had presided over the reopening of the coffin of King Charles I in the presence of George IV.[2] He had conversed with George III just before his death in Jan 1820 and would certainly have had interesting things to say, if royal prerogative had permitted, but perhaps KPR was not the one to bring out such conversation from him in 1822 even if it had been allowed. Should we give her a black mark for not managing to elicit anything interesting from her guest? Surely she knew of the Royal connections! Was she perhaps inhibited from speaking to such an elderly man with such very regal contacts? Speaking to a king's doctor about his patient's madness was certainly not an appropriate dinner table conversation, even if it had been allowed, and the young woman could perhaps be forgiven for failing to find an alternative topic. Sir Henry is reputed to have displayed at his Wistow dinner parties a section of the beheaded king's cervical vertebrae, with marks of the executioner's axe, which he took from the coffin of King Charles I, when he was supervising the disinterment of his body in the time of King George IV. Perhaps if he had shown that to Kitty, she would have had more to say! It was a display

[1] Sir Henry Vaughan, MD of Leicester, inherited and assumed the name of Halford by Act of Parlt 1809. Sir Henry who became President of the College of Physicians in 1820, held the office until his death in 1844, aged 78. He prided himself more upon his courtier-like bearing, and his elegant turn for writing good Latin verse, than upon his professional skill, and the general opinion of his contemporaries seems to have been that these were the principal causes of his advancement. He was liked by George III and he attended in succession George IV, William IV and Queen Victoria. Firth: *Highways and Byways of Leicestershire*.

[2] DE 5047 234 ST77/27 The Account of the opening of King Charles I's tomb

considered at the time to lack 'nice feeling' and was perhaps something reserved solely for male visitors.

At Gadsby (*A more vulgar dinner I never beheld*!!) she was seated next to Sir Francis Burdett (1770-1844), a rebel MP who had opposed corporal punishment in the army and had been imprisoned in 1819 for declaiming against the cruel repression at the massacre of Peterloo.[1] Kitty comments scornfully: '*The Patriot' hardly uttered*! It is difficult to know whether her hostility is based on a dislike of his political reputation or his personality. Perhaps she looked on him as a grumpy old fellow not worth social effort. Was she not good at social occasions or was he really so difficult to talk to? We have to remember she was very young and not well educated in modern terms. She took little pleasure in the entertaining*: March 1825, Lowesby... and I am happy to say the last for which it will be necessary to write a Bill of Fare this year.*

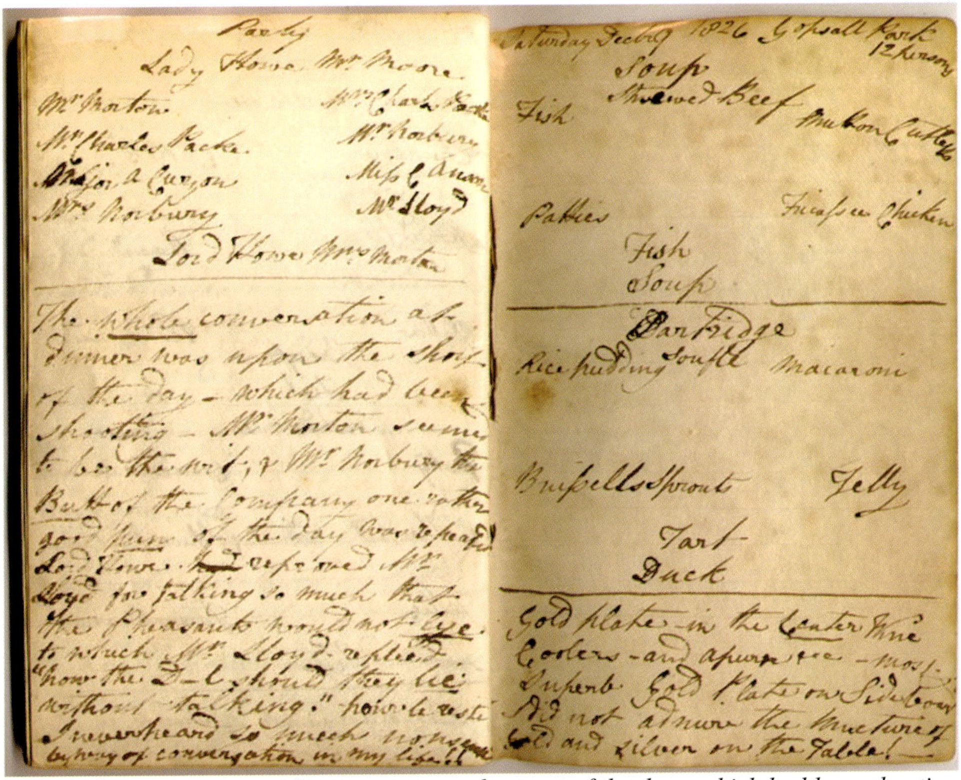
Party
Lady Howe Mr Moore
Mr Morton Mrs Clark Packe
Mr Charles Packe Mr Norbury
Major A Curzon Miss C Adam
Mrs Norbury Mr Lloyd
Lord Howe Mrs Morton

The whole conversation at dinner was upon the sport of the day - which had been shooting - Mr Morton seemed to be the wit, & Mr Norbury the Butt of the company one rather good pun of the day was repeated! Lord Howe reproved Mr Lloyd for talking so much that the Pheasants would not lye. to which Mr Lloyd replied "how the D-l should they lie without talking." [illegible] I never heard so much nonsense by way of conversation in my life!!

Saturday Decbr 9 1826 Gopsall Park 12 persons
Soup
Fish Stewed Beef Mutton Cutlets
Patties Fricassee Chicken
Fish
Soup
Partridge
Rice pudding Souflé Macaroni
Brussells Sprouts Jelly
Tart
Duck

Gold plate in the Center. Wine Coolers - and Epergne &c - most superb. Gold Plate on Sideboard. I do not admire the mixture of Gold and Silver on the Table!

The whole *conversation at dinner was upon the sport of the day - which had been shooting. Mr Morton seemed to be the wit and Mr Norbury the Butt of the company one rather good pun of the day was repeated! Lord Howe reproved Mr Lloyd for talking so much that the*

[1] "Peterloo Massacre" in Manchester 1819. The Lancashire militia charged into a crowd of people gathered to hear Henry Hunt demanding universal suffrage, and the ballot. Several people were killed and many injured.

Pheasants would not lye. To which Mr Lloyd replied "how the D----l should they lie without talking". I never heard such nonsense by way of conversation in my life. [Dec 1826 at Gopsall Park]

Her informal writing style with its lively punctuation, exclamations and underlinings, indicates her spoken voice for us and gives an insight into her character. (What a pity we have no notebook of hers to accompany CWP's Expenses Account of their Grand Tour of 1828-30. That would certainly have given us a different perspective!) One item she has left us is a useful summary of events at the time she and CWP inherited Prestwold in 1837. Written in diary form, on tatty little bits of paper, it records the dates for the death of CWP's father and their move into the Hall, allowing time for the widowed mother to pack her bags and leave: *Mr Charles James Packe, my father in law, died on Weds the 1st March at 2am 1837. His widow remained in possession at Prestwold by the permission of her eldest son Charles William Packe till Sept 12th 1837 on which day she left.*

During this time, Kitty was juggling with affairs in Prestwold, London and Glen. She records movements between her various establishments: *April 25th left Prestwold for Glenn. April 30th to London removed to 7 Richmond Terrace. Dec 14th 1837 Went to Prestwold for the first time after Mrs Packe's departure. 15th made inventory of the kitchen. 17th chose the site of new school house with G* [George Hussey Packe?] *18th returned to Glenn. Aug 13th 1844 went to Prestwold for the day and much pleased with all that has been done particularly the drawing room. Mr Packe[1] took a shooting party to Prestwold.[2]*

For 1849 and 1852, she lists visitors to the Hall, mainly Packe family members, and she gives details of the quarrel between her husband and his brother, George Hussey Packe over the Prestwold inheritance. Always a loyal wife, she supports her husband's decision to break with his brother and to abandon Prestwold: *Mr CW Packe did this simply that he might have the Power to do exactly as he pleased with his own But that he had not the least idea of leaving it away from his brother. April 3rd 1858 the Resolution of Mr CW Packe to leave Prestwold and to cease entirely to live there. He accordingly left Prestwold on 25th of August 1858.[3]*

When her husband died, in October 1867, Kitty continued to reside in Branksome Towers, the dream home they had built in 1854 as an alternative to Prestwold, but she took over the role of Lady of the Manor of Glen and kept up the account books and the survey of estates as CWP had done. To do so, she visited Glen from time to time and she continued the battle over the Prestwold inheritance. The *Husseyana*

---

1 CWP had inherited from his father and is therefore now *Mr Packe.*

2 DE 5047/20

3 The contents of Prestwold Hall listed in the sale document of Oct 1858 include *a 12' x 8' billiard table, a cottage pianoforte, a lofty mahogany four poster bed, double and single barrelled guns and twenty five tons of best Derbyshire coal.*

affair led to a very lengthy lawsuit and she harboured a great deal of resentment against George Hussey, which she poured out in letters to her nephew Charles Packe, who had been chosen by the childless CWP to inherit his estate after Kitty.

Her letters are in handwriting which is terribly difficult to read, unlike the elegant script of her nephew Charles. It is charitable to presume that some of the business letters are only the rough versions, kept as copies when the neat versions were sent, before the days of typewriters and carbon paper. The letters sent to Charles, however, are originals, with his inked in 'translation', when he has deciphered some of the words! Her letters to him are warm and affectionate and give a human touch to the family history. They reveal interesting details and are quite informative about her financial situation and her ideas for running the estate. She very much resented having to spend the money defending the *Husseyana* case. In 1867 she writes to Charles saying that she fears the money she wanted to spend on improvements will be swallowed up in legal fees: *It is astonishing how many things I should like to do with that 'residue' better than paying lawyers bills with it but I begin now to fear that it will prove 'Castles in the Air'. The only comfort I have is that if I have not the money neither you nor anyone else can blame me for spending it foolishly.*

She writes to him to say that all dealings with George Hussey should go through the solicitor Mr Miles: *I never depend entirely on the Character of anyone. There is more evil than we know of in the best and more good than one imagines in the worst but I certainly have a high opinion of Mr Miles's Intentional Honesty of Principle and of his positive clear judgement to see that 'Honesty is the best Policy'. I have very nearly the opposite opinion of your Uncle. Dec 12 1867. I should if possible wish you to avoid any personal communication with your Uncle Hussey on matters of business connected with me - you are too much interested yourself to pretend to go to him as an impartial arbitrator and it is always awkward for principals, especially relations, to argue together on money affairs.*

She obviously admires Charles' intelligence and ability but advises him against dealing directly with his 'wicked uncle' (George Hussey Packe). Her letters to him show the affection she and CWP felt for their nephew.
Thursday Dec 12 1867 Branksome,
My Dear Charles,
Many thanks for your letter which I think a very clever one, but remember that aunts are partial so do not let my opinion make you vain.

Dec 14th 1867. I believe your Intellect to be as superior to your Uncle Hussey's as that of your uncle Charles [CWP] *was but from your character being peculiarly free from anything like art or cunning you would be a mere baby in your Uncle Hussey's hands.*

She likes his confidence in and affection for her and is amused by the proverbs in French (and answers in the same language): *On revient toujours a son premier amour.*[1] She devoted time and attention to Charles' marital affairs, writing to him with real affection regarding his impending marriage:
Jan 25th 1868 Saturday,
My dearest nephew Charles
First of all I never received a letter that gave me so much pleasure as yours dated Jan 24th excepting those from your dear uncle [CWP] *which always were a delight to me!*

Her marriage allowance to him is generous and given in the hope that he will be able to stay in England: *I am very glad that you think you could marry without the allowance I have promised you of four hundred per annum because I hope that addition will enable you to live the greater part of your time in England. I shall be happy to settle that £400 per annum upon you in any way that may satisfy the young lady's parents; as of course it ought to be placed in a business like manner out of the possibility of being discontinued by any caprice or change of mine.*

She gives Charles general advice about marriage, full of capitals and underlining, and ends affectionately with an invitation to come and stay with her at Branksome. *Then I hope you will visit me for the winter months here for as long as your BETTER HALF may LIKE; to please her must be your FIRST object as it certainly will be your FIRST DUTY.* Her advice is to settle matters speedily: *Remember 'happy is the wooing that is not long adoing'.* (She is a great one for proverbs and quotations.) And she offers the young couple accommodation in Glen Hall: *If a House furnished and rent free for three months could enable you to expedite matters I could place Glen at your service during July and August and most probably September.* She has commitments at Glen: *I must be there myself in the month of May. I HAD intended to spend some time here* [at Branksome] *and if you would allow me to pay YOU a VISIT at Glenn Hall of a week or a fortnight between June and October that is all I should require for my parish business there...* And she has arranged to let the hall to tenants which means that *about the middle of October I should be obliged to turn you out as I should then want to propose the house for my Winter tenants who generally expect to come to it by the 15th November.* (In her account book of 1869 the hall is let to Capt Walmesley.)

She worries about his being settled in his bachelor ways: *Yes! Don't attempt to dispute that fact now! With all your ABSURD bachelor notions! You will soon find that il faut changer tout cela! If you make your wife happy -she will love you - if you don't - she won't – that's all!!* She remembers the early days of her own marriage to CWP, with his similarly doting aunts: *And now I'm not going to praise you up to the skies as is the fashion with aunts on these occasions for I remember*

[1] We always return to our first love.

being so alarmed at the encomiums your dear uncle received from all his female relations in reply to the announcement of his approaching marriage! 'How can they ever be pleased with me', I thought 'if they think him so very perfect'!

She makes sure she ends the letter on a note of high morality and instruction: *No! No! I am not going to make you vain and conceited! I acknowledge a great respect for your intellect because it is superior to mine but that is not saying much for you!! And I never did see you out of temper - but I never saw you provoked by a WIFE you know! and pray remember that no man ever can DESERVE the Love and Duty and self sacrifice of an amiable sensible high principled girl- but I do think you are as likely to make such a one happy as any man can be but never forget the gratitude you owe her for loving you enough to leave her parents and the friends of her youth FOR YOUR SAKE and to ADOPT and LOVE your family and friends which I hope and trust she will do - but it will be entirely for YOUR SAKE REMEMBER that she will try to love us all and make the best of us.*
PS. I fully intend you to show this to your 'Lina'.[1]

An undated page refers to her regret at not being able to attend their wedding because she is still in mourning for CWP and she refers to her sadness that no relations were at her wedding because, they told her later, they were not invited! She roundly declares that she would have invited herself to his and Lina's wedding *even if it had been in Ireland* <u>*if it had happened one year later*</u> *but nothing would induce me even to be in the church, as the queen* [Queen Victoria] *was, in deep mourning.* She would not like to relinquish her widow's weeds black clothing, even for one day, so soon after the death of her husband and would not be willing to attend any wedding while in full mourning but she sends best wishes and hopes the sun shines on them

Trivial domestic matters get a mention, too: sending him six postage stamps on Jan 2nd 1867 to repay the sixpence her (very honest) maid found in the room he stayed in when he visited her:
Dear Charles
My housemaid having given me such a good example of honesty I cannot chuse but to follow it and therefore enclose you six Postage stamps she having brought me sixpence which she says she found on the armchair in your bedroom. Mr Miles was the last inhabitant of that room and I think he is such a <u>*good man of business*</u> *that he would have written for it if* <u>*he*</u> *had left it.* (And then she also tells him off for not taking more care of his coughs and colds!)

Occasionally she writes of her plans for the farm and wanting pigs, and cows for cream and she mentions that people are sliding but not skating yet on Branksome lake. On Saturday Dec 14th 1867 she mentions her minor illnesses: *I was obliged at*

---

[1] Lina, Selina, wife of Charles Packe

last to send for Dr Bowlem after a week's doctoring of myself so of course he has the credit of curing me when with another day's patience I should have been well without him. We do not know whether Charles brought Lina to stay in Glen Hall with his aunt in 1868 but two years later he (without Lina) was at her side as she lay dying, in Branksome.

Even in the year she died, she was carrying out her duties for Great Glen and worrying about the court case over Prestwold. On Jan 7th 1870 the Christmas and New Year gifts of meat are recorded to the new schoolmaster, Paulson, and to all the schoolchildren.[1] (He received 16lbs of beef and the 71 schoolchildren shared 142 lbs of beef.) A fortnight later she died.

Her niece Louisa Emily Fellowes wrote details of her death: *Aunt Charles*[2] *died on the 22nd of January 1870, Saturday and was not buried till Thursday 3rd Feb. The arrangements for Consecration were nearly completed and her coffin was brought down to the dining room (from which room it was directed to be taken to the Mausoleum) before I left which was on the 31st. I was so ill dear Horace would not let me stay for the funeral but made me return and he went down the evening of 2nd Feb and returned 4th the funeral being the 3rd and I presume consecration the same day. I have record of these days in my short diary written at the time.*

Only Charles and I were at the death. Lina did not come till the following Monday or Tuesday as Aunt Charles particularly begged Charles to go without his Wife and sent for me. I went down on the 21st and she was up in the drawing room and was unconscious next morning and died Saturday evening. [3]

Matters at Prestwold had still not been settled. The problem of the lawsuit was now inherited by Charles. He returned to Branksome on May 1st to sort out the sale of Branksome Towers and communicated with his uncle from there: *Jan 23rd 1870. My Aunt Mrs Packe Reading died last night at half past eight. I was here for the last three days.* The reply from his uncle came, on the customary black bordered paper, to Charles Packe, Branksome Tower, Poole, Dorset. (The capital letters are somewhat haphazard.)

My Dear Charles
Your letter was forwarded to me and I recvd it just as I left Charles St. I am much obliged to you for communicating to me the Death of Mrs Packe Reading; we were not aware of her serious illness and therefore much surprised to hear of her death.

---

[1] DE 5047/5 1870 Jan 7th a present to Paulson from Mrs Packe Reading of 16lbs of beef (12s 6d) and to 71 schoolchildren 142lbs of beef (£5-12-4d).
[2] Aunt Charles is the family name for Kitty Packe Reading
[3] L E Fellowes in a letter to ECP on writing his family history DE 5047 205

as she had her friends with her at Branksome her end must have been I should think sudden.
With our kindest regards
I remain
Yrs Affecly
G H Packe

A second letter follows dated: *Febry 15/70*
My Dear Charles
I received your letter this Afternoon and hasten to reply to it to assure you of my anxiety through life, not to quarrel with any one, and particularly my Relations but I will not enter into details of what is past. I have endeavoured upon more than one occasion to try to come to a settlement thro my lawyers with Messrs Bouskell but we were repulsed and I had no alternative but to seek my redress in the Court of Chancery and I now should be very glad if could stay further proceedings. I understand if not it will come on in a few days Mr Bouskell had better confer with Mr Norton and prevent further Expense and Litigation. I am coming up to London on Thursday and will see Mr Norton upon the subject

And less than a week later: *Feb 20th 70*
My Dear Charles
I found your letter upon my return from London last night and I gave full instructions to Mr Norton to come to a settlement with Mr Bouskell, which would be much better than proceeding with heavy Law expenses If it is impossible for you and me to settle various points we have always wished an arrangement but Mr Bouskell Declined Should a settlement not be effected the case will come on Either the 7th or 9th of next month.

The three-day sale catalogue for Branksome Tower, May 19-22 1871, lists the furniture, the china and the contents of the library. It lists objects for sale with prices received. It was an end to an era.

CHARLES PACKE 1826-1897

As CWP and Kitty were childless, their nephew Charles inherited their estate in 1870, when Kitty died. He was then about 44 and his wife, Selina, was ten years younger. They, too, had no children. They lived in Stretton Hall from 1870-1896, having sold Branksome Towers when they came into the inheritance.

Charles Packe.[1]

Described as Traveller/Author in *Who's Who in Leics*.[2] His greatest achievements were in mountaineering. He was a keen climber and wrote his *Guide to the Pyrenees* in 1867.

One family story is of his honeymoon, in 1868, when he took his young wife Selina up into the Pyrenees and left her for several days in the care of a guide while he climbed higher up the mountain! (A dedicated climber is not always appreciated uncritically by his family and we are not told what poor Selina thought of this!)

The introduction to his *Guide to the Pyrenees* shows his practicality and his consideration for his readers, as well as his scorn for 'professionals'. He explains that his guidebook is specially intended for mountaineers and botanists and that descriptions of villages and beauty spots have therefore been curtailed: *Read at home this little book will have no interest but amid the mountains and the gorges of the Pyrenees it will, I believe, enable the tourist to be in a measure independent of*

---

[1] DE 3936/16
[2] L920

professional guides – those iconoclasts of the imagination and reverie- at all events to select for himself his own excursions with a fair notion of distances and the time to be consumed in them. In the face of Nature itself which speaks to its admirers in a language far more eloquent than pen or pencil, description is worse than useless. I have chiefly confined myself to the mere indication of the routes with heights and distances and the time to be allowed from point to point. Excursions have been computed from my own experience at a moderate pace including halts...but I thought it best to allow sufficient margin, remembering the proverb: chi va piano va sano, chi va sano va lontano.[1]

The book can apparently still be used[2] and modern climbers can still appreciate the work of the *dour Leicester squire, magistrate, geologist and botanist.*[3] His obituary in the Peterborough Diocesan Magazine in Aug 1896 sums up his achievements as a climber: *For more than forty years he spent his holidays in severe pedestrian labour, now among the familiar summits of Cumberland or the Highlands, now amongst the highest peaks of the Alps or Pyrenees, or in opening out new fields of achievement among the scarcely known ranges of central and southern Spain. Everywhere he carried with him a resoluteness of effort which never relaxed until his object was accomplished, and an absolute delight in bodily toil, privation and hardship, which his friends, not without reason, feared would prove too severe a strain upon his strength. He once told the writer of this notice that there was hardly a mountain top of eminence in Britain on which he had not passed the night, often with no shelter but a blanket or a cloak.*

By his intimate knowledge of mountain systems, aided by a singular accuracy of mind, he was able to furnish valuable topographical and geological memoranda, which were, from time to time, embodied in the transactions of the Alpine Club, of which he was one of the original members and for some years secretary. His valuable observations on the Pyrenean chain secured him the rare distinction of election to membership of the French Alpine Club, for which likewise he wrote occasional papers. He was a distinguished botanist, and was able to add several species to the flora of the Pyrenees; being also very successful in acclimatising rare kinds of plants in his garden.[4]

He was an active man throughout his life. In February 1888 when he was about 60, he mentions in letters to his brother that he has walked from Stretton to Leicester and back in the afternoon, to inspect the Infirmary. He makes several rather plaintive hints about wanting a companion to go with him to make *'one more*

---

[1] Who goes slowly goes safely. Who goes safely goes far.

[2] *A climbing friend of my son's went to the Pyrenees only last year (2002) and used this guide book, quite successfully.* (William Packe 2003)

[3] Alexander Maitland, *Country Life* April 11th 1985.

[4] Obituary, *Peterborough Diocesan Magazine*, August 1898

ascent of Scafell and if I had a companion I might run on to Skye...only they [the Cuillin mountains] *are rather severe.* A man of wide interests, he makes references to rare plants and to recent scientific experiments in electricity and photography as well as to nature and the seasons at home in Glen.

An article in *The Field* magazine[1] tells us about Charles Packe's part in introducing the Pyrenean mountain dog to Britain. At Stretton Hall his dogs were kept in an iron-railed grass enclosure which he called the dog park. He commissioned a lifesize model of a Pyrenean dog made of Dresden china: an expensive and vulnerable ornament.

Picture of Pyrenean dogs and a spaniel (all named) with a bowler hatted gentleman (unnamed) by the monument in Stretton Hall.[2] The dogs, as always, took priority!

My father (Col Packe) visited Stretton as a child and found his uncle Charles alarming. They, the children, were not allowed to eat breakfast until the dogs were fed. The ham on the sideboard, smelling delicious, was carved and given to the dogs first. (Margaret Packe.)

Margaret Packe, born at Stretton Hall, tells me that as a child she found many shards of blue and white pottery, the broken remains of this china dog, which had been removed to the dog park after Charles Packe's death, and put on a plinth, only to be knocked down by one of the boisterous dogs and completely destroyed.

While Charles was settling into his inheritance, many of his letters are concerned with money matters and the moving of stocks and bonds. In 1870, when he inherited, he began immediately building and improving and set about getting good tenants for Glen Hall, while he lived at Stretton Hall. Later letters dated 1886, 1887 and 1888 from Charles to his brother William, in the vicarage at Feering, are full of interesting references to the village and his activities in Great Glen. Many of the letters refer to his buying property in Glen[3] and he concerns himself with the

---

1 *The Field*, May 3 1956 article entitled *The Pyrenean Mountain Dog in Britain.*

2 Picture courtesy of Sheila Ball.

3 see Packes in the Village Chap 3.

school.[1] He worries about the effect of any loss of income from tenants but nevertheless offers to help with any expense his brother might incur in educating his son, young Christopher.[2] *Nov 16th 1887 pray recollect that I shall be very glad to help you in any way I can in the expense of it, always provided that Clements[3] does not give up his land. (It is not impossible that Clements at Christmas may give his notice which is tantamount to £900 a year off my income.)* He is pleased to have a tenant for Glen Hall: *Nov 16th 1887 My tenant at Glen, Mr Walker, wants to have a 7 or 14 year lease and to make the alterations in the house I spoke to you of. I think I shall let him have the lease . I suppose there is no chance of you or any member of the family wanting to live there in the next 14 years...I have let Glenn Hall and two fields to Walker for 7 or 14 years. He is a careful tenant and will I am sure keep up the place and grounds with which he is really pleased; so it is a good thing to have it off one's hands.*

The Hunt at Stretton Hall.

Never an enthusiastic horse rider, Charles Packe was apparently hostile to the hunt. Margaret Packe tells the story of how he once prevented the huntsmen following a fox into Stretton Hall: *He was not keen on foxhunting. On one occasion he stopped the hunt following a fox which jumped into the house saying, 'I will horsewhip anyone who goes after it there'.*[4] In one letter he mentions the weather in relation to the hunt. *We have snow on the ground and 5 degrees centigrade last night though it now thaws, to my grief, on the hounds' meet at Glen tomorrow.* Charles

---

[1] see Chapter 5 on the school

[2] ECP Edmund Christopher Packe

[3] Clements was his biggest land tenant. See chapter 3

[4] Margaret Packe

had been dismissive of hunting and shooting, even as a young man. In a letter to his uncle CWP in 1859 [1] he described how he went out shooting with Welby, a fellow officer who lived at Denton, near Market Harborough: *at his persuasion I consented to try shooting once more after four years intermission...But I am more than convinced that it is not half the pleasure and excitement of travelling in a wild country and climbing up mountains.*[2]

He was distinctly hostile to a lot of other things, too, and often sounds a very grumpy, curmudgeonly old man! He was, even as a young man, critical of society. In an early letter to his uncle CWP, when he was first appointed officer in charge, he had been scornful of army life. There was a lot of shouting to be done but very little activity to make him stiff: *I am a very little stiff but owing to have to give the word of command my voice is considerably affected.*[3] He obviously liked the action more than the socialising: *You know that our feet are under the dinner table almost all the time they are not on our horses' flanks, to say nothing of the time bestowed on dressing and undressing.* He described a formal army dinner as: *the same sort of thing as usual: everybody's health was drunk but the speeches were none of them worth reporting and I thought the grand dinner was the most wearisome proceeding of the whole week.*

It is the botanist in him which gives rise to Scrooge-like comments over Christmas: *Dec 28th 1887. We had a large Christmas party here. Our church is decorated as usual but I much grudge it and also the holly that they will stick about the rooms here...I hate mutilating the shrubs and robbing the poor starving birds of the berries which the almighty has provided for their winter keep.* On other occasions there is nothing to soften the impression! *Lina is mad about music and she and Mr Oddie are going to have a concert tonight at Glen in the schoolroom and I have consented to go to it, though it is neither enjoyment nor instruction and snow is on the ground.* Similarly in Feb 2 1888 he writes: *Lina and I were at a ball last night at the barracks; but we did not dance.* Perhaps the excuse for this ungracious behaviour is that he was tired: *I walked to Leicester and back in the afternoon to inspect the Infirmary and paid visits.*

In 1874 he refused to join the Conservative Association because he objected to unions of employers just as he objected to unions of employees ganging up against one another: *I have a very strong objection to associations for political purposes. I discountenance in every way the labouring men in Glen associating against their employers and it only appears to me fair and consistent to keep aloof from any league that might be worked against them.* He was certainly a man of principle and independent judgement! *I think that government by party is in these days carried*

---

[1] DE 5047/112 Letters from Charles Packe to his uncle CWP 1859
[2] ibid Oct 1859
[3] DE 5047/112 Letter from Charles to CWP from the Bell Hotel Leics Sept 1859

much too far.[1] He commented on a Protectionist meeting on Feb 7th as *a lot of twaddle.* At the same time he gives his opinion of the government: *I do not think much of the present govt. They are much given to blowing hot and cold. To gratify and retain the liberal unionists; they are going to give such a radical local govt bill as will astonish the country squires.* And in March 1888 he writes that: *Everyone here now anticipates war but I can hardly think mankind are such fools.*[2]

When he considers the position of his investments in Russian bonds, he makes sweeping comments on the whole nation: *I believe the Russians are too proud ever to repudiate their debt and Russia is an under populated and rising country, the reverse of England in both respects.* He has comments to make on scientific developments: *March 1892. What they call the new development of electricity seems to me nothing else than a blasphemous attempt to direct and create energy with which the Almighty works.*

Many of his later letters refer to his health. In March 1892 he mentions that he has been ill. For a man so proud of his survival in hard conditions, climbing in what we would consider highly inadequate clothes and sleeping out in the open in all weathers, it must have been galling to suffer the ill health of old age. He speaks bravely of improvement, but rails at the inadequacy of doctors and stresses his reliance on sunshine and fresh air. *March 10th 1888 with the warm weather I am getting better, decidedly better today but have been bad not able to sleep at night I should think Alfred will also mend with the approach of summer but every one must doctor himself in his own methods. I believe in neither doctors nor medicine but in Sun.* He pronounces himself *not at all well,* with a cough but rejects treatment and remains independent of outside authority: *I have not seen a doctor for 3 months, in law, medicine or religion. I prefer to rely upon myself.*

His independence in matters religious and his strong opinions with regard to his own burial caused a great final rift between him and his brother. He had been concerned for many years about the matter of his burial, writing to his brother William in 1882 that he wished to be buried in his dog park at Stretton:
In the will I made some years ago I have left all furniture and residue to you. The dogs would I think prefer to end their days here, I hope you will have acceded to my request and let me be buried in a wooden or wicker box in the dog park between the two cypresses behind the lion. I will endeavour to mark the spot. Perhaps you may not occupy the Stretton hall for very long after me but I hope little Christopher[3] *may enjoy it and keep up the family traditions. Do not let him forget the dog park.*[4]

---

[1] DE 5047/127/1-3

[2] The Crimean War had ended in 1856. Boer War battles in South Africa took place in 1880 and 1899.

[3] ECP

[4] DE 5047 146 Charles Packe letter to William Feb 21 1882

Charles Packe near the spot where he wished to be buried *'Between the two cypresses behind the lion'* in his dog park.

He was still on good terms with William in April 1890, asking for his help in finding workers for the estate: *Have you a good labouring man and his wife to send me to live in my lodge, 12/- a week and house and garden* and he reports to him the local news: *April 3 1892 We had a bad accident in Glen yesterday - a man tumbled into a well and got drowned.*[1] But by 1894, two years before he died, he sounds fractious and is distinctly ungracious about the kind gift from his brother of a stove for his room: *The stove is not the slightest use to me. I never intend to have my dressing room heated. I have just been protesting against an extra stove in the Church. How could I do this if I indulged those luxuries at home. I do not know what to do with the stove but hope you will not be hurt.* He decides not to waste it but to return it on Monday and then, on Feb 8 1894, writes that he will *give the stove to Oddie*[2] *as a present from you.* He goes on to boast that he is: *Like my mother for longevity etc no fire and open window all night.* A week later his wife has persuaded him not to act precipitously: after the stormy night of Feb 13 1894 he

---

[1] This may have been in High Street by the back of the cruck cottage.

[2] Oddie, the vicar. See Chapter 4.

records the fact that *strong wind blew down several elms* and goes on to say*: I have not yet given your stove to Oddie. L* [Selina] *wants me to think it over before doing so but I shall never have it in my dressing room.*

Selina's letters in 1895 show her worry about him: *God grant that a little time may be given him to turn to his saviour and face the awful fact of his precarious state. Charlie has seen his doctor H Butlin and he says he has no doubt that the growth in his throat is cancer.* References are made to food for the invalid: *Malt and cod liver oil and cream and milk.* In May 1895 *Dr Phillips of Glen* is sent for as Charles is ill again with flu. In Feb 1896 another doctor gives a more cheerful report: *Mr Marriott just been and gives a most satisfactory report and proposed not coming again. He has given him a medicine to pick him up a Phosphate of some kind and we are sending for it and oysters today. He can take Champaign and Burgundy as he prefers. He is to do just as he feels inclined about getting up.*[1] On April 10th 1896 Charles wrote to William: *I have not been very well the last few days. I have not left my room for 3 weeks but I hope one day to be carried out in a chair to see how the garden looks, and the trees. We want rain badly but the glass is so high it cannot come. I have been trying to eat some plovers' eggs but it is rather a shame to encourage the extinguishments of the poor bird, and I don't think they do me any good.*

The matter of his burial in the dog park remained unsettled. By April 10th 1896 Charles had taken positive action and wrote to his brother: *I have been obliged to apply to the Church Burial and Funeral Reform Association . I shall hear from them again but I believe they see no difficulty or objection in disposing of my remains in the manner I wish, in unconsecrated ground.* But William replied the next day, from Feering Vicarage: *I told you at the time I was sorry you should make the request.* In a further letter he goes on to say: *I do not see any great objection to burning the dead except for the danger of failing to discover crime but still I think the urn ought to be deposited where it is not likely to be interfered with and stolen, in consecrated ground.* Charles was furious at his brother's attitude and writes: *Your heart and mind are cast in a different frame to mine and it's no use appealing to you any more. I thought I could have counted on a brother's love in carrying out my last wishes in such a simple matter. In counting on your love I have leaned on a broken reed.*[2] The quarrel seems to have calmed down by May 1896 when Charles writes in a philosophic vein about his illness and the approach of death. *I have plenty of patience, perhaps too much for it is inclined to degenerate into indolence for nearly all day I lie in bed and console myself reflecting that this foolish and apparently to us ill regulated world is but a transitory one but I have many happy days spent in it to look back to.* He identifies rare plants for William and, practical as ever, plans gifts of bonds for Christopher *instead of waiting for my death when*

---

[1] Letters from Selina to William James DE 5047/148
[2] DE 5047/146 Charles to Wm James Packe

you would have to pay succession duty. He must have hoped to have the last word on the matter of his burial as his will declared his wishes. He died on July 16th 1896 at Stretton Hall *desiring to be buried in the dog park, trusting some clergyman willing to read the Church of England service although it is not consecrated ground.* The request was not honoured and he was buried in Great Stretton churchyard on the 20 July 1896. His friend Arthur Oddie officiated and the grave is unmarked.

Great Stretton churchyard.
Charles Packe's unmarked grave is near the corner of the tower.

THE REV WILLIAM JAMES PACKE (1833 – 1897- 1908).

It was under this cloud of disobedience to his brother's wishes, that in 1897 the Rev.William James Packe succeeded to his estate. Selina, his sister-in-law, did not stay in the hall after Charles died, and she, unlike Kitty Packe Reading, did not become Lady of the Manor. The title went, as CWP had decreed, to Charles' brother William, and Selina moved away from Great Glen.[1] William James was not a young man and was happily settled in his vicarage in Feering. Perhaps it is not surprising that, although he did much refurbishment of Stretton Hall, he never lived there. He obviously had no wish to uproot his family and leave the vicarage.

Nearly thirty years earlier, in 1868, he had been invited by Kitty Packe Reading to take the living of Glen,[2] but had chosen then to refuse and to stay in the diocese of Chelmsford. He told her how much he had enjoyed his visits to Glen: *I went up to the house and was glad to see Henry and Mrs Langley.*[3] *I thought the place looking very pretty and the grass very green owing to the late rains.* He obviously had some social contacts, too, and took the opportunity to call in on Sir Henry and Lady Halford at Wistow. But, although he liked Glen, he chose not to accept the job here. He did however make visits, with his family, when his brother lived in Stretton Hall and was kept informed about events in the village. But there seems not to have been enough to tempt him to live here when he inherited the estate. He was not prepared to move from his parish to settle in Glen.

After he inherited, the Hall was let to various tenants and Wm James was Lord of the Manor *in absentia,* doing most of his Great Glen business by correspondence. He was only a rare visitor to Glen[4] but kept in touch through letters and occasional visits. Clough Taylor acted as his agent and dealt with the tenants. The letters about the school finances and the site for the parochial hall are addressed to him personally[5] and between 1897 and 1906 we have letters[6] about the church bells, the water supply and the sale of Glebe Land.[7] In 1903 he made an agreement with the Foundation Managers to hand over the control of the school to them. His real love was for his parish in Feering, [8] where he died 'in harness' in 1908, aged 75.

---

[1] She did not die until 1920

[2] See Chapter 4.

[3] In the Lodge house. See Chapter 3

[4] His family mention that on one occasion Theodore Walker invited him to Glen Hall, and asked him to choose the hymn for grace.

[5] DE5047 150 See Chapter 4, The School and The Village Hall

[6] DE5047 154

[7] DE5047 161

[8] To illustrate his good relations with his parishioners, his son, Wm Packe, told me the story of the lady who asked the Rev WJP to take her false teeth to be repaired, as he was going into town!

EDMUND CHRISTOPHER PACKE, (ECP, later Col. Packe) 1878-1961

Born 1877 at Feering in Essex, the son of the Rev.W J Packe, Edmund C Packe appears in the 1881 census, aged 3, at 1 Stanhope Place, London, the home of his step grandmother. Mary Packe, his grandfather's second wife. He is listed there with a sister aged 2 and baby brother aged two months, and lots of nursemaids and servants. The family was presumably just visiting the grandmother in London.

In 1899 he joined the Royal Fusiliers and served in the South African war (1900). His determination to go to the war meant that he left Magdalene College, Cambridge before taking his degree.[1] He was severely wounded at the Relief of Ladysmith and we have a letter written to his mother from the hospital in Pieter Maritzberg in March 1900: *I was wounded by a bullet which took me in the left side of the chest underneath the left arm. I was lying down at the time and as far as I can make out the bullet ricocheted on to me from some stone. It was a jolly lucky wound for it just missed the heart and I don't believe did more than graze the lung rather badly. At present there are no signs of the bullets ever having come out but presently I believe they're going to examine me with the X-rays. By Jove, it's pretty good Cronje's defeat*[2] *and the Relief of Ladysmith having been brought off so close together, isn't it? I wish to goodness I could have been in at Ladysmith; they've been kicking up a tremendous row over it here and its very riling to have to lie and listen to them. The Doctor has just been in and told me that I am progressing far more favourably than he had anticipated, so I ought to, and do, feel very thankful to God for His great mercy.*[3]

His daughter gives the family version that *the Boers' 'slug' had missed his heart by being deflected by striking his silver cigarette case in his breast pocket.*[4] His nephew, William Packe, told me that[5] *he boasted of a bullet in his heart from the Boer war and showed the X-ray years later.* He was awarded the Queen's Medal from this war. He did twenty one years' service with the 2nd Battalion of the Royal Fusiliers and was in Cairo, Khartoum and Bermuda, as well as South Africa. In the Great War (1914-18) Major Packe, as he then was, served in France and Belgium and was mentioned in despatches three times. He was awarded the DSO. He served under Kitchener and was responsible for ammunition and then, *for a rest,*[6] he was

---

[1] *Some time in the 1920s he was notified by the College authorities that because of his determination to play his part he could go down to Cambridge and sit his finals for a degree, which he did and was awarded a BA! (He must have been pretty rusty by then.)* Margaret Packe

[2] Piet Cronje, Boer general

[3] DE5047/168

[4] Margaret Packe still has the bullet, in a display cabinet.

[5] William Packe interviewed 2003

[6] *The Leics Mercury* 25th April 1953 recounting these achievements puts the phrase in inverted commas, to show the irony.

given a staff job in Ireland during the Sinn Fein rebellion! He had one more spell in India before retiring in 1920.

He married Olivia Rachel Nora Maclean in 1908 (in Pretoria). His first son, Charles William Christopher Packe, born in 1909 while they were abroad, became a talented cricket player. His second, Arthur James, was born in 1910[1], and the third, Robert Julian, was born in 1913. His fourth, Michael, born in 1916, was the only son to outlive him. Margaret, his only daughter and only remaining child, was born in 1921, at Stretton Hall.

The whole family were cricket supporters and at various times all four of the men were players, captains or secretaries, of Leicestershire County Cricket Club. William Packe, remembers that when he visited his uncle Christopher (ECP) at Stretton Hall: *We all played cricket. ECP would get twenty two boys and we'd all have a game in the park.*[2]

63. THE PACKE FAMILY

Picture from *The History of Leicestershire Cricket Club* of ECP with his three sons, Robert Julian, Michael St John and Charles William Christopher, and Margaret, his daughter.

ECP inherited the Stretton estates when his father, William James Packe, died in 1909 but he did not move in to the (still rented out) hall until he was retired from the army, aged 41, in 1920. Life was hard when the 1918 war ended. He had no

[1] Arthur died of tubercular meningitis at the age of 10, while he was at boarding school.

[2] Margaret remembers how much she would have liked to play. But when they needed an extra 'man' her playmate, Arthur Haines was put into overlarge gear and sent out to bat!

money beside his army pension. *My father was 41 when he went to Stretton* [Hall] *to live, in 1920. He had just retired from the army to rejoin his wife and young sons who had moved in before him. His wife had got very fed up with trailing around the world in the heat with the small boys.*[1]

They used to say there were 6 Rolls Royces in Glen before the First World War[2] but times had changed by the time Col. Packe arrived in Great Glen. He was not one of the Rolls Royce owners: he seems only to have driven an old Morris.[3] The estate was short of money and many of the Packe-owned houses and plots of land in the village were put up for auction. We see from the 1919 sale documents that many of the plots and buildings did not bring in much income. He had to sell off many lovely things in the house as well as farm-buildings and farmland belonging to the estate. When Theodore Walker, died in 1929, Col.Packe decided to sell Glen Hall, with vacant possession but at some point he changed his plans, and moved into Glen Hall, selling Stretton Hall instead His daughter Margaret was about ten when they moved from Stretton Hall into Glen Hall. Stretton Hall was then sold as a hospital.[4]

The Packes lived in Glen Hall from 1930 until 1953. The early years there must have been traumatic for the family. The Colonel's wife died in 1933, leaving him with his young daughter Margaret, who had developed poliomyelitis when she was about five in 1926.[5] His son Michael was at boarding school and the others had already left home for army careers. In 1935 his son Robert Julian, a promising cricketer, died of dysentery in India when he was only 22. His firstborn son, Major Charles William Christopher, died in the 1939-45 war (and is named on the village war memorial). As Wm Packe put it: *All the boys died unnecessarily young: Arthur aged 10, Julian 22, Charles 33 and Michael, the author of a very fine book on John Stuart Mill, died of cancer, aged 50 or so, on 21st December, 1978.*[6]

During the 1939-1945 war Col Packe was, of course, beyond active service age but became involved on the 'home front'. Soldiers were billeted in his outbuildings at Glen Hall and he also welcomed evacuees from London, going down to the distribution point himself and choosing brothers with sisters, '*because he thought they would be happier together.*[7] Many people living in Great Glen today have memories of Col Packe and he is universally spoken of with affection and with gentle amusement at his old fashioned and unworldly ways. *He was a real gent.*

---

[1] Margaret Packe Dec 2002-

[2] Fraser Gilbert.

[3] Joe Goddard remembers: *A shabby shooting brake driven at rural speeds.* Margaret Packe disputes the shabbiness and mentions how well Mr Haines looked after the car.

[4] To the Leics and Rutland Joint Board for the Mentally Defective.

[5] Five children in Glen village developed polio at about the same time.

[6] Wm Packe, interviewed in 2003.

[7] Margaret Packe. See Chapter 3.

Everyone respected him. They all knew him when he walked around.[1] They remember him with kindliness as a gentle man without pretensions. It is clear that they knew he had no wealth, they knew he did not live extravagantly, they knew he did not pay well but they liked him and understood his position: *Col Packe was a gentleman. He was very well liked but didn't pay his employees well.*[2]

There are many anecdotes of his somewhat absent-minded manner. Walter Allen tells how the colonel would always stop on his way to church to talk to the bell ringers about the cricket *and he'd do all the actions with his stick and it'd get to twenty or half past eleven and he'd say, 'Oh well, I'd better go. Never mind! I'll be in time for the collection.' He had a dog that'd silently be chewing your coat and people went away with their coat all frayed and chewed by his dog, a Labrador. He didn't know it was doing it!* We hear, too, of his eccentric attitude to traffic, both in his own driving and his way of crossing main roads: *When he walked he had no idea of crossing the road; he used to put up his stick and just cross. The colonel had a car with a dickey seat.*[3] *He always drove us back from the Hall to the lodge at Christmas. Christmas at the hall was our treat. We all had to go at a certain time, say 7 o'clock in the evening. They'd have a huge, huge Christmas tree in their beautiful drawing room and the colonel used to present us with a gift, and it was usually a book. Very nice, a beautiful present. I remember having the same book bought for three years running and my mother told him it would be a good idea if we could have a book voucher or token!*[4]

People still speak of his kindness to them: *My brother actually lived at the hall when he was married in 1948 and waiting for a council house. The colonel said if they wanted they could live there with him in a separate room and bedroom and pay rent. So they did for quite a long time. The colonel was lonely and liked the company. Margaret was away at college.*[5] One resident described his kindness to her when she was little and suffering from polio. He provided a place to store her wheelchair for her: *I was on m' back for two years with polio (his daughter had it, too) and I had meningitis and he used to come and see me. I remember one day he come in and me Mam said—she knew who he was—he brought me a big basket with about three little kittens in, real kittens, 'cos I like cats, he brought them in and he were ever so nice. He had a hut, near Thorpe's, he kept my wheel chair there.*[6]

The latter years must have been a sad and lonely time for him. His gardener and housekeeper served him loyally and when he left Glen Hall in 1953, they moved

---

[1] Lilian Haines, later Gash, daughter of Col Packe's gardener and housekeeper .
[2] Tommy Clarke, interviewed by JP-A 2003
[3] A dickey seat, a folding seat at the back of a car (originally for servants). Margaret Packe says the car with a dickey seat belonged to her brother Charles.
[4] Lilian Haines
[5] Lilian Haines
[6] G Moody, interviewed before she died, in 2003, by J PHA.

with him to a matching house opposite Dell House, the smaller and more convenient modern home, designed by his friend, the architect Goddard. Joe Goddard, the architect's son, described ECP as: *very interesting to talk to. He was articulate and an elegant reasoner and speaker, very much of his time and class. He wrote that history of Glen.*

The *Leicester Mercury*, announcing the production of his book *An Empire Building Battalion*[1], describes him as the '*youthful 75 year old living in Dell House, with his Labrador and enjoying a five mile walk every day.*

---

[1] *The book traces the history of the 3rd battalion of the Royal Fusiliers from its formation in 1898 to its disbanding in 1922. ECP spent 10 years in compiling the book and writing it in longhand… A triumph of perseverance due to records being destroyed in the blitz and to Col Packe's failing eyesight. Much was drawn from his own personal diaries.*
Leicester Mercury 28 11 1956

An article in the *Leicester Mercury* for Remembrance Day Nov 8th 1958 notes the attendance of *'probably the oldest person at the festival, 81 year old Lt Col Edmund Packe DSO, OBE, DL, a much bemedalled veteran of three great wars. Col Packe and other older veterans (including 4 Chelsea Pensioners) marched forward as the band played the 'Boys of the Old Brigade'. Proud, standing erect, they were once more 'ON PARADE'.*

The colonel dressed up in all his medals outside Dell House, with the similarly styled house built for the Haines family in the background.

The picture is from the album of Joe Goddard, whose father designed both houses. ECP has signed it, very modestly naming Canaan, his dog, before himself.

Canaan and myself, ECP

The colonel lived at Dell House, until he died, at the age of 83 in April 1961, in the presence of Mrs Haines. He is buried in the churchyard with his wife and young son, Arthur.

CHAPTER 2 THEIR HALLS

Seats are the dwellings of the rich and opulent; in them kings and nobles and the order of the gentry reside. To their owners the Peasant bends his humble knee and approaches with fearful steps the stately mansion.

Throsby, *Excursions 1790*

Glen Hall

The story of the Packes in Great Glen begins with Glen Hall, built by 1830 for William Burton and bought by CW Packe in.1837.There is no mention of Glen Hall as a Packe property on the 1835 estate map, where the Stretton Estate land is coloured green.

The field on which it stands (in the centre of the picture) is labelled as belonging to Mr Wm Burton. In 1834 Glen Hall was *now in the occupation of the said Wm Burton.* CWP had bought the mill (at the bottom right of the map excerpt) by October 1836, from Sir Henry Halford, and acquired the green coloured areas later, in 1846, when he bought the Stretton Hall estate.

William Burton, who died in 1821, had bought the land from Sir Henry Halford in 1817. His son, another William,[1] had built the hall on the land in 1830 and started negotiations to sell it to CWP in 1835. It is described in the sale document as: *all that newly built capital messuage or dwelling house with stables, coach house and other outbuildings yards Gardens and Plantations near or adjoining thereto (18 and a half acres or thereabouts).*[2] By March 1837 he had purchased Glen Hall, for £2,550, and lived in it for a time.

A letter from Edith Lawson, one of CWP's nieces tells us: *In 1846 he lent my Father*[3] *the house at Glen for the summer months and we were all taken there and thoroughly enjoyed ourselves. He and Aunt Charles*[4] *lived at Glen when not in London while they were making the alterations at Prestwold to which we all went at Xmas time 1848 for a sort of house warming.*[5] In the 1848 Post Office Directory, Charles William Packe is recorded as being at *Glen cot* (a name for what is now Glen Hall). Edith Lawson confirms that it was afterwards rented, but does not remember the name of the tenant: *I think Glen was let after they went to live at Prestwold but I never heard who was there.* In fact it was leased to Anna Raymond by December 1848 for seven years at £130 per annum. She is named as resident in *Glen Hall cot* in the 1851 census, and is described as a landed proprietor living here, though born in France, in about 1806 (in the time of Napoleon!) a British citizen and now a widow aged 45.

The lease agreement, between Charles William Packe of Prestwold and Anna Raymond of Harrow Weald House, Middlesex, lays out the conditions *with regard to all that capital, Messuage or Mansion House with outoffices, stables, coach house, yards, gardens, pleasure grounds, paddocks, plantations, fish pond and other appurtenances adjoining and belonging and lately occupied therewith by the said Charles William Packe...And also that cottage at the entrance from the turnpike road now occupied by Henry Langley.*

She is to prune the fruit trees and *Protect the spinneys from cattle...And is to paint in a proper and workmanlike manner the woodwork and ironwork in the external part of the said Mansion house cottage and outbuildings and greenhouse or conservatory And to insure against fire* [with a reputable firm] *And not plough, dig up or break any part of the lawn, paddock or Pleasure Grounds And not mow or suffer to be mown for hay, nor fell lop or top any of the trees and not permit or suffer the fishponds or waters to be fished or drawn by nets or otherwise than by*

---

[1] born 1804, died in 1856, buried in Glen but described as resident in Thornton Heath, Surrey.

[2] DE 803/22 sale document March 1837

[3] Edmund Packe, CWP's youngest brother.

[4] *Aunt Charles* is the name used by the family for Kitty Packe Reading

[5] DE 5047 171 letters written to EC Packe by his aunt Edith Lawson when he was writing his history of Glen, answering questions regarding CWP, her uncle.

angling therein. She may enjoy the right to game but may not make any alterations to the said messuage or Mansion House or outbuildings or stop up any of the windows without the consent in writing of the said Charles William Packe.[1] And if she pays up and obeys these rules he promises *not to molest her as a tenant*![2]

She stayed about ten years and in 1858 Archibald Finnie, of Stackley Lodge, took over the lease of Glen Hall. Finnie was still there in 1861 but in 1862 his rent is recorded as due from his executors. (He had, presumably, died.) His place was taken by James Baillie, who is described in the 1861 census as a retired Naval Officer, aged 28, with his brother and five servants, resident at the hall. James Baillie appears as tenant in CWP's Account Books of 1862 and was still there in Nov 1865 when Packe took out a further mortgage for £6,500 on Glen Hall, *a Mansion House with offices, stables, Entrance Lodge, gardens, pleasure grounds, fish pond* ***now in the occupation of Capt Baillie*** *with Water mill, farm house with barn stables, cattle sheds and other agricultural buildings and a malt office and 13 acres of grass land adjoining in the occupation of Mrs Clements.*[3]

By 1869 a Captain Whitmore rented Glen Hall from November to April for £200 plus a cottage and stables for £41. He was succeeded, during Charles Packe's ownership, by Oswald Part, who left in 1886, explaining that he was now looking for a place with good shooting on site, as he is *too heavy to hunt and needs exercise.*[4] The next tenant, Theodore Walker, was not a hunting, shooting and fishing man but a successful industrialist. He began his long tenancy in 1887, initially with a lease of seven years, and proved to be an excellent tenant, improving the house and grounds beyond recognition. Charles Packe wrote enthusiastically about his new tenant to his brother William in1887[5]: *I think Walker seems to be a good tenant at Glen and, unlike the others, one who will keep up the place and is protecting trees.* Walker's lease was extended to fourteen years and he actually remained in Glen Hall until 1928, when he died.

Theodore Walker's father's firm, *R Walker and Sons* was the forerunner of Wolsey's. *In 1830 the late Mr Robert Walker, the founder of the business ... came to Leicester from Glasgow and entered the firm of Ann Wood and Son, whose business had been in existence since 1755. Mr Walker eventually succeeded to the business. In 1864 he erected a handsome block of buildings on the corner of Rutland St and Charles St. They also have a large mill at Abbey Park, Leicester and another at Fleckney with everything up to the very best modern standard.* The family firm was known for its modern methods and philanthropic attitudes, making

---

[1] Lease agreement Dec 15th 1848. DE 803/26. The wording is similar to that of other lease agreements.

[2] This is quite normal terminology!

[3] DE 803/24

[4] Letter Sept 28th 1886 DE5047/131

[5] See Chapter 1 part 3 page 5

careful provision...*To secure health, comfort and personal safety of their employees whom, it is pleasing to note, are not regarded as 'hands' but as intelligent servants of their employers, and are treated as such...Most amicable relations exist between employer and employees...Just and considerate dealings (from employers) and respect and confidence (from employees)...They employ 1,000 workpeople plus work given out to be done by others at their homes.* They *introduced the manufacture of Scotch lambs' wool hosiery into Leicester. In every respect the house stands in the very first rank in the hosiery trade.*[1]

The article goes on to tell us that Theodore and his brother Ralph were both born in Leicester and educated there and at Amersham Hall, Reading: *Both do a great deal of good and useful work of a religious and philanthropic nature. Their grounds are frequently placed at the disposal of temperance societies, Sunday schools, treats and entertainments – to advance social, religious and intellectual welfare of the busy workers of this great industrial centre. Mr Walker took great interest in what was to become the Salvation Army... until his health broke down and he had to go to live in the country. He toured the world with his wife to visit their son in India and wrote a detailed account of the journey in one of the local papers. He mounted and presented the first ten cases of British birds and nests to the Natural History Museum at South Kensington.*[2]

The Leicester Guardian praised Theodore Walker for his philanthropy. *Mr Theodore Walker, one of the best known gentlemen in the town, always to the front in social, religious, philanthropic and temperance work helped to found Melbourne Hall church and was its first Sunday School Superintendent (and stayed for ten years).*
He was a member of the Royal Geographic and other learned societies and had a deep interest in natural history: *Only this year he has conferred a benefit in the Abbey Park. He laid out that pretty rock garden at Glen station, so attractive a feature on this section of the Midland Railway...He delights in flowers and gardens and at Glen Hall he has laid out a Japanese garden, in which no expense has been spared to make it look like a real bit of Japan.*[3]

---

[1] LRO L920 *Men of the Period* 1897
[2] ibid
[3] LRO *Leics Guardian* (Wyvern) May 28th 1904

Theodore Walker's Japanese garden.[1]

The beauties of Mr Walker's landscaping are mentioned in a book of rambles written in 1911 where a walk from Glen to Burton Overy is described: *A finger post near Glenn church mutely endeavours to send people to Burton Overy by road but, disregarding its advice, continue as if for Kibworth until the lodge and drive to Glenn Hall (the residence of Mr Theodore Walker) is reached on the left.*

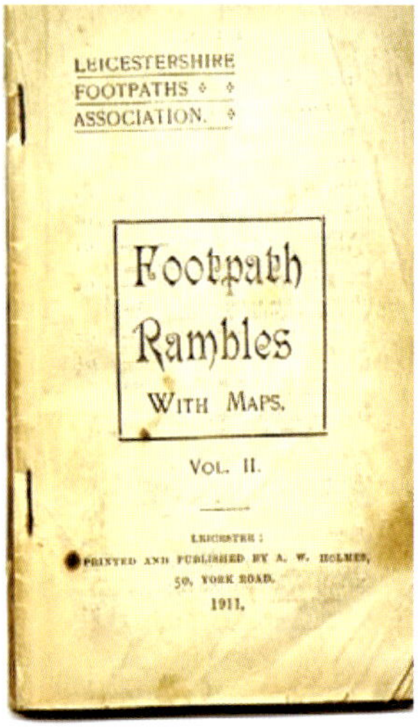

A footpath commences at the lodge gate to the road – it turns right by the fish pond and here discloses a pretty scene. The pond is fringed and screened from the road by lofty trees. The silver stems of the birch (the lady of the forest) are reflected in the water, and the cut-leaved elders seem amphibious with their roots apparently from the lake and branches overhanging. See, on an islet, a Shinto temple, flanked by stone lanterns, repeated in the wave as though nature loved such things of beauty. On a larger island is a red Toru – a Shinto symbol of nature worship. Chinese geese, with their pretty striped necks, are swimming about and carefully watching over their new-hatched brood.

Between the gates by the spinneys is an old icehouse

[1] Photo courtesy Margaret Packe. from Theodore Walker's album. The Japanese exhibition in London 1862 gave rise to much interest in things Japanese and inspired Gilbert and Sullivan's comic opera *The Mikado,* 1885.

formerly with a bed of nettles on top, now converted into a Swiss chalet with broad roof, outside stairs and carved balustrade, a faithful copy of a Bernese Oberland chalet. The wide overhanging roof is intended to keep the snow off, and the brick building below is an imitation of the hovel where the cows are kept in the winter. It has been the endeavour of Mr Walker to make the ugliest spots the most beautiful: take this walk and judge how far he has succeeded in his happy quest.
After feasting our fancy and imagination on this tranquil scene, return to the road and continue for 200 yards until the picturesque cottages known as Glenn Mill are reached.[1]

In 1871 Theodore married Anne Roberts (the eldest daughter of Alderman J K Roberts JP, who was Jubilee Lord Mayor of Manchester and one of the principal founders of the Welsh University at Aberystwyth. He appears in the 1901 census living with Theodore and Annie at the Hall, when he was a widower aged 83). William Ralph, brother of Theodore, married Anne's sister Ala four years later. Theodore and Annie had three sons (Ernest, Herbert and Robert) and three daughters. One daughter, Frances Evelyn (Fanny), married the Rev. Mr Anderson and was godmother to Col Packe's daughter Margaret. Theodore bought Rupert's Rest[2] for Fanny in 1915.

Theodore played a full part in village life, was a member of the school governors and when he died it was as a tenant and friend of Colonel Packe. Great Glen church has a stained glass window dedicated to Theo's wife, Annie Walker, who died in 1910 and another to Mrs Ernest Walker, his daughter in law, who died in 1927. He also presented half an acre of ground to be used as an additional burial ground, in memory of his son Lt. Robert Walker.

Walker family gravestones near the London Road churchyard entrance.

[1] Leics Footpath Association Footpath Rambles p 259
[2] Ruperts Rest see chap 3 part 1

When Walker died, in 1928, Col. Packe put the hall up for auction:
For sale by Auction Tuesday May 7th 1929 at Three o'clock. Messrs Warner, Shepherd and Wade and PL Kirby 16-18 Halford St.
One of the best known of the lesser Country Mansions for many years the residence of the late Theodore Walker, Esq, protected by a Substantial Entrance Lodge.

General Notes and Stipulations. Stone Japanese lanterns and other ornaments in grounds will be left by the tenant free of charge if Purchaser requires. If not, the tenant will remove same. Viewing by card from the Auctioneers for presentation at Main Entrance Lodge.
5 receptions. Billiard room. 13 bedrooms and dressing rooms. Top floor 2 maids rooms. Bathroom. Electric light. Central heating Robin Hood Junior Independent boiler. Stabling for 12 horses. Stable block surrounds Spacious Yard with walled manure pit in centre. Cow sheds for 5 cows. Spacious tennis and pleasure lawns.

Ornamental lake Japanese and alpine gardens Woodland walks. Entrance Lodge, 2 cottages and land. Vacant possession after June 25th 1930. Tel Gt Glenn 5.

On the north a sunk Japanese garden laid out by Mr Walker in a picturesque dell, originally a disused gravel pit. Oriental temple and Japanese House. This garden is at present time submerged.

Ornamental lake *2.75 acres in extent with wooded islands, walks, boat house, Swiss chalet summer house and another wood built arbour. Lake stocked with pike, perch and natural haunt for Wild Fowl.*[1]

In those days that pond used to freeze up solid and they used to floodlight it and go skating on it and my wife's brother (Harry Smith) went through the ice and had to be rescued and he was taken up to the hall and slept there all that night. (Stan Gibson, speaking of about 1920.)

[1] DE 4674/263 Glen Hall sale particulars. Picture of Glen Hall lake c. 1900 courtesy Fraser Gilbert

Miss French, our infants teacher, used to take us on rambles through the gate opposite your house[1]*, into the spinney and all round the back of the lake and there was all these Chinese and Japanese houses, past the ice house and through another gate at the back of the hall, where there was more Japanese garden. It wasn't a right of way. She had permission. And then we turned round and came back down the drive.* (Stan Gibson.)

Glen Hall lake today. The swans have gone but the herons remain, with ducks and geese, and children to delight in the scene.

In fact, Col Packe did not sell Glen Hall, but decided to keep it as his family home and to sell Stretton Hall instead. The family lived at Glen Hall, from 1929 to 1953, when the Colonel moved to Dell House, newly designed and built for him by his friend Goddard.

Dell House, newly built in 1953 *a much more modern, manageable and comfortable house than Glen Hall.*

[1] Gamekeepers Lodge

Dell House 2004

Mr Gill, owner of Dell House in 2003.[1]

From Dell House, the Colonel was able to see many changes to the hall.
Mr and Mrs Fox, the new owners in 1953 made substantial alterations to the house and to the lodge house. Margaret Packe recalls that her father was worried that the hall would collapse when Fox knocked down the back half.

Margaret Packe remembers the hall as a wonderful place for children to play! It was twice the size it is today, having sizeable farm buildings, with stables and tack rooms and a pigeon loft and dovecote, a cobbled yard and a midden. She remembers the massive back door and the laundry and a big clock on the buildings at the back of the house. *There were dingy kitchens and back stairs to the second*

[1] Mr Gill died in 2004

floor with two maids bedrooms and a bathroom (the Haines family[1] *came for baths), two back bedrooms and two more bedrooms and a big nursery with two windows next to the colonel's bedroom. The stable block was converted into a scullery and butler's pantry with a stone flagged corridor to the colonel's study and the billiard room. There was a meat safe in the wall into the kitchen garden, a coach house, stables, pumps, rats and a tack room with a side saddle.*[2]

The hall was sold again in 1975 to Bruce Fletcher, the builders, and again in 1977 (for £55,000) and in 1979 to Invicta Plastics. It was left empty and became run down, to be sold again in 1981. The sale description of the hall demonstrates a sad fall from its former glory: *Great Glen Hall sale by private treaty 1981 Shakespear, McTurk and Graham by direction of Invicta Plastics with vacant possession upon completion. Magnificent Regency House.*

The agents understand it to have been built about 1839[3] *under direction of the Packe family,*[4] *requiring further modernisation. Ground floor windows boarded up. Viewers are advised to take a torch. Boating lake. 2 redwoods. Stabling suitable for several horses. Listed building Grade II. Boiler room with Robin Hood boiler. Not now in working order. At the entrance to the hall is a small gate lodge which again requires modernisation and improvement and this could be made into a delightful separate cottage.*

The hall is now a family home, but without the wealth and servant power which originally gave its grounds such grandeur.

[1] The housekeeper and gardener's family.
[2] Margaret Packe
[3] Factually incorrect. It was built by 1830.
[4] Not true. The agents understood wrongly.

Stretton Hall

The seat of Sir George Robinson, not now used as a family residence; it was formerly the dwelling of the respectable family of Hewit. The hall was built by the Hewits.
Throsby, *Excursions* (1790)

Stretton Hall 2004.
The 1715 date stone is low down to the right of the front door.

Dame Dorothea Hewitt, who inherited the property, was married to Sir George Robinson and they leased it in 1836 to John King. In 1846 CWP bought Stretton Hall, paying £30,000 to the Rev Sir George Stamp Robinson. He thereby became Glen's Lord of the Manor but did not, in fact, live in the hall.

The block on the left, with the ballroom/billiard room, is a later addition, from the time of Charles Packe.

The hall was never lived in by CWP but was let out on lease, to John King. Many rich and famous people rented rather than bought residences in this period and John King remained as the Stretton Hall tenant for over 35 years.[1] In the 1851 and 1861 census he is described as a magistrate aged 69, with wife and two unmarried daughters aged 38 and 34, and a lot of servants. He lived in Stretton Hall until 1870 and in the 1871 census his two daughters were still resident there.

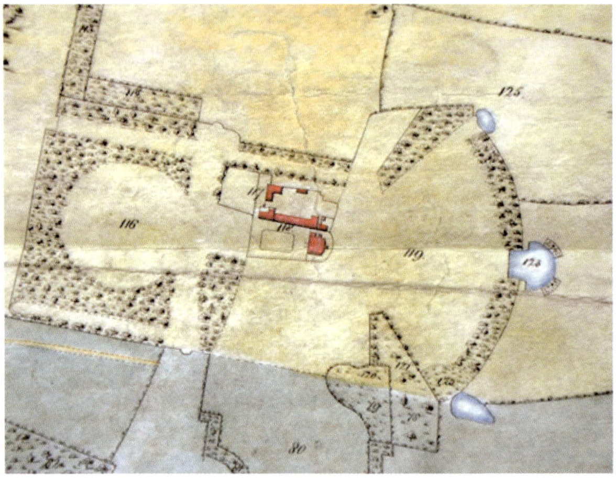

A plan of Stretton Hall with its pleasure grounds at the time of its lease to John King. From the 1835 Robinson map. DE 1215/2

CWP still had his main residence in Prestwold Hall at this time as well as his 'cot' at Glen Hall and after 1854 he also had his 'custom-built' Branksome Towers in Dorset, where he died and was interred in the mausoleum in 1867. His widow Kitty Packe Reading also died at Branksome in 1870, leaving their estate to their nephew, Charles Packe. He took on the inheritance with enthusiasm and immediately decided to sell Branksome Towers and to settle in Glen, where he had the choice of Glen Hall or Stretton Hall as his main residence.

His first intention[2] was to let Stretton Hall (to a Mr Farquhar) and he wrote to Mr Miles, his agent in Glen: *There is no time to be lost in putting the house in repair as no one can inhabit it in its present state, neither is it fit to receive furniture. I have pretty well made up my mind that new offices must be built on the ground floor extending into the yard on the east side: that is a kitchen, scullery, pantry and housekeeper's room: the servants hall might remain below stairs but I am sure that no family would like to go there with the offices as they now are. The range of stabling, domestic offices, cottage, barn might stand over for the present till I see who is coming for a tenant. Let me know if you have heard from Mr Farquhar: but I want the repairs to be commenced at once and to be done in a substantial and thorough manner. Please answer to the above address. I go to Branksome on Fri May 6th*

---

[1] DE 1215/3 Lease to John King 1836

[2] In a letter from 1 Stanhope Place, Hyde Park (April 29 1870)

He gives the same information again to Mr Bouskell, his Leicester solicitor, on *May 6 1870. I have written to Mr Miles to give orders for putting Stretton into repair at once; and have no doubt if it does not suit Mr Farquhar we shall find another tenant at Michaelmas but Branksome must be off my hands as I cannot undertake the expense of keeping that up, beyond the autumn.* Mr Bouskell replied on May 2nd 1870: *When you spoke to me as to residing at Glenn or Stretton I told you I thought the former was preferable. Since then from what I hear as to the large outlay required for the stables before a gentleman would take it for hunting I have altered my opinion.* Charles took his advice and then leased Glen Hall to various tenants including Oswald Part and Theodore Walker. He undertook the improvement of Stretton with gusto and paid promptly for all the services. Knowledgeable and well informed as a botanist, he planted a number of unusual trees at Stretton Hall. He and his (long suffering) wife Selina lived in the hall until his death in 1896. From his letters we get a good impression of his interest in the place and we know of his desire to be buried (with his dogs) in the dog park at Stretton.

When Charles died, his brother, the Rev William James Packe, inherited. He refurbished the hall again but remained living at his vicarage in Feering, Essex. In correspondence with his clerk of works he says he is too busy to visit Stretton and receives the reply on Nov 16th 1899: *I am pleased to say the work is progressing satisfactorily and by the time you pay us your next visit you will see a great change.*[1] In Nov 1900 there is correspondence with Halford the builders on the subject of water closets and cisterns, rods and water. In another letter, Charles Dixon, the incumbent tenant, writes for expert opinion on the latest mode of lighting and for permission to change the billiard room: *The billiard room is very useful for dancing as it has a door into the garden. The place is looking very pretty and I hope you will be able to find time to come and see it. I shall leave Peake in charge with some servants. Peake, as you said, is a splendid old fellow. I wish there were more men like him.*

William Packe was resistant to the idea of Mr Charles Dixon's moving the billiard table from the billiard room as *the floor is supported by piers on purpose to take the legs of the table.* He is also dismissive of the idea of 'a gas engine to pump water from the well'. *I am told a lad can quickly do the pumping. There is a prospect of a scarcity of water over a bit and I fear Mr Dixon will have to be a little less lavish in his use of it or these wells will soon be dry.* Clough Taylor, Packe's agent, explains that Mr Dixon wants the oil engine not only to pump water but to generate electricity so that he may light the house and W J Packe replies that he doesn't want to be involved in the expense of a pump for a boiler and certainly doesn't want electricity for lighting in the house. *Sorry I do not like the idea of the electric lighting. I cannot have the walls and ceiling pecked about for the wires and fitting*

---

[1] DE 5047/9/1-21

which at the end of his lease will not be required. (WJP was known to his family as 'Mr No' for his initial reaction to any suggestion! There is however a receipt from Wm Freer dated Dec 1901 for heating apparatus fixed at Stretton Hall, so presumably WJP relented a little. He paid his London solicitor £251 for discussing plans, visiting the site, surveying buildings and drainage, preparing plans, meeting and discussing and sending altered plans and estimates, working drawings, obtaining tenders etc and in Feb 1902 he paid the architect £75 for increasing the stable accommodation.)

When WJP died in 1909 his son, ECP, inherited, but continued to lease out both halls because he, a captain in the army, newly married and with a young child, was living and serving abroad. Capt Packe (later a major and Lt/Colonel) did not come to live in Stretton Hall until he retired from the army in 1919. Margaret Packe, who was born soon after her father came to live at Stretton Hall, remembers the huge ballroom, where she and her brothers played games of cricket! Her great friend, Arthur Haines, the son of Mr Haines, the gardener, lived with his family in the lodge adjacent to the hall.

Stretton Hall lodge, adjacent to the back of the hall. Margaret Packe and young Arthur Haines were neighbours and playmates here.

Margaret remembers going as a little girl, down the long drive to the South Lodge with messages to Mrs Adams who lived in the lodge house. (Her brothers were friendly with Arthur Adams and the Capell boy, who worked on the estate.)

Stretton Hall Lodge house, rented in 1930 by Mrs Adams (for £7 16s 0d per year). The house has been much enlarged, with an additional porch in 2003. The drive to the hall was moved from one side of the lodge to the other.

The house is marked as the Lodge house, plot 119, on the Conveyance map of 1930.

Peake's Cottage is marked with a dot on the Conveyance Map, near plot 73. Peake was described as *a splendid fellow* looking after the hall and grounds in 1900. *I shall leave Peake in charge.*[1]

In 1930 the cottage was let to Mr James Williamson on a weekly tenancy at a rent of £13 a year.

Peake's Cottage in its woodland setting

[1] Correspondence re tenancy of Stretton Hall between WJP and Mr Dixon. .

Conveyance map of Stretton Hall1930.[1]

Much of the land was rented to Mr W H Heard[2] for £122 10s 0d per annum. Stretton Hall farm was let to Mr Heard and Mr F C Hallam at £242 10s 0d a year. A road opposite the farm drive now leads to Peake's cottage.

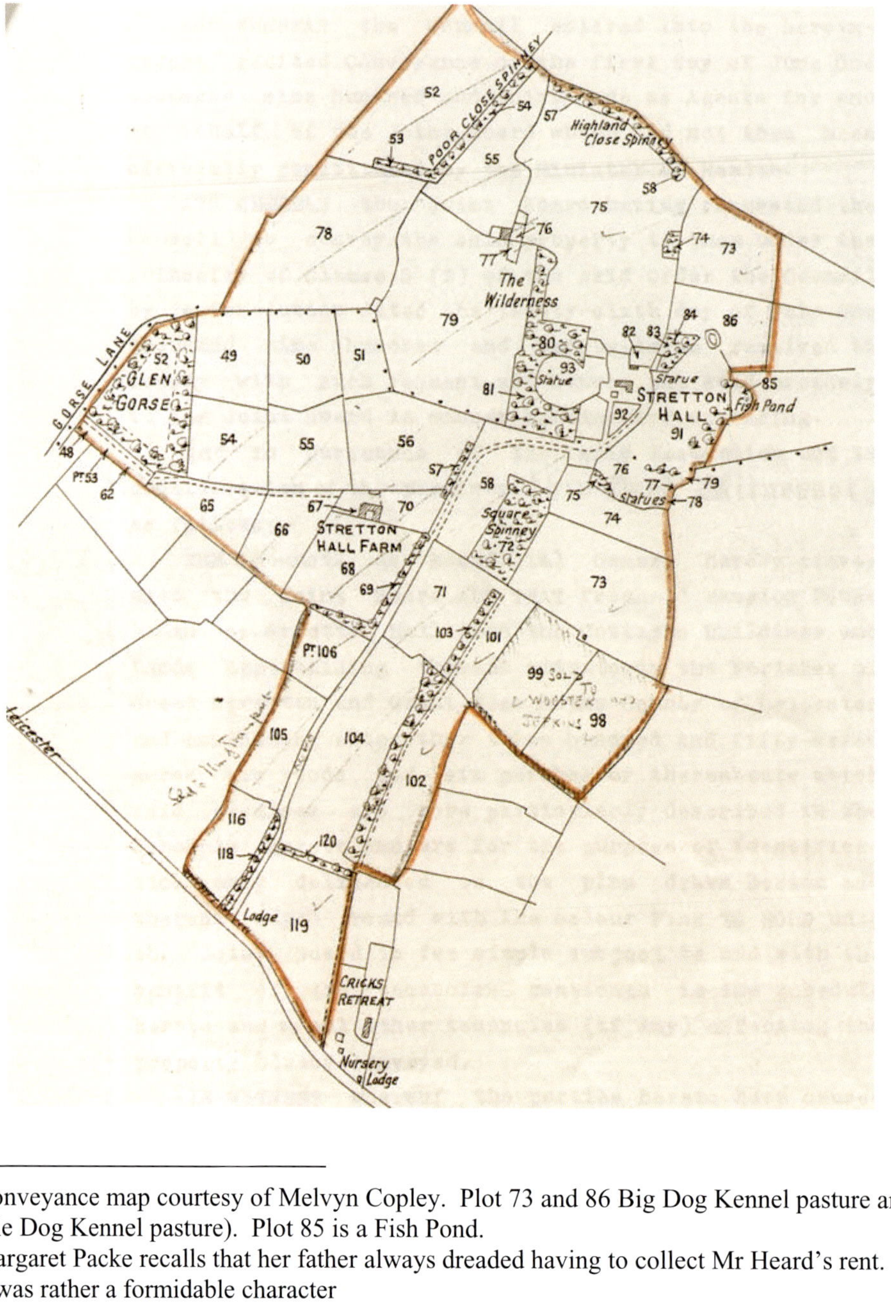

---

[1] Conveyance map courtesy of Melvyn Copley. Plot 73 and 86 Big Dog Kennel pasture and Little Dog Kennel pasture). Plot 85 is a Fish Pond.

[2] Margaret Packe recalls that her father always dreaded having to collect Mr Heard's rent. He was rather a formidable character

Stretton Hall and grounds taken from the air. [1]

The front of the hall looks out to the right of the picture. Stretton Hall Lodge is slightly left of the hall. The circular lawn top left is plot 93 on the conveyance map. It is now a housing estate.

Stretton Hall stood facing a field with a small pond (not a lake as at Glen Hall) at the bottom, the dog park would have been within sight on the left of it. [2]

When Stretton Hall was sold to the Health Service it became a *Hospital for the Mentally Defective.* Many residential buildings were erected within the grounds and this naturally detracted from the beauty of the original layout. But the grounds to the east of the Hall remained undamaged and the gardens continued to be well kept. *Don Spencer, the groundsman was the best in the county. In the walled garden we grew flowers for all the hospitals in the area.* [3]

The hall has been recently converted into three dwellings and the gardens have been lovingly cared for. But the rest of the land has been sold to David Wilson's building firm, which has built an estate of mini-mansions and a network of roads

---

[1] Photograph courtesy of Nigel Hurst, who worked on the estate for some years

[2] Margaret Packe

[3] Melvyn Copley.

beside the listed building. The hall remains standing but has lost, on its western and northern sides the glory of its original setting in extensive and beautiful grounds.

View over plot 76 towards the *statue*, 78 (obelisk) which can be seen beside the pair of trees in the background to the right of the cedar tree by the bridle-gate

CHAPTER 3 PACKES IN THE VILLAGE

Great Glen consists of 80 dwellings. The principal landowner is Sir George Robinson, Baronet. Robert Hames Esq lately high-sheriff for the county, and Mr Cooper, residents here, own each of them a portion of the lordship.

Throsby, *Excursions,* 1790. No.XXII p.319

Charles William Packe and Kitty Packe Reading

Great Glen was an important settlement long before the Packes arrived. It had been granted a market when the Martells were Lords of the Manor[1] and the village was called Glen Martell. In 1495 the Martell Manor House was sold and by 1660 it had disappeared. We do not even know where it was situated. By 1711 Stretton Hall, possibly built on an older site, had become the base for the Lord of the Manor.
When the Packes became Lords of the Manor, by buying Stretton Hall in 1846, they touched upon every aspect of village life: the church, the school, the parish councils, the workhouse, the water supply. They built and bought houses and acquired many tenants. Glen was a thriving village, served by two coaching inns, The Crown and The Greyhound, on the Turnpike road. It had about 160 houses and 743 inhabitants (in the 1831 census) and 190 houses and 795 inhabitants in 1841. It was served by an ancient church, a new Wesleyan chapel (built in 1827), various schools, several pubs and beerhouses, shops, trades, a framework knitting industry, a local policeman and a Workhouse (The House of Industry, which closed in 1846) with 17 inhabitants and a master and matron.

We do not know if CWP played much part in the village before he became Lord of the Manor but he was an MP, living in Glen Hall, and Glen residents were his constituents, even though most of them did not have the vote.[2] Nor do we know if he had time or inclination to consort with his near neighbours in the fine, recently improved or restored, houses on the Green or in The Nook and Orchard Lane. Sir Henry Halford, his fellow MP, lived at Wistow Hall and could have been on his visiting list[3] but Sir George Robinson who owned Stretton Hall, was not resident there. The landed gentry of Glen were not of Packes' class, although some were landowners named in the Enclosure Award and many of them became CWP's tenants when he bought the Stretton Hall estate. CWP had bigger fish to fry and although he entertained his family in his *cot* (Glen Hall), his other visitors went to the more impressive Prestwold Hall, when he lived there (late 1837-1858).[4]

---

[1] John Nicholls: *History and Antiquities of Leics* 1798. Vol ii The Gartree Hundred. Roger de Martivall 1303

[2] Universal male suffrage did not arrive until later, in 1867, and even then the vote was only for men living in houses valued at more than £10 per year in rent.

[3] Halford's predecessor visited the Packes at Lowesby Hall. See Chapter 1 KPR

[4] Chapter 1. KPR notebook

Looking at the maps of the Stretton estates in Glen in 1835, reading the Valuation lists of 1837 and the account books of CWP and KPR (1862-1870), we see the way the Packe property expanded in their time. It continued to expand under Charles Packe, who also built houses and who helped in the restoration of the church and concerned himself in affairs of flood and drought. His brother Wm James did not take up residency in Glen when he inherited the estate and we can then detect a falling away in the Packe expansion in Glen. By the time his son, Col EC Packe, inherited, money was short and times were hard. We can see the fall in the Packe fortunes in Glen after the War of 1914-18 by looking at the sale in 1919 of their houses,[1] many of which failed to reach their target price. There were further sales in 1929-32. ECP sold Stretton Hall and moved into Glen Hall, which was in turn sold in 1953. He then moved into the much smaller establishment of Dell House.

It is a story which mirrors the rise and fall of many upper class, wealthy or aristocratic families in the nineteenth and twentieth centuries. It is also a story of the contrasting fortunes of the working class villagers, many of whom moved from the utter poverty of agricultural labouring and framework knitting, through wars and unemployment into the improved standards of living we see today in the houses of Great Glen. Our interviews with people who remember the village as it was in Col Packe's time and with people who live in houses built, bought or sold by the Packes show us the changes which have taken place in our lives and expectations.

We gather a great deal of information about ownership and occupation of houses in Great Glen, at about the time of Charles William Packe's arrival by studying the 1837 Valuation list.[2] This gives names of Occupiers and Owners of houses and land. The biggest house-owner in 1837 is Robert Haymes, who has twenty eight cottages. The other wealthiest landowners do not seem to have invested to such a degree in houses for rent. George Cooper, for instance, is listed as having ten cottages for rent, and Sir George Robinson is listed as owning only six dwellings.[3] The Parish owned twenty four dwellings, mainly cottages, rented out at about £2 10s or £3 per year. Bigger houses were rated as worth £10 a year or more in rent. The most expensive houses in the village were privately owned and lived in by George Cooper (£32), Robert Haymes (£45), the Rev Corrance in the Vicarage (£25) and CW Packe in Glen Hall (£55).

Other quite wealthy people rented, rather than owned, their houses. Benjamin and William Cooper did not at this stage own their own houses but rented them. Many

---

[1] See Chapter 5

[2] QS 27/2/193. See Factfile at the end of the chapter for selected examples from 1837 Valuation. It lists houses above and below £10 a year in rent and it gives the Gross Estimated Rental per year and the Rateable Value.

[3] including Stretton Hall rented to Sir John King. Others are rented to Wm Clements at £14, Wm Oldacres at £16 and Wm Edgely at £5 per year. He has only two smaller cottages, rented by Wm Storer and Thomas Thompson at £2.10s a year. (RV £1 10s)

other people renting expensive houses also owned cottages which they leased out to others. James Lewin, the butcher, rented his home in Orchard Lane and owned nine cottages. Frances Burton (widow of Wm Burton) is listed as owning seven dwellings, mainly cottages. Abraham Wright lived in a house with an estimated rental value of £14 a year and he rented out cottages at £2, £3 or £4 a year.

Packe property, edged in red line.
Land acquired by CWP in 1835 coloured pink (Glen Hall)
Land acquired by CWP in 1846 coloured brown (Stretton Estate)
Land acquired later coloured yellow.

In the 1837 Valuation CW Packe is listed as owning only one house (Glen Hall).

The 1830s

When CWP bought the newly built Glen Hall and the old mill from Wm Burton in 1837, he would have had as near neighbours various impressive houses and two prosperous coaching inns (The Crown and The Old Greyhound) bordering the Turnpike Road. Since its opening in 1726 this road had cut the time of travelling. In 1811 the mail coach leaving London at 8pm was scheduled to arrive in Leicester (a distance of 98 miles) at 10.20am. By 1835 with speeds of 10 mph it arrived at Leicester (via Northampton and Market Harborough) at 5.48 am.[1]

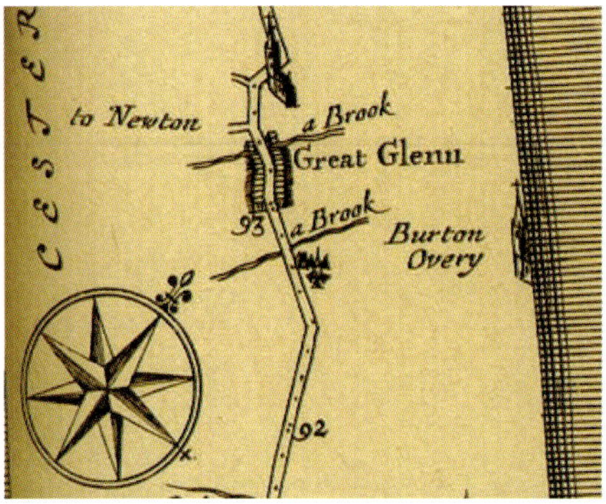

Ogilby's map of 1675, shows the road pre-Turnpike, with houses centred round what is now the Green. The church is top centre. The mill is marked with a symbol just below the Burton brook. The houses are indicated beside the main road between two brooks, the River Sence, and the Burton Brook. Mileage from London is numbered.

The Turnpike Road with easy access to London would have been a great advantage 'for CWP as an MP, commuting between Glen and the Houses of Parliament. Improved coach design and better road making techniques had led to increased speed, not entirely to everyone's satisfaction. The Leicester Chronicle reported on March 3rd 1827 the overturning of the Manchester to London coach at Great Glen with catastrophic consequences resulting from *the extremely quick mode of travelling adopted by the mails at the present time.*[2]

CWP himself complained, in his scrapbook[3] about the rumble of the heavy coach traffic waking him! *Lucubrations in the night of the 12th of Nov 1836 when the author could not sleep and listening to the coaches*[was inspired to write a riddle about the coaches]...*Passing night and day through Glenn.*

The Turnpike Road 1790

---

[1] Arthur Cossons, *The Turnpike Roads of Leicestershire and Rutland* 2003

[2] John Soer: *The Royal Mail in Leics and Rutland 1997*

[3] From the scrapbook of CWP, in Margaret Packe's possession

OGILBY'S ROAD MAP, showing Great Glen half way between Kibworth and Oadby and half way between Market Harborough and Leicester, 93 miles from London. 1675.

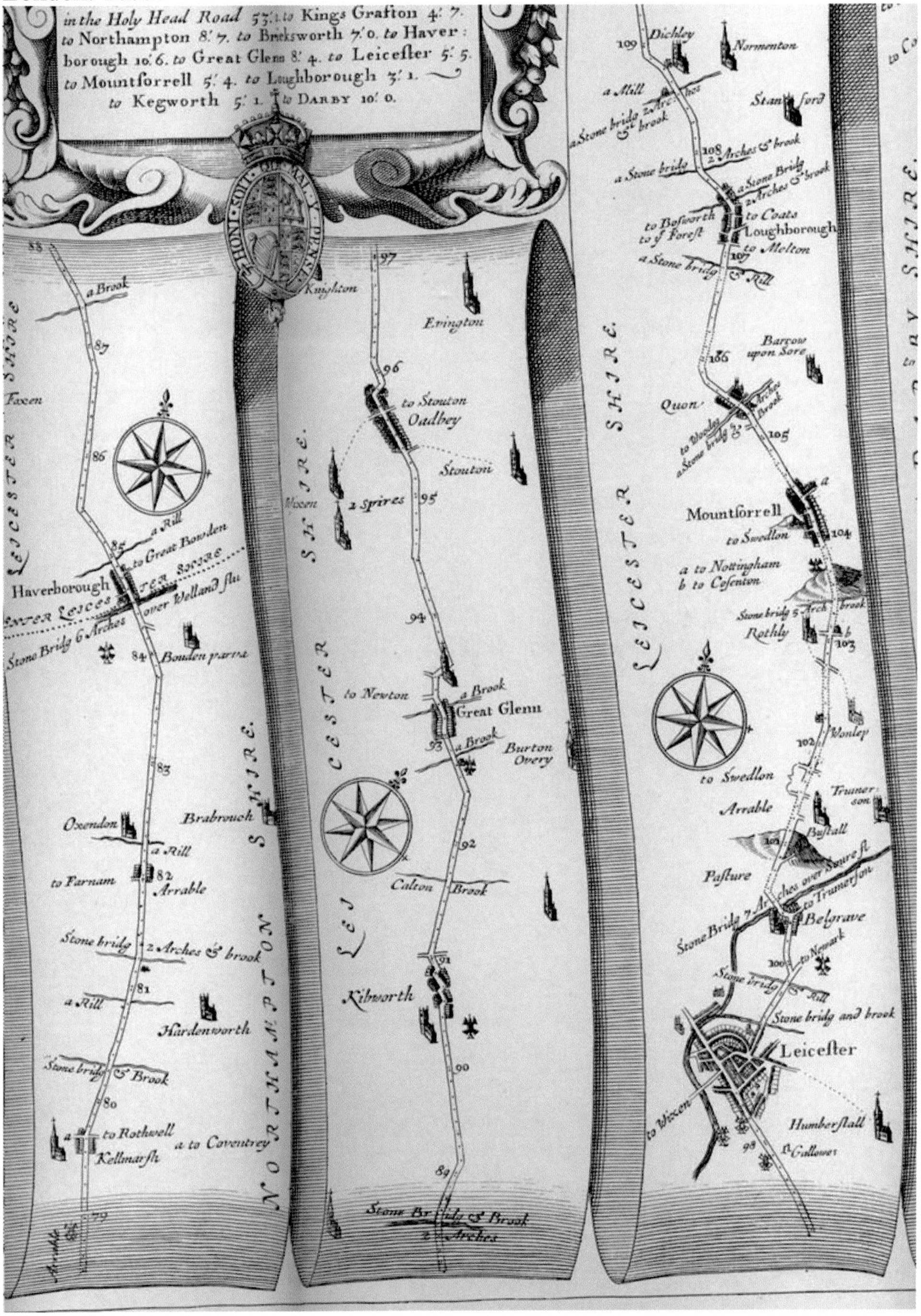

John Prior's map of 1777[1]

This shows the turnpiked road (with miles numbered rather differently from Ogilby's map) and the mill and the houses which were here before CWP arrived: buildings by the Green, and on Orchard Lane, Main Street, High Street, and Stretton Road. It depicts two roads going north to the Strettons, on either side of the river Sence. The one that continues from the end of High Street is now merely a bridleway but was formerly a main route.

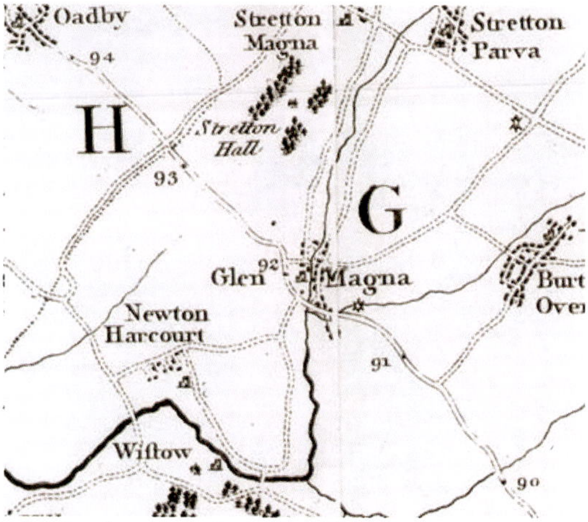

The buildings shown on Prior's map include the inns on the turnpike road:

The Crown, (confusingly referred to as 'The New Grayhound' (sic) in the 1837 Valuation) was owned by Beardsley and occupied by the Landlord, Green Hodgkin,

[1] John Prior: *Leicestershire in 1777* ed J D Welding

a widower with two daughters and a servant. By 1870, the inn had a landlady, Sarah Gilbert.

The Old Greyhound, owned by Burditt in 1837. The landlord, throughout the time of CWP, was Wm Norman, named in Pigot's Directory of 1830, the Valuation of 1837 and the census of 1861. By 1870 Jane Pick was the landlady.

The mill is, of course, marked, as another important village landmark. It was owned by Sir Henry Halford in 1837, with Wm Oswin as miller, and tenants Sam and Job Sturgess.

The mill houses would not have had this mock Tudor façade in CWP's time.[1]

[1] picture from Theo Walker's album, courtesy Margaret Packe

Prior also marks some houses on Orchard Lane, including Glen Farm, owned by Sir George Robinson in 1835. (See Chap 5 Lot 11)

Orchard House is on the left and Glen farm to the right of it.

Orchard Lane c.1900.[1]

Bridge House, dated 1748[2] is marked. It was originally three cottages, and remained as two separate houses into living memory

The building was bought in 1800 for £200.

[1] Picture courtesy Terry Sharp
[2] according to Jeffrey Whitelaw, *Hidden Leics and Rutland.*

Another pre-Prior building is Carlton Lodge. Parts were built about 1640.

The present house is a combination of two houses. The mansard roof was added much later.

Prior's map also marks The Yews, on the main London Road. The Yews built about 1760, described by Throsby in 1790 as *Mr Cooper's house, a neat dwelling but perhaps too near the road for a summer residence.*[1]

The Coopers were well-established landed gentry in Glen. George Cooper (1751-1831) had been allotted land in the 1790 Enclosure Award. He was an influential Dissenter and gave land for the building of the Methodist Meeting House in 1826. There are memorials to him and his wife Mary in the chapel.

Various branches of the family lived in The Yews, The Sycamores and Ruperts Rest and many of their gravestones can be seen in the churchyard. The Coopers were the top landowners and the biggest ratepayers in Glen until about 1900 when the Sprigge part of the family had taken their place among the top gentry.

On the 1835 Stretton Estate map,[2] Mr Cooper owns the land by Rupert's Rest, Mr George Cooper owns the land at The Yews and Mr W Cooper owns the land on the opposite side of the road. They also rented land from Sir George Robinson. When George Cooper senior died in 1831, his son George (a wealthy bachelor grazier)

---

[1] Throsby, *Excursions* 1790

[2] See Factfile at the end of the chapter.

inherited. The Yews was then valued at £32 rental per year.[1] It was later bought by Henry Coleman, another rich landowner. The auction sale document[2] of Oct 1871 announces the sale of the house, *under the will of the late Henry Coleman, deceased formerly in the occupation of George Cooper*. The Yews has had a mixed history since then, both as a billeting recovery home for soldiers in the first World War and later as a hotel and public house/restaurant.

The adjacent row of cottages and stables, formerly part of the grounds, have now been converted into one house.
Cottages and stables beside the Yews (now Wizards Haunt.)

A second branch of the Cooper family, Benjamin Cooper (1758-1823) and his wife Harriet Cooper (1775-1845), lived on the opposite side of the road in The Sycamores. Their son, William Benjamin Cooper inherited and lived here in 1851 with his wife and daughter, both called Elizabeth. After William's death in 1883 (aged 73) Elizabeth stayed in the house with a female companion and servant until she died in 1899 (aged 84).

The Sycamores[3] c 1900

Benjamin and Elizabeth Cooper's daughter Elizabeth (born in 1839) married a Dr Sprigge. The Sprigges are listed among the chief landowners in Glen.[4] Wm Benjamin Cooper Sprigge, died in a motor bike accident in 1924, aged 21.

---

[1] William, the younger son, rented a house at £20 a year but he bought Rupert's Rest from his brother George in 1838, rebuilt it and lived there until 1850 when he died. Neither of the brothers had children.

[2] 21D56/1

[3] Picture courtesy of Elizabeth Carr, a descendant of the Cooper Sprigges.

[4] Sprigges are listed with EC Packe and Sir Maurice Levy in directories of 1932 and 1941.

Another house which is marked on Prior's map is opposite the church on Church Lane. Throsby described it in 1790 as *a gracious house* and calls it *Mr Hames's house, situate at a little distance from the (London) Road.*

Hames's house as we see it today. The grand façade was added in 1874.[1]
(In some census documents the house is called Glen Hall but is not to be confused with the present Glen Hall, which was named in the census as CWP's *mansion* or *cot.)* The older parts of the house are behind it.

In 1837 it was valued at £45 rental per year. Robert Haymes, (1768-1855) lived here, opposite the church, in 1841. He was a big landowner named in the Enclosure Award of 1790 and became sheriff of Leicestershire in 1813. He was still here in 1851, aged 83, employing seven labourers, two carpenters, a stableman and boy. There are monuments to his family in the church, where he is described as *friend to the poor, the fatherless and the widow*. He gave funds to the framework knitting cause and in his will he made a charitable bequest to the village: *I give and bequeath unto the Vicar and churchwardens of the parish of Great Glen the sum of £100 on trust to invest the dividends and interest thereof to lay out annually in the purchase of Bread to be distributed to such of the poor people of the parish not receiving Parochial Relief ...on every Christmas day either before or immediately after Divine Service.*[2] It was this Robert Haymes who bought a couple of buildings in 1785 from someone named Strickland and converted them into the nine cottages now known as Peep Row, on Main Street.[3]

By 1937 the house was owned by Col. (or Doctor) Jamie, who made considerable alterations, adding a bathroom and demolishing stables and coal sheds.[4]

---

1 Architects plans for alteration of the house for the Rev R Haymes house. (11D58/4)
2 DE849/42 14/34-35 Robert Haymes' Will .
3 See Chapter 5 Lot 32 and 33.
4 DE 1388/P/348 See p109 for Miss Aston's account of working here for Dr Jamie.

Also marked on Prior's map, north of the church, is The Vicarage, described in such unflattering terms by George Boyle when he rejected the living in 1855.[1]

Drake's Directory of 1861 describes it as *a good residence near the church* when Henry Luke Dodds was vicar.

Also marked on Prior's map of 1777 is Chesterfield House,[2] standing on the Green. It was formerly called The Firs and lived in by Dr John Fewkes, official medical officer for the Workhouse and Medical Officer and Public Vaccinator in 1900.

Other buildings are farmhouses and a cruck cottage on High Street.

[1] see Chapter 4.

[2] Chesterfield House, picture beside the war memorial, page 102'.

Prior also marks houses on Main Street and on London Road.

Ruperts Rest, originally a much smaller house, was owned by George Cooper senior in 1786 and occupied by Mrs Burton, widow of William Burton, who built Glen Hall.
Wm Cooper bought it (for £700) from his brother George, and had it enlarged and rebuilt in 1838. In 1837 the house was valued at £15 a year in rental. In 1878 it was £37 per year. The romantic name of Ruperts Rest is not recorded in early documents. It appears in deeds after Thomas Crick bought the house.

Ben Moffat, a descendant of the Coopers, gives evidence for the name of Rupert's Rest: *There were Coopers already living in Great Glen at the time of the Civil War, and my mother (1904-1977) remembered her father sending for sale a gold watch that was believed to have been handed down through the family since Prince Rupert had given it to a Cooper ancestor in return for some favour. That Cooper was a yeoman farmer who then lived where a house called Rupert's Rest now stands in Main Street, hence its name.*[1]

The deeds of Rupert's Rest describe the house as *all that Messuage or tenement with the barns stables outbuildings yard garden orchard or backside and appurtenances in possession or occupation of the said Wm Cooper (by whom the said messuage had been lately enlarged and in great part rebuilt).*[2] We are told that: *When Wm Cooper departed this life April 5th 1850 his heirs put [it] up for auction at the Lion and Lamb Hotel, Leicester but no adequate bidding was made for the same.*[3]

The house remained unsold until bought by Thomas Crick. By 1910 the owner of the house (GER £45) was Robie Russell Goddard, a glove manufacturer. He sold it in 1915 to Theodore Walker of Glen Hall for his daughter, Fanny Anderson. The deeds refer to the house as: *known by the name of Ruperts Rest formerly in the occupation of Thomas Crick deceased then of Daniel Woodruffe or his under-tenants and now of Theo Walker or his under-tenants.*

---

[1] from a document kindly lent by Elizabeth Carr, sister of Ben Moffat.
[2] Deeds of Ruperts Rest kindly loaned by Alison Tasker 2004.
[3] Feb 1860 Conveyance to Thomas Crick

When the house was sold in 1979 the sale document[1] mentions *the imposing driveway entrance through double timber gates…hung from brick pillars with ball pediments, rendered brickwork with Swithland slate roof, exposed oak beamed ceilings and full length sash windows and early Victorian conservatory and stabling for three horses (with planning permission for conversion into two four bedroomed houses).* This planning permission resulted in the conversion of the stable block adjacent to Ruperts Rest into housing.

People living in the village today remember the stable arch between the two cottages next to Ruperts Rest before they were converted into one house, now 41 Main St. The central section was formerly a great arched stable gateway between

separate cottages, one being a butcher's shop and yard. The deeds include the names of the tenants of *those two cottages with the butcher's yard, formerly in the occupation of Thomas Batchelor and Widow Woodcock and now in the occupation of Green Achurch and George Ellson.* Green Achurch was the butcher here in 1848 [2] and George Elson ran a post office from his cottage in 1861[3] before his widow moved to Post Office Row.[4]

The White House was also standing when Prior made his map.

The White House, 25 London Road, was originally a smaller building. The chimneys mark the earlier extent of the house. The porch is a much later addition. Formerly called *The Cottage*, it was sold by the Halfords of Wistow, in 1780.

The story goes that in 1830 richly decorated pistols were found in the attic, which later led to the notion that Prince Rupert had stayed here when escaping from the battle of Naseby in 1645. Harwood Hill, however, states[5] that the house where Rupert rested was destroyed. The land was owned by Wm Horton, a carpenter with a son and an apprentice working for him, and his property was

---

[1] L333

[2] Post Office Directory 1848 (He appears as Green Haychurch, spelt with an aitch!.)

[3] Drake's directory 1861

[4] See Chapter 5 Post Office Row.

[5] Harwood Hill, *History of Market Harborough* 1875

valued at £50 GER in 1837. In the 1878 Valuation, Thomas Crick owned the house (GER £35) and rented it to Josiah Armitage.[1] In Kelly's Directory of 1888, Wm Throne Crick, a surgeon, was resident in *The Cottage*. It was owned by Frederick Crick and leased in 1910 to Dr Robert James Bonis, for £40 a year.[2] In Kelly's Directory of 1932, the owners were two Misses Thompson.

There are other houses which were certainly in existence when CWP came to the village, although they are not marked on Prior's 1777 map. He does not, for instance, mark the small houses in The Nook. Before they were improved and extended they may not have warranted his attention. They were not gentrified and enlarged until after his map was made.

The new frontage of number 5 The Nook, built in 1784 hides the much older cottages behind.[3] The bricks on the façade are inscribed with the date and the initials OW, TC, RH and WB. The initial WB refers to William Burton (born in 1748) who lived in this house and who built the new frontage.

William Burton was obviously a man of wealth and a respected figure in the village. His name was inscribed on one of the new church bells in 1783. He was a churchwarden (1785-1789) and an Overseer of the Highway (1790-91) and in 1817 he took out a mortgage for £500 to buy, from Sir Henry Halford, the land (costing £1,500) on which Glen Hall was built. He died, aged 73, in 1821 and it was his son, another William, who took out a mortgage to build Glen Hall in 1830. Young William then lived in the Hall before selling it to CWP soon after.[4]

---

[1] Josiah Armitage is described in the 1881 census as aged 68, with a wife called Ann Beaumont and a 25 year old daughter Elizabeth, all born in Yorkshire. There is no other census entry for Jos Armitage but his name is mentioned in various documents in 1830/34.

[2] (This is less than the figures quoted for The Sycamores, for example and both of these houses have a low value compared with Robert Kaye's Manor House, £176, Robert Rowley's house, on Church Lane, £104 and Stackley House £104.)

[3] The present owners found a wide cobbled way between their house and Bassetts, next door. Under the floor boards were bills for leather hides and receipts for leather work for EW Burton dated 1701 and 1705. They also discovered a delivery ticket label addressed to Miss Burton.

[4] William Burton's mother, Frances Burton, is included among the gentry in directories of 1835 and 1854.. She owned several houses and went on to live in Rupert's Rest. Her unmarried daughter Sarah continued to live here in The Nook. In 1851 Frances (aged 85) returned to live with Sarah until she died (aged 92). Sarah remained the householder until she died in 1866 (aged 64). Frances's granddaughter, unmarried still lived here in 1891

Bassetts, number 3, The Nook. (GER £26 in 1837.)

Here, too, the façade was added, in about 1840, to older cottages, seen at the back. The present owner points out the partly illegible date with initials inscribed high above the left front window. The present house was *formerly three tenements or dwelling houses, formerly used as a curriers shop, now one, with yard and homestead thereto adjoining and used as a bakehouse.* The bakehouse is described as having been newly built in 1775, converted from a currier's shop.[1] Wm Burton was a currier (leather tanner).

The original owners were the Beaumonts, followed by Franks, who married into the Beaumont family and owned ten houses in Glen in 1837. In 1804 the house was owned by John Bosworth and in 1809 by his son William Bosworth, an Overseer of the Poor[2] and a *constable* (an important office) of the House of Industry. In 1843 CWP paid Mr Wm Bosworth £850 for this *messuage or tenement with bakehouse and yard,* but Bosworth continued to live in the house.[3] (In the 1851 census he is described as a baker, aged 55, with three grown up children and two servants. Thomas Linthwaite, also a baker, aged 60, lived at the same address.)

The bakehouse can still be identified at the rear of the house. By 1878 CWP was no longer the owner: the Sykes family[4] leased it to Wm Allen the baker. The ownership came down eventually to a Miss Sykes who in 1909 let the bakehouse to Hubert Davis. When she died in 1913 she left *the house and bakehouse at Great Glen* to her niece, who sold it in 1946 to Kate Jefkins, of The Mount, for £1,360. Miss Jefkins sold it three years later for £2000 and in 1952 it was sold for double that amount.[5]

These are houses we know to have been in the village in 1835 when CWP arrived, either because they are marked on Prior's map or on the 1835 Stretton estate map.

---

[1] The conveyance of Dec 1886 gives the past history of the house.
[2] DE1667/16 Vestry Minutes
[3] DE 803/25
[4] The owner of the adjacent land is named as Robert Sykes on the 1835 map.
[5] I am indebted to Anthony and Penelope Simpson for this information.

Houses which were too late for Prior's map, do appear on the OS map of 1835.

The church, the hall and the mill are clearly shown. The Lodges are the Mount and The Sycamores. *Glen Industry* is the workhouse, before it was moved to Billesdon. The pubs and houses on London Road, Orchard Lane, The Nook, Main Street, Church Lane, High Street and Bindleys Lane are all indicated.

The 1840s.

We have information from the census about people who lived in the village in 1841. This gives us the ages (usually rounded down to the nearest 5) of all residents and the occupations of the men[1] with the names and ages of their children. It tells us whether the residents are male or female but does not give us the relationship of people in the house (whether husband, wife, son, daughter etc.) but it does tell us the names of the servants, and whether they are male servants (MS) or female (FS). Unfortunately, the addresses of their dwellings are not given and because the enumerators did not necessarily walk round the village in a set order to collect the census papers on the night of the census, it is not easy to discover where their houses were. We are told of a few and can work out some others. We learn which people had servants living in their houses, and can presume that these are in the houses of the wealthier families.

Houses with servants.

CWP's name does not occur in this census, which indicates that he was away from Glen Hall, possibly in his London house or at Prestwold Hall, but Henry Langley, the servant he brought from Hoton, near Prestwold, is recorded as being in the

---

[1] Very few married women are recorded as having occupations. Widows and spinsters like Martha Newton, schoolmistress and Mary Dencher, FWK, Sarah Hodgkin, haberdasher and Elizabeth a laundress aged 60, and Sarah Clement, farmer grazier, are recorded. The rest are wives and daughters.

Lodge house.[1] CWP doubtless had other servants living in the hall when he was at home, as did most of the local landed gentry.

Households with resident servants belong to: Robert Haymes, Frances Corrance the vicar, Sarah Clements, George Cooper Benjamin Cooper and Hannah Cooper. Their houses can be identified from other documents: Robert Haymes, aged 73, lived in the big house opposite the church with his son Thomas, a surgeon, and four servants. In the Vicarage, Frances Corrance (aged 55) with two young children, has four servants. Sarah Clements, farmer and grazier (aged 31, with six children under 12) has two male servants and one female living in North House. (We know from later documents that she was a widow, and that she was also the village postmistress,[2] so she really did need servants!) George Cooper (aged 50), living in The Yews, has two servants and Benjamin Cooper (aged 30), living at The Sycamores, with a wife and year old child has one female servant. Hannah Cooper (aged 60, of independent means), living with John (20) and Harriet (36), also has one female servant in the house.

Many of the other prosperous farmers had servants: Thomas Hobson (aged 40), a grazier living at The Mount, has three young children and two male servants; John Easom, farmer, with his wife and three children under 10, has a male and a female servant; Wm Higginbottom, a farmer aged 75 has two female servants and Wm Oldacres, another rich farmer with an elderly relative and a very young child in the house, has two male servants and one female; John Chapman a grazier (aged 30) has a male and female servant; Wm Bosworth the baker (in The Nook), a widower with three grown up children has one female and one male servant; William Horton, a carpenter (aged 58), has a son and an apprentice and a male and a female servant; James Lewin, a butcher (aged 35) with a wife and three children under 8 and a 15 year old apprentice, plus a 20 year old agricultural labourer, employs two female servants, aged 10 and 15. (It doesn't sound an easy job for such young girls!) Phillis Brake, the ex-teacher (aged 70), of independent means, lives with her daughter Elizabeth aged 37 and Grace Hodgkin (her sister) and one servant, to run her boarding academy for three children under 10.

It was not only the rich people in the biggest houses who had servants. Some of the professions and trades also had them. Martha Newton the schoolmistress, for instance, has a female servant, Sarah Dickman, living with her. The publicans, as we would expect, have servants. Wm Norman (aged 65), the publican of the Old Greyhound Inn, with seven children ranging in age from 35 to 6 months, has two

---

[1] We are told that Henry Langley is aged 35 with his wife Elizabeth and two children, William, aged 11 and Jane aged 9. Henry Langley is still there in 1848 in the '*cottage at the entrance to Glen Hall from the Turnpike Road*'. See Chapter 5 part 3.

[2] Hagar's Directory of 1849

resident male and two female servants. Green Hodgkin (aged 50) makes do with one servant and two daughters (aged 21 and 11) at The Crown.

We can pinpoint quite accurately where some of these people lived because they became tenants of CWP and are recorded on the 1835 Stretton estate map, which CWP acquired when he bought Stretton Hall. The deeds include the map and a list of Sir George Robinson's tenants, enabling us to see where some of the people lived, because the buildings they rented are coloured in red and the plots are numbered to correspond with the tenants' names. We know from this document[1] that Thomas Thompson was the tenant of a cottage at 33 (nearly opposite the old Fox and Goose), John Glover rented a cottage on plot 37 (near where the village hall now stands), Wm Storer lived at plot 38, Mr Cooper rented plot 36 (where CWP's school was built) and Wm Oldacre rented plot 31 (the corner of London Road and The Nook). Wm Burton lived at number 29 (in The Nook), Robert Sykes had plot 30 (a hovel in the field behind it) and James Lewin rented plot 25 (Glen Farm, Orchard Lane).

Trades without servants include several shoemakers, bricklayers, two carriers, two young surgeons, a farm bailiff, two tailors, blacksmiths, wheelwrights, a straw bonnet maker, two dress makers, a haberdasher, carpenters, a grocer, bakers, and a laundress (aged 60) living with a plasterer (aged 25) and his wife and young children. Green Achurch, a butcher with a wife and four children under 8 has no live-in servants. As for the rest of the inhabitants of the village, they are mostly framework knitters[2] and agricultural labourers.

Framework knitting.

Great Glen was a centre for Framework Knitting, formerly a profitable trade, which had fallen upon hard times. Framework Knitters' wages had fallen and we know that in the 1840s they were in a parlous state. By 1844 FWKs in Glen were earning only five shillings a week[3] and living in extreme poverty. As early as 1812 the poet Lord Byron had made an impassioned emotional maiden speech in the House of Lords on the plight of poverty stricken framework knitters. There had been uprisings and breaking of machines by Luddites, a massacre at Peterloo in 1819 and further riots in 1826. The poverty of framework knitters was a burning political issue.

---

[1] See Factfile at the end of the chapter.

[2] One framework knitter, Wm Chambers, lives in a house with Ann Flint aged 20 and Mary Elliott, who is described as a female servant but it is unlikely that she was the servant of the other two. They are all three aged 20 and Mary Elliott might work outside the home, as Henry Langley did for CWP.

[3] W Felkin, *Statistics of the Hosiery Trade*

In 1833 William Jackson, secretary to the FWK Society, had pointed out the contrast between the rich and the poor.[1] He speaks of *The Higher classes of society, that are possessed of capital* and points out that, in contrast to the FWKs, *They are not content to dwell in miserable habitations, to be clothed in rags, to have no bed to lie on and no clothing to cover them. You see that they occupy commodious mansions, that their houses are filled with elegant furniture, their persons adorned with costly apparel, and their tables furnished with the choicest food. To enjoy and perpetuate these blessings to their posterity is the constant aim of the higher classes.* He urged workers to copy their 'betters' in such matters: *We* [workers] *ought in this respect to imitate their conduct...to use every lawful means to live in comfort by* [our] *industry.*

This was pretty revolutionary stuff, despite the emphasis on 'every lawful means'. Poor people at this time had no voting power. The Reform Act of 1832, which had proposed universal suffrage (with votes for all men over 21) had not fulfilled the hopes it had raised. Most working men were excluded because they did not reach the £10 residency threshold.[2] The gap between the rich (with a vote) and the poor (without) was causing dissension, particularly in industrial towns. In Leicester and Hinckley there were meetings of Chartists to demand the vote for working men.

CWP had arrived in politics at a difficult time. He was, according to his obituary in the *Leics Chronicle*, a man *deeply attached to conservative principles* and his party was not sympathetic to the idea of votes for working men. *Household suffrage must have seemed to him synonymous with anarchy.*[3] Jackson lists the names of several of CWP's neighbours as *Gentlemen who have come forward as treasurers* to help the knitters. He has *a list of subscriptions already entered into to improve your condition.* These donors include Robert Haymes, who had donated £10 and Henry Halford, who had given £25, along with the Duke of Rutland (£311), Lord Robert Manners, MP (£25) and Sir George Beaumont (£10). This was two years before CWP came on the scene in Glen and it is difficult to know whether he would have wished to be included as a subscriber, had he been asked.

In 1844, when CWP was Member of Parliament for South Leics and resident in Glen, but before he became Lord of the Manor, Wm Felkin published his *An Account of the machine-wrought hosiery trade; its extent and the condition of FWK* and in 1845 the Hosiery Commission Enquiry investigated the state of the trade. The report of the Enquiry gives a picture of the social conditions of this major industry in the Midlands. There are over 400 pages of evidence for Leicestershire

---

[1] *An Address to the FWKs of Leicester* 1833 in *British Labour Struggles: Contemporary Pamphlets*

[2] The vote was only allowed to men owning or renting houses worth £10 a year or more.

[3] *Leics Chronicle* Nov 2nd 1867. See Chapter 1.

alone.[1] We can read the transcripts of the evidence given, by '*ordinary people speaking in simple language clear enough for children to understand.* It is heart-wrenching stuff.

There are two entries for Great Glen. Wm Grain, Parish clerk of Great Glen, a Frame Work Knitter for 53 years, gave evidence*: I went into the frame at 10 years of age. I have had good prices in my time and I have a very bad one at the present time; they are dreadful prices now. I am forced to work 5 days a week for 7/-. I am older than I was some years back and cannot do so much work. The General Conditions of people in the village are very bad.* He speaks of the decline in the number of knitting machines, which has dropped to 100 frames from the 175 of fifteen years earlier. As for the workers: *Part have left the village and part have gone into agricultural work.*[2] He is comparatively fortunate in that he gets paid in cash but finds the deductions for supplies very hard: *I work to Messrs Biggs direct, not through any undertaker [middleman]. We get the wages in ready money, with deductions: Frame rent 1s 6d, needles 2d, candles, half a pound at least, 3d.* (A shilling and eleven pence is a lot to deduct from a weekly wage of seven shillings!) He works in his son's shop: *My son takes them [the knitted goods] in every week or fortnight or whenever they order.*

The other witness is Wm Hutchings[3] who says: *I am a widow man. I have been in the trade 30 years. He has a shop with eight frames in High Street, where his daughter helps him occasionally. The rest are journeymen [day workers].* He has seen how rents and rates have risen, while wages have fallen: *I used at that time for the little house I have, to pay 9d to the rate and now these premises cost me 25 shillings a year.*

One topic of investigation for the Enquiry was the importance of allotments or gardens to help counteract the effects of poverty and unemployment. Witnesses are asked whether the situation of poor framework knitters could be improved by having allotments. Wm Hutchins replies: *I am of the opinion if every man had a piece of land for his cultivation it would bring him out of the trade when trade was bad instead of driving him into the market* [and having to sell goods below cost price]. *They would be occupied on their own land and they would bring the produce from that land into consumption by their own families. If they had a piece of ground to cultivate it would be a great benefit. It would help those men with families to bring them up to a useful occupation. Getting pigs and potatoes are of great use to a family.*

---

[1] *The Guide to Information contained in the Report on Conditions of FWK* 1845

[2] ibid Page 369 no 6921

[3] William Hutchings, FWK manufacturer, owned his own house in 1837 and one other (RV £6). Aged 50 in 1841, he lived with 3 daughters, Ann, a FWK aged 25, Mary, 9 and Elizabeth, 5, in North End (High Street).

When asked **What allotment have you in Gt Glen?** he replies*: About four acres allotted to us through Sir George Robinson and we have sent a memorial* [memo] *to him. I did it myself about 4 months ago and he sent a very civil answer back and now we expect by the latter end of the year he will introduce the allotment system in the village to a greater extent.*
The reference to Sir George Robinson, the Lord of the Manor, is interesting. Great Glen allotments are marked on the 1835 map, which CWP acquired at about the time of the Enquiry. On it, plot 39 is described as *Lower Town Close, set in gardens for the Poor.*[1] The allotments remained there for many years.

To the question: **If there was a sufficiency of allotments would the poor men be able to pay a moderate rent and cultivate it properly?** Hutchings describes how the friendly society works in Glen. *There are 140 members in our society. We can guarantee payment when due. We have a society paying by instalments of 1d a week, according to a man's circumstances some pay more, and consequently when we get our money together enabling us to buy seed. We hope to get 35 acres.* He explains how the rent money is paid to the Lord of the Manor: *Our society is incorporated and we have a committee managed for members. No allotment tenant is allowed to pull up his crop until the rent is paid to the committee secretary They lock the money up and the managers take the money to Sir Geo Robinson's steward to save him the obligation of collecting it from each allottee. We have two committees, one of Superior Gentlemen of the Parish and one of artisans and workers of the land.* It would be interesting to know if this system continued under CWP's lordship of the manor. There is no indication that the poor people got their thirty five acres from either Sir George or CWP.

The Workhouse
The Poor Law Amendment Act of 1834 had adversely affected the poor framework knitters. Conditions became worse for them because the system of poor law relief by the parish had been withdrawn in favour of centralised 'new improved workhouses' with stricter controls designed to have a deterrent effect for the able bodied poor. The parish was not encouraged to subsidise the idle. The workers, understandably, dreaded the idea of the new workhouses. Witnesses to the Hosiery Enquiry in 1845 are asked how the new Poor Law affects them. Wm Grain replies that because a worker cannot now get any relief from the parish*: A man is compelled to take out work even at a reduction because he cannot get anything from the overseer of the Parish. Scarcely a single man can get a living, much less a man with a family. He must either have relief or starve.*

Great Glen parish had maintained a self-sufficient workhouse with its own farm but the 1834 Poor Law Amendment Act declared that parishes should band together to form Poor Law Unions and provide a strictly governed workhouse for the

[1] DE 1215/2 See Factfile at the end of the chapter.

unemployed to limit the demands of the poor on the parish rates. A House of Industry was built in Glen to replace the old workhouse farm cottages. In 1835 Wm Horton, Thos Batchelor and Samuel Bettony were engaged to repair the walls and windows and John Glover was paid to provide new furniture. In 1840 the walls were made higher for greater security with greater separation of the wards.[1]
The 1841 census lists the inmates of the workhouse in a separate section, away from the main entry for Glen, although the buildings were part of the village and not physically moved from Glen until some years later. The master was Deene, with his wife as matron. The inhabitants were: Thos Thickpenny (aged 70), Harrison, Atkins, Boothesay, Underwood, Wm Hall, Robert Newton (blacksmith), Mary Ann Newton, Goode, Martha Holyoake (aged 25, with George aged 4 and Eliz aged 2), Wignall, Holmer, Johnson, Browett and Browett, a married couple. They were not necessarily all Great Glen families, but the case of Martha Holyoak (a Glen name) sounds particularly sad for her and her two young children.

Wm Hutchings speaks movingly of the system of separating men from wives and mothers from children: *Men out of work used to be supported by the Parish and given so much a day. The new system beats the prices down because the only alternative for workers is a ticket for the Workhouse. There is no other relief. A steady man would not like to break up his home, if he has got any spirit; he loves his wife's company and that of his little children and to have his wife and little children and those whom you are to love and respect taken away from him - those are heart rending cases. So a man will sooner submit to any prices his master will offer rather than submit to such usage, and of course that the hosiers know. Rather than accept a ticket for the workhouse he will take any price offered him. And then his poor wife and children suffer under the greatest privations of life, because when he has done his work he has nothing to support his wife and children with...And his lot becomes a mass of wretchedness and ruin.*

Great Glen's small workhouse was sold and the vestry meeting of Aug 27th 1846 records that the mortgages were paid off.[2] White's Directory of 1848 confirms that the sale is under way: *The old House of Industry built many years ago for Glenn Magna and several neighbouring parishes, used by Billesdon Union till 1846 but will shortly be sold.*

In 1847 Sir Henry Halford, CWP's near neighbour and fellow MP, felt concerned enough to write *A Plea for the Frame Work Knitters with a View to the Amelioration of their Condition.*[3] In it he summarises the speeches and essays of

---

[1] DE 1667/16 Southwell museum provides a vivid re-creation of workhouse conditions. See also Julie O'Neill, *The Life and Times of J T Becher,* of Southwell, Notts

[2] The original lessees were: Henry Coleman, Robert Haymes and John Ragg and John Grain. DE 849/16

[3] DG 24/1074 17/81 Henry Halford, *A Plea for the Frame Work Knitters* Oct 2nd 1847

famous Leicester reformers like Robert Hall and Wm Felkin[1] and he praises the 1845 Hosiery Commission Enquiry, as *a very able report.* He speaks of the intolerable distress: *the low and scanty wages of the workmen frequently incapacitates them from receiving an adequate supply of wholesome and nutritious food...whole families sleep in the same room.* And he reminds his readers that *workmen are totally unable to afford the means of educating their children as they cannot spare their labour. All the education they receive is at the Sunday school and they are frequently kept from attendance there by want of clothing.* He concludes that: *The duty of society is plain – to raise all its classes to as high a position, physical and moral- as may be.* His essay was published after the bill had been rejected by parliament. CWP was his fellow MP at the time but we do not know what he thought of all this. He did not commit his thoughts to paper (as Halford did) and did not speak in Parliament, as far as we can tell. We have no evidence of his involvement in the matter, and can only presume that he hoped and prayed that sleepy Glen would not rise up in revolt and that rich and poor would continue to co-exist as before.

The 1850s

The decade began with the great fanfare of the 1851 Great Exhibition, which celebrated the wealth, power, progress, trade, cotton and woollen mills, steam, steel, science of the British Empire. The population of Glen was 780 (398males and 382 females). This is an increase of nineteen from the 1831 figure quoted by Wm Grain, the parish clerk.[2] There were 189 inhabited houses plus one uninhabited. CWP had added to the number of buildings with his schoolhouses built in 1846 and Bott Stone cottages, proudly initialled and dated 1851.

The 1851 census gives names, ages, jobs and relationship to the head of household. Most of the same people are in the same jobs and the same houses as ten years before, but we can detect certain changes. Some new names appear, like that of Sharples Adcock, *farmer and agent for CW Packe.* There are a couple of ex-soldiers, who are listed as Chelsea Pensioners (though that may be merely a courtesy title given to any ex-soldiers at the time). Women are labelled as *DD* (domestic duties) or *Pauper,* as are all old people without an income. There are a dozen or so in d*omestic employment,* presumably working for other households, and there are about 30 wives who are also FWKs, glove stitchers or seamstresses (for the trade). A couple are dressmakers. Widows work as FWKs or charwomen and one is a laundress who takes lodgers while her unmarried daughter does the Domestic Duties. Young girls of 11 and 12 appear as seamstresses and 13 and 15

[1] Wm Felkin *An Account of the machine-wrought hosiery trade; its extent and the condition of FWKs* 1844

[2] At the FWK Enquiry, Wm Grain quoted the census figure for 1831 as 769, see previous section

year olds appear as FWKs. A score of unmarried young women are in the hosiery and glove trade. It is the main source of employment for them.

There are still about sixty men in Frame Work Knitting, some as masters employing several men. But we note, too, those who are listed as *former* FWKs like Stephen Burdett, *late FWK now pauper.* The lot of the poor was probably not much improved. The Highways Accounts books[1] give us the names of day labourers working on the highway. In 1851 James Glover, George Grain, John Allen and Elias Tailby, were together paid a total of £1 9s 4d (about 7s each for the week's work). In 1853 John Allen, George Grain and Abraham Folwell are listed as labourers and in 1854 Wm Scott, Wm Allen, Henry Johnson, Joseph Jayes, Wm Harrold, Howard Capell, John Vann, John Bindley, Joseph Peberdy, John Harrison, Humphrey Lambert and Samuel Burdett all appear, earning three shillings each. Wm Allen *on contract* earns 7s [a week]. In Oct 1856 John Jarvis is contracted for stone breaking at 5 shillings a week and in December this goes up to 6 shillings. In January the contract goes to John Peberdy for 2s 6d.[2] (FWKs earned on average 5s a week in 1845.)

Materials and expenses seem by comparison very costly: John Bindley gets 2s 0d for materials. A *stone hamer* cost 9d in 1851. Magistrates' fees with a journey to Leicester cost eight shillings. The Clerk's fees were one shilling. A year later the magistrate's fees have gone up to 8s 6d, a hammer costs 1s 6d and a carriage shovel cost 6d. Stones for repairing the highway are provided by Mr Lewin who is paid 18s, Mr Hobson 6s, Mr Norman 5s, Mr Achurch and Mr Langley 6s. These are all familiar names to anyone who has studied Great Glen documents. Many of them appear in CWP's rent books[3] (and some of the names still appear in families in the village today).

CWP was able to enter the newly re-opened Houses of Parliament in 1852 By 1854 CWP had started on plans to build a great new mansion at Branksome; he must have viewed world news with some alarm. In the Crimean War against the Russians, 1854-6, the Earl of Cardigan[4] led his Light Brigade into the 'Valley of Death'.[5] Presumably CWP followed the graphic and gripping newspaper reports which came in the *London Illustrated News.* We do not know whether any of his tenants went to fight in the war but his nephew Charles was in the Yeomanry[6] in 1859, some years after the war, and wrote letters to his uncle describing how his brigade was nearly inspected by the terrifying Lord Cardigan: *the adjutant has been*

---

[1] DE 24/6 and DE 24/15 Highways Accounts 1850 - 53 and 57.
[2] It is not clear why John Peberdy was awarded less pay.
[3] See the following section
[4] James Thomas Brudenell, Earl of Cardigan (1797-1868) commanded the cavalry brigade in the Crimean War 1854. He became Inspector General of Cavalry 1855-60.
[5] The poet Tennyson's words
[6] The Volunteer Unit of Cavalry, later absorbed into the Territorial Army.

very fierce this time under the terror of the inspection of the Inspector General of Cavalry but today the news arrived that Lord Cardigan is not coming to us and we are to be reviewed by a simple colonel. [1]

After 1854, his building and his charity work at Branksome were possibly of more immediate interest to him than the affairs at Glen but he did continue to carry on his duties here. Throughout the years there had been mortgages and remortgaging. He had received rents and been paid for land bought by the Midland railway[2] and he kept his financial affairs in order. By 1859, however, he was complaining of increasing age and failing health in the letters he wrote when claiming a peerage. He was feeling he needed a quieter life in Parliament: *My health is now not up to the hard work required there.* He mentions *a doctor's note to this effect.*[3] In the 1860s we have fewer documents referring to his activities, so perhaps he really was slowing down in his buying and selling and dealing in mortgages for village property.

The 1860s

For this period we can zoom in to CWP's own account book for details of the rents collected from his tenants in Great Glen. We do not know why his account book begins at this particular date. It may be that his earlier notebooks had just become too scruffy to use, or it may be that he felt time's winged chariot at his back and wished to tidy his accounts for Kitty. Whatever his reasons for making it were, we must be grateful for the information it gives us.

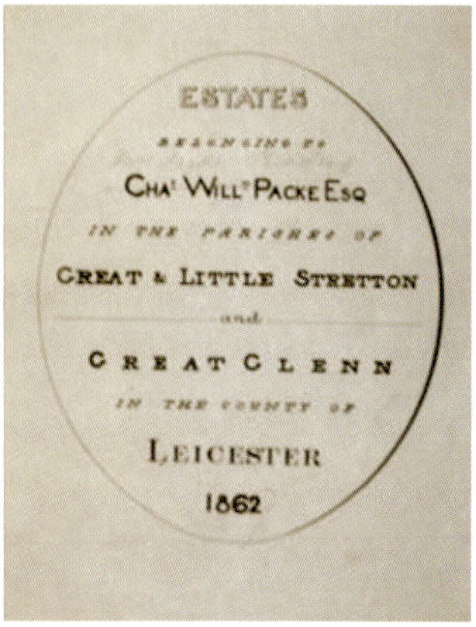

The accounts book of Estates belonging to Charles William Packe in the Parishes of Great and Little Stretton and Great Glen 1862[4] is a little notebook with beautifully written lists of tenants, with the acreage of land they rented (in acres, rods and perches) and sketch maps to illustrate the plots.

---

[1] DE 5047/112 Letter of Charles Packe to his uncle CWP Sept 1859.

[2] DE 1215/4 He received £2,175 from the Midland Rlwy 1845. The company had opened the Leicester to Hitchin Line, in 1857, passing through Great Glen. The station was opened in May or June of that year. CWP made some profit from it because it went over his land. The line did not, however, go as far as London until the Bedford-London section was opened in 1868. It is not clear whether CWP ever used the train, but FPR certainly recommended it to George Boyle in 1855. (See her letters to him p.126)

[3] DE 5047/201 Claims for peerage letters quoted in Chapter 1.

[4] DE 5047/4

The first page lists his own holdings, *In Hand.* He then goes on to list the property leased to other people. The pages are cross-referenced to numbered plots, based on the Stretton Hall estates map of 1835[1] and most of the tenants are those listed by Sir George Robinson.

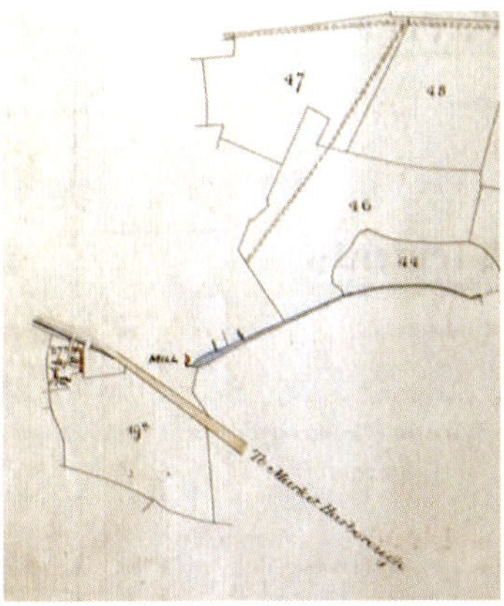

On this page Glen Hall is not marked, though it had been built by 1830 (in the unnumbered field just north of the mill). This is because the land was not part of Robinson's estate. The land belonged at the time to Wm Burton.

On another page, the hall and the mill are included. (CWP must have had the map specially drawn.) The hall is listed as Plot 41 *Mansion House with lodge and outbuildings, plantations and pleasure grounds* and rent is due from the executors of Archibald Finnie. (Anna Raymond's lease had ended).

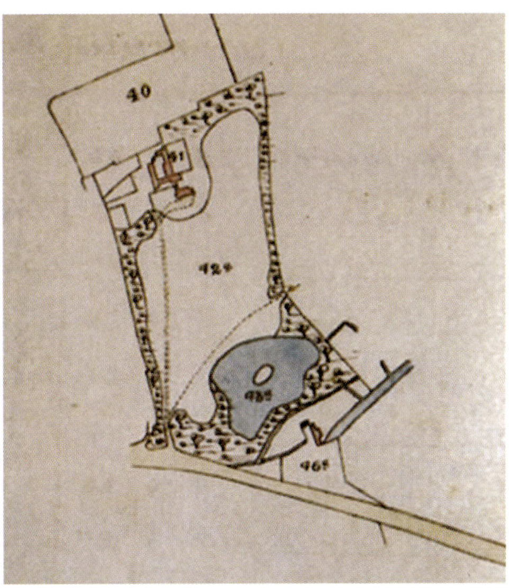

Plot 46a is the mill with garden and orchard, rented to Joseph Freeman, the miller. Numbers with an additional *a* indicate a plot not having belonged to Robinson's estate. It was not bought by CWP until 1840.

From the summary at the end of the book we see that CWP himself has the biggest holding of land (In Hand). Sarah Clements at North House has the second biggest holding. Lewins have the third biggest.

Only ten houses are listed in his accounts and it seems strange to find no mention of the school houses, built in 1846, and Bott Stone House, built in 1851, or the lodge houses for his two halls.[2] The lodge houses were probably tied cottages (Charles Packe lists seven cottages which were rent free) but for the houses built by CWP it is more likely that he kept a different account book.[3]

[1] See Factfile at the end of the chapter.

[2] There is no mention of Peep Row, either. Robert Haymes owned the cottages until 1860.

[3] These houses were, in fact included in a separate supplementary page when ECP submitted his accounts to the tax office in 1920.

Kitty Packe Reading

Changes in tenancies.

When CWP died in 1867 his wife took on his role of Lord of the Manor and her estate accountant started a new book, dated 1869-70. This is based on CWP's book, but rearranged to fit in with the changes in the tenancies. In her Summary page the land recorded as 'In Hand' goes down from 338 acres to 57 acres. More land is rented out to tenants.

One new tenant is Richard Benskin who leases 188 acres. William and Sarah Clements are still the biggest land-tenants with more than 170 acres each. Sarah Clements has the same acreage as in 1862 and her son William now holds an equal amount.[1] Morley Hodges Lewin appears instead of his father James Lewin and he now farms the land his father rented plus his own.[2] The mill is still rented with 15 acres by Joseph Freeman and his executors. Joseph Forman has increased his holding (from two acres in 1862 to about 14 acres) and now rents plot 29, the *Homestead and Hovels* (behind 5, The Nook). John Easom at plot 35, just north of Ruperts Rest, has slightly increased his holdings. (The pencilled note under 36, *School and School house* is added later.)

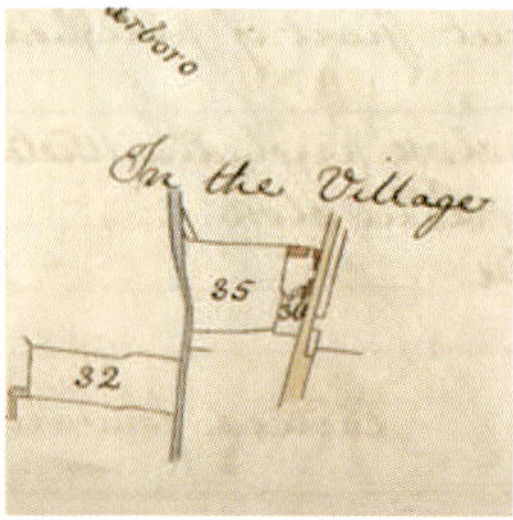

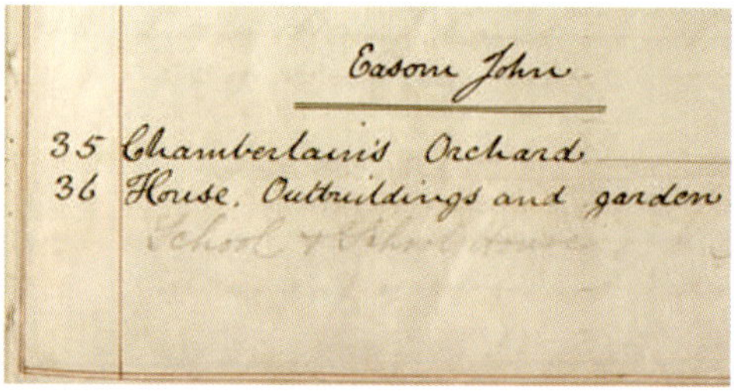

Sundry Cottagers includes plot 31, described as a house (once divided into two) with outbuildings, gardens and a croft, rented by Richard Benskin, on the corner of The Nook and London Road.[3] The cottages of Marriott, Bland, James Norfolk and Robert Sykes are lumped together as 'sundry cottages' with a small total acreage. John Carver still has plots 33 and 34 cottage and wood yard, with a very small acreage. William Ragg disappears (from Trent House) and a new tenant, Joseph Lovatt rents the butcher's shop and Round Close (The Green).

---

[1] The Clements are at North House farm 27a and 26a. (see Chapter 5 lot 12)

[2] Morley Hodges Lewin's house is at plot 25, with fields 26 and 27 opposite, on the corner of Orchard Lane and London Road. His lands extend down to the railway and canal (see Chapter 5 lot 11)

[3] Sold in 1919. See Chapter 5 Lot 3

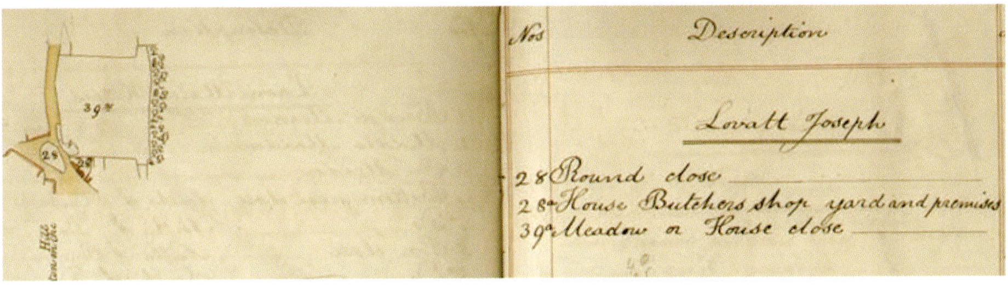

Glen Hall (*Mansion House with outbuildings plantations and pleasure grounds and fish pond*) is listed as *In Hand.* We know, however, that KPR was in fact accustomed to lease the hall in winter months. (It is about this time that she offered the hall, rent free, to her nephew Charles for a couple of months, and hoped she could visit him here.[1]) Although she continued to live at Branksome and in her London home, she did visit her Glen estate regularly.

Charles Packe

In 1871 when Charles Packe moved into Stretton Hall there were 198 houses, nineteen of them empty, in Glen. There were 767 inhabitants (374 males and 393 females).[2] Many of these residents were born and bred in Glen. In some families every single member has been born in Glen. (A minority of couples sought their partners by going further afield, to places like Burton Overy or Oadby.) The same family names recurred through generations[3] and we find many members of the same families in different parts of the village. First names, too, recur, very confusingly, in families like the Batchelors, the Lewins, the Coopers and the interestingly named Green Achurch, father and son. All this makes it difficult to decide where each particular family lived. Easier to deal with are those people like the Burtons whose family lived in the same houses forty years earlier, in the time of CWP.

The 1871 census gives us some street names for guidance as to where the people lived (though street names have changed over the years and some have disappeared altogether). The Nook[4] had very many more dwellings than it has today. The residents were: Wm Allen, a baker aged 34, with apprentices and lodgers; Daniel

[1] See her letters in Chapter 1.
[2] Cf 795 in 1841: 782 in 1851 and 785 in 1861.
[3] Recurring family names include: Allen, Lewin, Dencher, Elson, Gilbert, Jarvis, Grant, Clarke, Bland, Nosely, Jayes, Pywell, Middleton, Muddimer, Faulkner/Falkner, Gamble, Rowe, Thompson, Coleman, Coulson, Newton, Grant, Grain, Wormell, Burdett, Achurch, Batchelor, Easom, Elsom, Peberdy, Barsby, Collier, Dickman, Bird, Hubbard and Peake.
[4] The Nook is called 'NEWARKE' in the census

Nosely, a FWK employing other people in the outhouses and hovels which were behind the posh frontages of the malthouse (now Bassetts*)*; Goodacre, a carpenter; and Ann Jayes, a charwoman aged 40, with four children of her own and little Emily Goodacre as her boarder. Living near them are Sarah Bland, a 37 year old widow employed as a stitcher (with five children and a lodger), Middleton, a tailor, Muddimer, a farm labourer, Jos Faulkner and other lowly paid FWKs[1] and farm labourers.

The Nook seems to have been one of the FWK centres in the village. Daniel Nosely, aged 53, employs men and boys. John Nosely (a FWK aged 58) lives next door to him and three other men employed by him as FWKs including John Why (aged 76), William Why and John Rowe (both aged 50) and two Faulkners, Joseph (aged 40) and Maria, a 62 year old widow, a stitcher. All these people live in The Nook. Not far from them, on the London Road in the two cottages next to the entrance to Glen Hall,[2] Harriet Clowes and William Thompson, are both FWKs. But the majority of the knitters dwelt at the far end of the village.

High Street (*Top End*) has Thomas Wormell (aged 62) in Allens Yard and Thomas Clarke (43), William Woolner (46) and Daniel Allen (aged 58) with three sons also FWKs. (One of his sons has the name *Hutching*, probably named after the William Hutchings who gave evidence at the Hosiery Enquiry of 1845.) William Hutchings, now 84, lives in the house next door with his daughter Ann, a seamstress, and his son in law, a tailor. Next to them are a 38 year old FWK widow, Eliz Grain, and Joseph Grain, a widower of 70, still recorded as a FWK, so still presumably working. Further along High Street, next to the Royal Oak pub, is Thomas Denscher, a 41year old FWK, employing eight men, two women and two boys, including his own two sons aged 17 and 15. Isaac Clarke, next door, is described more specifically as a stocking maker and, on the corner of the road, in Bott Stone House, Thomas Capell has a FWK son aged 14.

In *Stretton Road* (Main Street) there are more people in the knitting or hosiery trade. William Rowe, a cotton weaver (aged 77), William Weston (aged 71), Thomas Wormell (aged 33) and Martha Scott, a seamstress, all live near the Co-operative stores and Samuel Burdett, William Neale (aged 21), William Dencher (73) and Fanny Grain a 39 year old unmarried seamstress, live in Peep Row.[3] John Achurch, living near them, has a wife who is also a seamstress. Other names of FWKs appearing in the same street are Mary Coleman (aged 22), Daniel Nosely (30), William Coleman (71), Charles King (55), William Grain (63), Henry

---

[1] Numbers recorded for FWKs are lower than they were in the 1840s but there are still about forty two of them. Some employ men and boys, while some have their wives and children working with them. Many of the wives who are not recorded as in gainful employment doubtless did their share of the work and some women are listed as stitchers or knitters.

[2] Owned by Halford and not bought by the Packes until 1897

[3] Peep Row see chapter 5 plots 32 and 33.

Thompson, whose son aged 14 is also in the trade and Daniel Allen with his unmarried son of 22, also a FWK.

In *Burton Lane* (Oaks Road) there is another cluster of FWKs: Wm Rowe (39) with five young children all born in Glen, Henry Carver, a widower of 54, Henry King (aged 32, born in Newton Harcourt) with a wife called Bridget from Dublin and two young children, one born in Burton on Trent and one in Glen. His neighbours are Isaac Faulkner (aged 45), Francis Burdett (49) and John Dickman (59), from Smeeton with a FWK son Henry, born in Arnesby. Four more knitters live in *Mutton Square:* Thos Rowe (aged 52) and Ezra Coleman (22), a newcomer to the trade, Mary Morris, a widow of 55 and William Coleman (45). In a road called *Weaver Street* in the census, there is another Rowe (Henry aged 49) employing the three oldest of his children and eight other hands, and William Dickman (31) Isaac Bird (45) and his 16 year old daughter, a seamstress.

Some young men whose fathers were FWKs must have seen that there was no future in the trade and we note in this census the appearance of railway workers. On the whole they are young men in their 30s, with families to support. Thomas Hyde, was a platelayer aged 37, living with his father in law, George Coulson, a labourer aged 74, in the 'railway cottages, known as Post Office Row.'[1] Their neighbours, George Newton (aged 40), Abner Folwell (aged 35) and Nathaniel Grain also worked on the railway. Abner is recorded as having five daughters and a son and Nathaniel has three young daughters, all born in Glen. Both men were from long-standing Glen families. Other railway workers include Jonathan Clarke (30) on Oaks Road, Charles Green, the 24 year old son of an ag lab, Henry Johnson (41) at *Top End* and Robert Grain, a brewer's 15 year old son with five younger siblings.

Servants

At the other end of the social scale there are, in 1871, about fifteen houses with live-in servants. Glen Hall had about ten, Eliz Beardsley in Glen House had four, Sarah Clements in North House had one and Elizabeth Robey employed four in the big house opposite the church.[2] The vicar and rich graziers like Thos Hobson at The Mount had two servants, but one servant per household seems more usual. Beadman, who owned his own house (valued at £117 annual rental), Sarah Gilbert (landlady of The Crown), Jane Pick (landlady of The Old Greyhound), Parsons, a retired chemist, Horton (The White House), George Coleman (The Yews), Elizabeth Cooper (The Sycamores), all have one servant. Most of these servants are young unmarried girls aged between 15 and 18. Ann Easom, the grazier who lives near Ruperts Rest, employs Hannah Coleman, aged 16, as a maid of all work. But

---

[1] Post Office Row see chapter 5 Lot 31.

[2] Haymes' house, Dr Jamies' house, Church Lane, opposite the church. See Chapter 3 part 1.

some unmarried or widowed men have older servants or relatives as housekeepers. Thomas Crick for instance has, at Ruperts Rest, two nieces as housekeepers, plus a 40 year old woman servant and a gardener (Wm Cobley, aged 27) to look after himself and Henry Davy, a 77 year old retired last-maker (presumably a relative or former employee).

Lodgers and Boarders

In the smaller houses, the less well-off took lodgers and boarders to eke out their existence. In The Nook, Middleton the tailor has two lodgers and Ann Jayes has little Emily Goodacre, aged 6, (probably her neighbours' grandchild) as a 'boarder'. In Main Street George Coleman has a young schoolboy, Robert Grant aged 11, as a boarder. Thos Grant, an ag lab, has three grooms lodging with him and John Grain, at the co-op stores, has Mary Morris a widow aged 76, as a boarder

Apprentices

The tradesmen often had apprentices. Allen, the baker in the Nook, has an apprentice, John Wilford, aged 14. Francis Clarke, the 16 year old son of an ag lab, is a bricklayer's apprentice. On Stretton Road, George Coulson's grandson, Arthur Hyde, aged 13, is a carpenter's apprentice.

When Charles Packe's uncle (CWP) first came to Glen in 1835, he bought one dwelling (Glen Hall). He is listed as owning only one in the 1837 valuation. By 1862 he had at least 10, including Glen Hall and Stretton Hall. When Charles Packe inherited the estate, in 1870, he acquired these dwellings and he went on to acquire many more.

John King has the same 62 acres at Stretton Hall. Henry Langley, CWP's servant who lived in the entrance lodge to Glen Hall in 1848, has a cottage and garden (15 perches at no 37) on Main Street (the road *to Little Stretton*). James Norfolk is his neighbour, at plot 38. These cottages (on the site of the existing doctors' surgery) no longer exist.[1]

[1] See the 1835 map in Factfile at the end of the chapter.

The 1878 Valuation[1] lists Charles Packe as owning 45 houses, nearly 20% of the total in the village, and more than any other property owner in Glen. The other main landowners were Thomas Crick (owning 38 dwellings), Lewin and Osbourne (together owning 26) and William Edgeley (owning 14). Most of the dwellings were small cottages with low rents of between £3 and £5 10s a year but men like Thomas Crick also owned houses that brought in considerably more income. (He owned two houses with rental values of £28 and £14 a year. He also owned The Royal Oak pub, leased to Elias Bland for £19 10s a year.[2]) Robert Sykes owned the bakehouse in the Nook, leased to Wm Allen for £20 a year. Benjamin Cooper owned one house which he lived in, and rented out another of the same value (GER £25). Frances Burton rented, for £15 a year, a house belonging to Augustus Hunt.

Charles Packe had inherited some houses valued at more than double this amount. The mill house was leased to Joseph Freeman at £70 a year, Glen Hall, leased to Henry O'Brien, had a Gross Estimated Rental Value of £100, Trent House was rented by Joseph Lovett at £46 5s per year, and one on the corner of The Nook and London Road was rented, with a lot of land near Stretton Hall by Frank Sutton Hodgkin for £270.

KPR's account book, with additions in pencil by Charles Packe. The name of Richard Benskin is pencilled out and Frank Hodgkin's name[3] is inserted in Charles Packe's annotation

[1] See Factfile at the end of this chapter
[2] By comparison,, The Greyhound, owned by Catherine Norman and leased by Richard Roberts, was valued at £50, The Crown, owned by Beadman and leased to Chisholm, £24 and the Fox and Goose, owned by Flint and leased to Burditt for £18 a year..
[3] Frank Hodgkin does not appear in any Glen census but may have been related to various Green Hodgkins, born in 1718, 1754 and 1791. One is named in the 1759 Enclosure Award and another named as a publican, aged 50 in the 1851 census. His wife is buried in Stretton Magna churchyard. But by 1878 the Hodgkin lands in Glen had been acquired by the Packes and the only Hodgkins in the village are poor people: John Hodgkin, for instance, is an ag lab and Grace Hodgkin is a tenant of Crick's Retreat.

Charles Packe also owned Bott Stone cottages (with Thomas Capell and Wm Grain as tenants paying an estimated yearly rent of £3 15 shillings), the two houses built for the school teachers (with rents of £4 10s and £2 10s a year) and Glen Hall lodge house (with Henry Langley as tenant at £5 a year). These are houses which did not appear in CWP's account books.[1] Peep Row cottages are listed as Packe property, with a yearly rent of £3. (Charles must have acquired them at some time after 1860, when they belonged to Robert Haymes.) He also built houses in High Street.[2] These were built to a very high standard, in 1874. He must have felt financially confident, as in 1876 he paid for the restoration of the church.[3]

A note on Thomas Crick (1803–1879)

It is appropriate at this point to speak of Thomas Crick, who emerged as an important rival to Charles Packe as a property owner. In 1872 he built his row of almshouses, Crick's Retreat, in memory of his wife Elizabeth, to provide free residences for his relatives *and other poor persons of good character and advanced age, who have led honest, sober and industrious lives and have not been reduced to poverty through any fault of their own.* Strict rules were laid down: *None to marry without permission, no absences for more than three nights in any one month, no trade or business, no pig, fowl, cat or dog. Front porches and steps to be kept in good order. No abusive language. No uncleanly or dirty habits or inconvenience or annoyance to other inmate.*

A man and wife were employed as gatekeepers to live in the lodge house and to keep the gates closed *except for times of illness or other sudden necessity.* They were in charge of pumping water for the tank, keeping roads and paths and trees and shrubs in order and the wife was to help nurse any sick inmates. A copy of these rules was to be given to all inmates.[4]

The centre of the building proudly boasts a plaque bearing testimony to Crick's footwear production. *Thomas Crick's boot riveting invention revolutionised boot making and was the true start of shoe manufacturing in Leicester.*[5]

---

[1] The supplementary account book which CWP probably kept for these houses is not extant.
[2] See Chapter 5 Lots 35 and 36
[3] see Chapter 4
[4] DE 3225/33-36 Indenture Crick's Retreat 1871
[5] DE 2148/114-5. *The Leicester Advertiser* March 3rd 1961

Crick's Retreat provided *free residences for relatives of the founder and other poor persons of good character and advanced age. The present building holds 20 inmates but it is proposed to erect a chapel and houses for a similar number. Rule 14 states that 52 cwt of coals and 14 pounds of candles or the value of such candles if required for artificial light shall be allowed and supplied per annum for each house and each inmate who shall be a relative of the founder or of his wife shall receive an allowance of 2/6d a week and each inmate who shall not be such relative shall receive an allowance at the rate of 2/- a week.* [1]

These buildings must have been of interest to Packe, as the back of the row is visible from the drive to Stretton Hall. I suspect he viewed them with mixed feelings!

In 1874 Crick had built Console Cottages, adjoining the Royal Oak on High Street and Wharton cottages, near Peep Row.

He went on to buy up houses elsewhere in the village. It seems that by this date dwellings could be considered a profitable investment. And Crick was going up in the ranks of house ownership. As well as the houses in High Street and in Main Street, he owned the co-op stores (GER £19.10s) and a score of cottages. By 1878 he owned 38 houses, compared to Packe's 45. And he lived in the prestigious house of Rupert's Rest.

---

[1] Kelly's Directory 1876

We know that as early as 1876 Charles had debated with himself whether to buy a row of cottages (Post Office Row) even though he thought it might be more nuisance than it was worth: *There are eight cottages and will soon be a small field adjoining Glenn Hall which are to be sold by auction on Sept 5th. They are very desirable additions to the* [Packe] *property as being in the midst of it and the row on the opposite side*[1] *belongs to me but really I have had worry enough about purchasing land for the benefit of the property. It is not a* *<u>profitable</u>* *investment but the question is whether if Crick or some building company bought them they might become a thorn.*[2]

Charles felt that Thomas Crick might be a thorn in the flesh if he were allowed to buy these cottages, so close to Packe property, and he worried that he might regret letting slip the opportunity to acquire them himself. He seems to have been somewhat wary of Crick, a comparative newcomer to the ranks of property owners in Glen. (Do we detect a certain rivalry and disdain for the man with new money and no aristocratic background, to boot?) Charles bought the cottages in 1877 and thereby acquired eight new families as tenants.[3] The 1878 Valuation names 28 other of his tenants in cottages valued at about £3 a year[4] as well as the tenants of the more expensive holdings inherited from CWP.

By 1889 the Packes had acquired the lands originally allotted in the 1790 Enclosure Award to Wm Hewitt, Sir Henry Halford, Green Hodgkin, King, Franks, Matthew

---

[1] He must be referring to Peep Row, though it is not exactly opposite Post Office Row, merely on the opposite side of the road!
[2] DE 5047/144/1-41
[3] see Chapter 5 Plot 31. Post Office Row. Wm Bromwich (or Bromage), Samuel Crick, Jonathan Rowe, Mary Elson, Daniel Allen, Thomas Coulson, James Allen and John Achurch.
[4] Nathaniel Grain, Richard Sidenton, Fancourt and Elizabeth Hall (in the school houses), Ann Easom (opposite them), Wm Neale, George Coleman, George Coulson, Widow Newton (former school teacher), Thomas Grant, John Grain (co-op stores) Wm Rowe, Wm Barnes and Wm Achurch (in three neighbouring houses), Chas Overton, John Hodgkin, George Grain and James Morris (three neighbours in Weaver Street in the 1871 census), Thomas Capell, Wm Grain, Isaac Clarke, Isaac Grain (in High Street near the Royal Oak) John Pywell, Isaac Muddimer, Wm Peberdy, George Hubbard, John Wise, and Enos Atkinson (who seems to be a newcomer to Glen, not named in the 1871 census.)

Harrison, Thomas Blackwell and Dorothy Campion. By the time he died, Charles Packe was the biggest landowner in the village.

Packe property in Great Glen bounded in red.

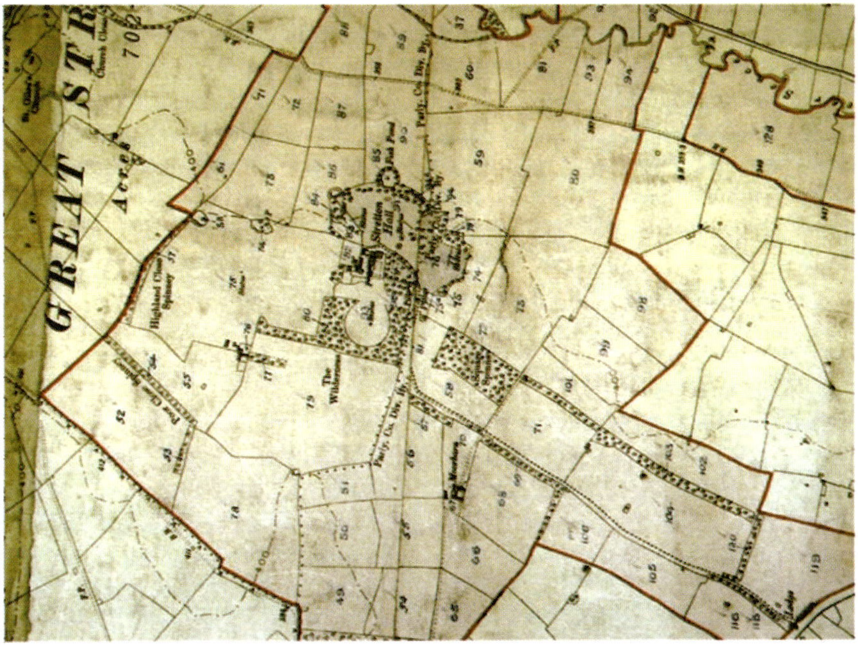

William James Packe

Floods and Drought.
The story of Great Glen inevitably has to include the supply of adequate, clean, pumped or piped water. There are constant references to the need for water from pumps, wells and springs. It is a case of 'water, water everywhere' when it floods but 'ne'er a drop to drink' at other times! The floods endangered the water supply. In June and July 1839 the floods not only totally spoiled the hay crop but also contaminated the water: the *Constable Waywarden* was empowered to collect a sanitary rate to pay for the effects of flooding in Burton Lane. In 1877 the Vestry Minute Books recorded a resolution: *to send a memorial to the Sanitary Authorities calling their attention to the very unsatisfactory state of the water cours* [resulting in] *the frequency of Floods – and the adopting of such means as they shall think proper for the prevention of the same.*

One of the functions of The Town Lands Charity[1] was *providing needful supply of water for the use of inhabitants of Great Glen.* Charles Packe was one of the trustees. In 1882 the water supply was discussed and it was remarked that *before the floods two years ago there had been no complaints of water nor had there been illnesses occasioned by it.* But water pollution and defective sewerage were now apparent. Charles was active in the Vestry affairs and the village water supply was a matter of concern to him. In 1893 a vestry meeting was specially summoned to consider the question of water supply in the parish *with immediate reference to the spring discovered at the back of Glen Hall.* It was decided: *That the water be brought down from the spring at Mr Packe's expense to a stand pipe at the base of the Allotments and there be allowed to stand for general use for six months and after that period, if the supply is found to exceed the demand the Sanitary Authority is to be at liberty to add two extra standpipes at their own expense and to carry it away to convenient stations always on the condition that sufficient water is left at the original standpipe.*[2]

Writing from Stretton Hall to his brother William on July 3 1893, Charles complains: We have a terrible scarcity of water both here and in the village. In the village I have spent £100 in putting up a pipe and stand-pipes. Here in Stretton we are obliged to drink Apollinaire [mineral water] and dispense with our running baths. I am afraid many of the young trees will die and the cattle suffer. In

---

[1] DE 503/15 The Town Lands Charity 1875 The other major considerations were the management of *church maintenance and insurance v. fire, the Benefit of deserving and necessitous poor (by providing clothing, bedding, fuel, medical aid, food etc or by assisting such persons to emigrate). Any Leftovers for the children of the poor at school, if diligent and meritorious, provided that such children shall conduct themselves to the satisfaction of the managers of the said schools. Keeping in good and sufficient repair the bridges, causeways and highways within the parish.*

[2] DE 849/16 Vestry Minute Book 1869-1880

August 1893 there is scarce a drop of rain and as late as Dec 28th he writes: The scarcity of water is terrible.

By 1898 there were plans for a piped water supply. On Jan 17th 1898 Arthur Oddie, the vicar, wrote to Wm James Packe (at Feering rectory): *There seems to be every prospect of a general* [water] *supply from Leics Water Company. They have surveyed the ground and estimated the expense of laying the main through Main Street at £2000. This would mean 6d in the £ on rateable value. The Parish would charge water rents to those houses supplied. It seems to me that this will be a very great boon to the parish generally.*

In the meanwhile, there was a pressing need to seek out safe wells. On Jan 28th 1898 the vicar went on a fruitless search for one: *There is a spring up the Stretton Lane about half a mile from the centre of the village which is never dry but when I went to look at it and see whether it could not be utilised I was disappointed to find that it would be utterly inadequate as regards quantity.* Existing wells, always in danger of running dry, did not always provide safe drinking water. The vicar wrote to WJP warning him of one dangerously polluted well on his property: *I must say that Capell's condemned well* [at Bott Stone cottage] *is being freely used as ever and it is not safe that it should be, but poor people will never believe it is harmful if it tastes well.*[1] Ten days later he writes more urgently: *It is attached to one of your cottages and is being used now in breach of the law. I would press on you that you should at once stop its use. I am aware that its stoppage will cause inconvenience to many but better that the position should be faced.*

There is no record of what was done or how people felt about it. Their washing water still came from the 'dippy holes' in the brooks. People carried drinking water in buckets from the best places they could. Wells were very important. *My dad used to talk about the very deep well down the Orchard Lane.*[2] Some villagers still remember using the river and *deepy holes* for washing because water from pumps and wells would run dry.[3] Not all could afford 'Apollinaire' as Charles Packe did! When the tenant of Stretton Hall suggested the purchase in 1899 of *A gas engine to pump water from the well*, William pointed out the need to conserve water[4]: *There is a prospect of a scarcity of water over a bit and I fear Mr Dixon will have to be a little less lavish in his use of it or these wells will soon be dry.*

Piped water and sewerage came to the village much later. In June 1914 Billesdon Rural District Council made an agreement *with Edmund Christopher Packe, a captain in the Royal Fusiliers,* about a sewage tank *in a garden belonging to the*

---

[1] DE 5047 154
[2] Sheila Allen
[3] Chapter 5 Tommy Clark plot 21
[4] DE 5047/9/1-21. See Chapter 2 Stretton Hall.

said ECP and now occupied by Ezra Mason situate near the brook in Church Lane,[1] *Great Glen, for the reception and discharge of sewage from the village of Great Glen and pipes for ventilating their sewers at each end of a row of cottages called Packe's Row and a pipe fixed to a tree in the hedge bounding a field now occupied by Robert Henry Lewin.* The RDC had put in these pipes *sometime since* and now agreed to pay ECP 4/- and 2/- for pipes every Dec 31st *and not permit the tanks to be a nuisance or injurious and danger to health and thoroughly clean the tank three times at least every year.*[2] It was a start!

Flooding of course did not cease. There were floods in March 1955 and in 1960. The River Sence has since been dug out and deepened to alleviate the recurring problem. Even recently, when the bypass was being planned, one of the main worries was the likely increase in flooding from the extra hard surface areas and it is still a main factor in the fear of increase in building within the village. Glen residents have many memories and stories of the floods in the centre of the village.

Floods near the old Fox and Goose, 9/11/1957.[3]

Floods near The Old Greyhound and Bridge House.9/11/57.

[1] See Chapter 5 plot 35 for Ezra Mason's house.
[2] DE 1215 7
[3] Pictures courtesy of the *Leicester Mercury*

The Village Hall

The village in the time of William James Packe is mainly covered in the chapters on Stretton Hall, the church and the school. But it is appropriate perhaps to mention here the other matter which he had inherited: Charles Packe's endowment for the building of a Village Hall. On Jan 28*th* 1898 Arthur Oddie, who had been vicar and friend of Charles Packe since 1886, wrote from Great Glen Vicarage to Wm James Packe: *Has anything been done as to the Village Hall? It is time that the matter was proceeded with and architect's plans obtained. If you could see your way to giving me a site on the allotments almost opposite the school there is no other site that would compare with it. Batchelor who occupies one of the pieces which is gardened by several of the Men at once pointed out that site as the most suitable site.*

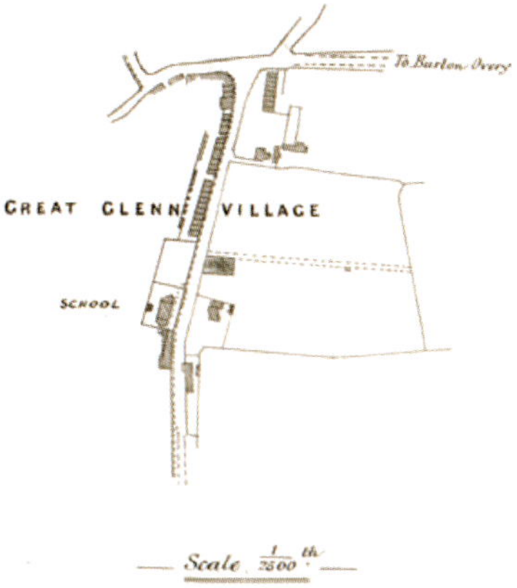

The village hall deeds map marks the hall beside the path through the allotments.[1]

On Feb 10th 1898 the vicar followed this up with another appeal: *Your brother's name will be connected with it for generations to come.* Oddie, perhaps aware of WJP's reputation for saying 'No', used Clough Taylor the land agent to press the matter. Clough Taylor then wrote to WJP,

From Friar Lane, Feb 21st 1898.

Mr Oddie tells me you agreed to give a site for a village hall at Glen and has asked me to go over to Glen and decide on a site.

When Oddie received no reply, he wrote again, on Feb 23rd 1898, thinking that Wm James had refused the first suggestion: *The next best site is on a piece of ground out of a field which I and another hold as trustees of St. Cuthbert's Charity. It would have a frontage about opposite to those new cottages of yours that your brother built.*[2]

---

[1] DE 849/74

[2] The Trustee land on the corner of Church Lane, opposite houses built by Charles Packe on High St.

The Trustee Land proposed by the vicar for the village hall would have been behind the house in the centre of the picture, on the corner of Church Lane and High Street nearly opposite the houses built by Charles Packe.(see Chapter 5 lots 35 etc) [1]

The vicar pressed for swift action: *The spring, the time for building operations is now before us and we are all anxious to see your brother's legacy begin to take shape in bricks and mortar so that next autumn it may be available. Indefinite delay provokes questions as to what is going to be done about the bequest. Some of my people, especially Mrs Walker*[2]*, are impatient and look upon me as supine in not pressing the executors to commence operations.* He still hoped that his first choice of a site would be acceptable to WJP: *Possibly you have not definitely decided against the allotment site.*

The allotment site was in fact accepted. The Village hall was built in 1899 and part of the allotments were sacrificed. The hall, owned by the executors of Charles Packe and tenanted by the trustees in charge of running it, was rated at £9.6s per year in 1909. It proved a great success, much appreciated by the village residents.

In July 1917, Mr Robert Rowley donated a sum of money in memory of his wife: *Eliz Hastings Rowley deceased, late wife of R Rowley was much interested in the Parochial Hall and was much concerned as to the annual cost of heating, cleaning and maintenance thereof in the future. Robert Rowley wishes to provide for such cost and has transferred to the Trustees £400 and War Loan bonds to sell or invest,*

---

[1] Photo c. 1900 taken from a point near the old Fox and Goose. The left half of the house was later removed for road widening and the road was bridged over the ford.
[2] Wife of Theodore Walker of Glen Hall

To be called the Rowley Trust Fund And offers the suggestion that a minimum charge of ten shillings including the use of the piano be made when such hall is required by the parishioners of Glen Magna and the sum of fifteen shillings when hired to non-residents of the village.

Many villagers remember the Parochial Hall from their youth. Margaret Packe was delighted to know it was still being used: *I am surprised it is still standing. It was quite a focal point in our time. Little concerts and 'beanos' were held in it and my brother Michael organised dramatic events, when he was 17 or so. Many villagers and Packe friends came. There was a fee and the proceeds were for District Nurses. During the war there were weekly dances at the Parochial Hall (we called it that). They were very popular. The Parochial Hall doubled as a school for the evacuees. The Men's Institute next door had a billiard table.*

Ray Pickard remembered his father walking up to Glen Hall (c.1940) to see Col Packe about a booking for the Village Hall.

Fraser Gilbert recalls that it was later decorated with stuffed animal heads: *When Col Packe moved out of the Hall (in 1953) he gave all the wild animals' heads from a shoot in Africa...lions and tigers, crocodiles, antelopes, all sorts of animals, mounted on boards. They were all put up round the village hall, on the wall above the door. I don't know what happened to them now.*[1]

The hall is still used for a variety of events and has recently been given a face lift!

The Village Hall 2002

[1] Fraser Gilbert.

E C Packe

When he inherited the estate in 1908, EC Packe had little experience of living in Glen. Born and brought up in the vicarage at Feering: *He had, reluctantly, paid duty visits to his uncle there as a child.*[1] For a long time afterwards he was a 'king in exile', in the army and living abroad. He had inherited at a difficult time. There was a tide of sales of land in 1900, as agricultural workers moved to other work and settled in towns. *Country house owners who were almost totally dependent on agricultural economy had to improve incomes by investment in stock markets or were forced to retrench after 1879.*[2]

In the Valuation of 1910 he is still the biggest landowner in Glen, owning about 45 dwellings, but the income from their rents was small. Cottages had a Gross Annual Value (GAV, formerly called the Gross Estimated Rental) of between two and five pounds a year.[3] Glen Hall's was £146. The other most lucrative properties were: Glen Farm, Orchard Lane (Harry Cramp), Trent House (Henry Lewin), The Nook corner house and shop (Elson) and North House Farm (Wm Clements).[4] (For details and pictures of these houses, put up for sale in 1919, see Chapter 5.) The substantial houses in High Street, built by Charles Packe in 1874 were rated more highly than his other cottages but nevertheless only reached a gross annual rental value of six or seven pounds a year.[5] A couple of cottages on the London Road, opposite the Yews, brought in rents of £8 annually.[6] The schoolhouse (where Fancourt lived) was a more substantial property (£9 15s) but the neighbouring house (lived in by Laura Davis) was rated less highly (£5). Alfred Clowes and Arthur B Clarke, living in cottages near the entrance to Glen Hall, paid about £5 10s rent per year. Most of the Packe properties were smaller dwellings, with a Gross Annual Value of £5 a year.[7] We learn more about these houses, including what rents were actually paid in 1919, in Chapter 6.

The more expensive houses in the village, lived in by owner/occupiers, had a considerably greater rental value. Those rated at over £100 include Stackley House (Braithwaite, GAV £130), the Manor House (newly built for Robert Kaye, £220), Glen House (lived in by Rowley, £130). The other substantial houses are The Yews (Hannah Brown, £90), The Mount (R J Aspinall, £60), a house owned by

---

[1] Margaret Packe 2003

[2] *Researching the Country House*, Batsford Local History Series, 1992. Elton, Harrison and Wark

[3] See Factfile, Valuation figures 1910.

[4] Glen Farm, Harry Cramp, GAV £12 10s; Trent House, Henry Lewin, GAV £20, Elson, The Nook, GAV £18 15s and Wm Clements, North House, GAV £17.

[5] Harriett Capell, £7 16s, Ernest Bland £6 10s, John Achurch and Ernest Mason £6 10s.

[6] Tenanted by Malvina Spriggs and Harry Hayward. A smaller nearby cottage, tenanted by George Shephard is rated at £4.

[7] See Factfile.

Clara Pochin and J Brown, (tenanted by A Whittle, £55), The White House (Frederick Crick, rented to Dr Bonis, £40), The Sycamores (owned by the executors of Eliz Sprigge), Ruperts Rest (R R Goddard, £45), The Vicarage (£30 12s) Chesterfield House (Theresa Fewkes, £22) and the old bakehouse in The Nook (Miss Sykes, tenanted by Hubert Davis, £20).[1]

The names of the people in these houses appear in various roles in the village. From 1908 until 1920, when ECP returned to take up residence in Stretton Hall, his position as lord of the manor was in many ways taken by wealthy industrialists like Robert Rowley, Robert Kaye and Theodore Walker, his tenant in Glen Hall. It was they who sat on the various committees and governing bodies, dealt with problems and handed out prizes and saw to the maintenance, while he was abroad as a fighting soldier in France and Belgium

Properties in the village as numbered on the 1908 Valuation.[2]

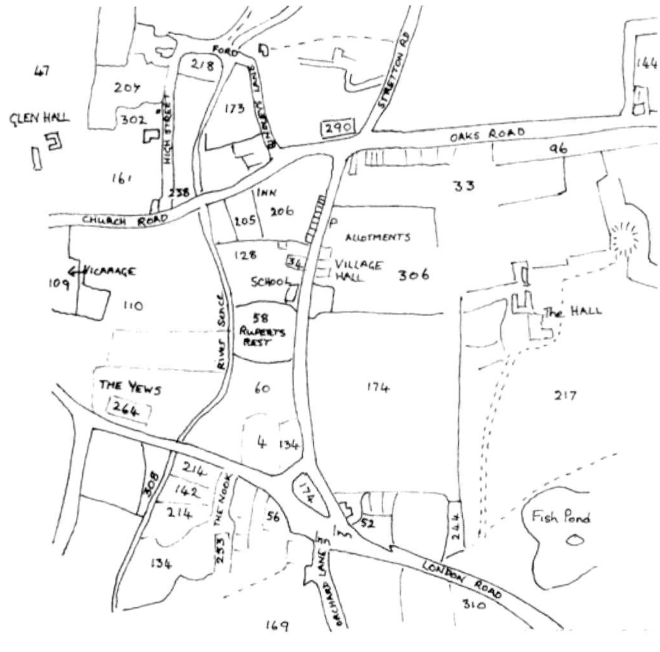

47 Glen House (Rowley
109 the vicarage
264 The Yews
214 The Nook (Elson)
142 Miss Sykes
314 the school
306 the village hall
58 Ruperts Rest
4 The White House
134 Chesterfield House
174 Trent House
52 The Crown
56 shops (Wand and Warner)
169 Glen Farm
217 Glen Hall

By this time the Lordship of the Manor had lost the significance of former years; it brought in no wealth. Manorial courts were no longer held and with them went the income which had formerly come to ECP's predecessors from land deals in the village, when each contract and sale brought a fee for the Lord of the Manor. Even

---

[1] Cf. The Royal Oak, GAV £15.12s; The Crown, GAV £40; The Greyhound, GAV £32.

[2] Hand drawn, simplified extract of the 1908 Valuation map. The local copy of the original has been lost. A copy can be seen in the Public Records Office, Kew. IR/130/4/90.

when, after the war, ECP returned to the village, he apparently took no interest in the title. *I don't think my father ever cared about being Lord of the Manor, nor would he have taken any notice about it.* [1]

The First World War (1914-1918)

The first World War had a tremendous impact on the economics and structure of society. It gave a blow to the feudal and hierarchical system still in operation when it began. Men from the upper classes and well educated public school boys like ECP, expected to serve their country and were accepted as natural leaders of men. They achieved high ranks in the armed forces, leading their troops into actions requiring great courage. ECP played his role bravely and well, gaining medals and honours to add to those he won in earlier battles and other wars. Poorer men and less well educated people rose mainly to non-commissioned ranks of sergeant and corporal. Poets like Wilfred Owen, Edmund Blunden, Seigfried Sassoon and Robert Graves, who fought in this war speak movingly of these humble people suffering from the effects of gas and wounds, or going to their deaths in foreign places, often unhonoured and unsung.

On Nov 11th we honour the Unknown Soldier as representative of these men. Those of us with relatives who fought in this war remember them on this occasion. For me the reference is my own father, twenty years younger than EC Packe, and from a very much lower social class. He was one of the few who returned safely from fighting in France. He often spoke to me of his experiences, when as a young lad of sixteen he had seen the death of other young men while they were in the squalor of the mud, with rats running over them in the trenches. He was, like ECP, one of the fortunate few who returned safely, counted his blessings, and mourned for the many friends and companions who had died.

The War Memorial, Chesterfield House and Main Street.

The war memorial on the village green shows the impact the war had had on Great Glen. The names listed on the base are of young men who went to fight and did not return to their families. Many of the names are familiar to us from census returns of generations earlier. Some of their families were Packe tenants. The dead are listed in order of rank.

First on the list of those who died is W.

[1] Margaret Packe 2002. She does not even know what became of the title when Stretton Hall was sold to the Ministry of Health in 1930.

Allen, who reached the rank of Second Lieutenant.
Walter Smith Allen, the son of Walter Allen the blacksmith, born and bred in the village, aged 7 in the 1901 census, with an extended family of cousins and uncles, died in France in March 1918. Many of the villagers would have known him and mourned with his family.
Second on the list is the sergeant, David Warner.
David Warner, killed in action in Palestine in 1917, was not named in the 1901 census but William Warner was the grocer in the shop near the Greyhound in 1904.
Then come the Lance Corporals**:**
Sidney Easom, born and brought up in Glen, the son of a bricklayer Thomas Easom and Edith, a dressmaker (who had both signed the petition[1] to remove children from religious instruction at school and to be provided with secular instruction instead). Sidney would then have been 10. He died as a soldier aged 20 in France in March 1918.
Harry Jenkins, the son of George and Ada Jenkins, does not appear on the 1901 census list. Perhaps the family were comparative newcomers to Glen. Harry died aged 19, a soldier in the South Staffs regiment.[2]
John Henry Neale was aged 11 in 1901, the youngest son of William and Elizabeth Neale. The family of five children all born in Glen, lived in Post Office Row on Main Street.[3] He was in the London Regiment and died on Sunday Sept 10th 1916 in France at the battle of the Somme.
Next on the list is:
John William Bennett, a sapper in the Royal Engineers. He died aged 19, killed in action in Flanders. He was the youngest of five children of William (a coal carrier) and Hannah Bennett of Burton Lane, all born in Glen.
He is followed by the Privates:
Arthur Bland, killed in action in Aug 1917 aged 26. He was aged 9 in 1901, one of the six children of Elizabeth Bland, a widow, living at 24 Post Office Row.
Joseph Clowes, died aged 32 in Oct 1916 in Flanders. He was the son of the widowed Ruth Clowes, who had lived with her husband Alfred in the cottages by the entrance to Glen Hall and who had also signed the parents' petition for secular education at the school in 1904. There were seven children in the family and Joseph was ten years older than his youngest brother and eight years younger than his oldest brother. Joseph was a hosiery hand aged 16 in 1901.
Bert Coleman has no entry in the Glen census for 1901. He enlisted in London and died on July 1st 1916 at the Somme. There were Colemans in the village in earlier times.

---

[1] presented to the school managers in Oct 26th 1904. See chapter 4.
[2] The men are from various regiments, following a deliberate policy of separating soldiers from the same area so that the death toll should not fall too heavily on any one district when one regiment went into battle.
[3] See chapter 5.

Benjamin Gupwell, the son of parents from Crick, near Rugby, has no entry either. The family must have been comparative newcomers to the village.

Herbert Folwell, the son of Mrs Annie Folwell, Stretton Lane, is from a long line of Folwells in Glen. Annie's husband James had been the coal agent in Glen and their three children were all born in the village. Herbert died aged 19 and was killed in action, serving with the Manchester Regiment, formerly The Sherwood Foresters, in Salonika in 1917.

John Edward Grain was also from a long line of the same name in Glen records. The family lived on Stretton Road and Wm Grain rented two fields from Packe. John was one of four children. He was in the 3rd Leicestershire Regiment and died in Flanders in 1916.

Edwin Victor Harris, the middle son of three, all born in Glen to Edwin (a joiner) and Hannah, living in Stretton Road. A neighbour of John Grain, who was eight years his senior, he died like him in Flanders field, in Oct 1917 aged 19.

Reginald Arthur Peberdy, the son of Alfred and Emma Peberdy of St Thomas' Road , born in Glen, died in Flanders in June 1917, aged 24. The Peberdy name occurs frequently in Glen records.

It is a sad roll call, echoed in almost every village in England at the time.

The extra plaque shows names of people who died in the second war. It includes EC Packe's son, Major Charles William Christopher Packe, of the Royal Fusiliers.

Theodore Walker, ECP's tenant at Glen Hall, was also bereaved. He gave a plot of land to the church to make an extension to the cemetery in memory of his son. The school managers showed their homage by giving the school a half holiday on Jan 23rd 1917 *when the tablet in the church on which the names of soldiers from this parish who have fallen or may fall in this war are to be inscribed or engraved.*[1]

Great Glen itself did not come under enemy attack and the war references appear in village records, like this one, incidentally, without drama. There must have been many widows and unmarried girls whose lives were made difficult by the loss of

---

[1] DE 849/52 School Managers Minute Book 1903 - 1938 Dec 1917

their menfolk. and many who took over the men's jobs and the roles of providers. This is not recorded in the documents. (The 1921 census will reveal such details.)

During the 1914-1918 War, EC Packe, as a major serving in France and Belgium, had little contact with Glen. Before he had finally returned from the war, he arranged with his brother James, who lived in Rothley, that land and property in Glen should be sold in order to cover running costs of the estate.[1] In 1919 houses and land were put up for auction in an attempt to raise money. Individual items brought in amounts ranging from £50 to £370.[2] There was no bid for the *fertile land* allotments on Main Street and the present memorial green was withdrawn from sale (as a *building plot*) when it failed to reach a price. ECP then gave the plot to the village as a war memorial site. The results of the sale must have been a great disappointment!

The 1920 and 30s

There was unemployment and agricultural depression after the war ended, the value of land had decreased and framework knitting in Glen had come to an end. By the time ECP came to live with his family in Stretton Hall, he had sold off much of the land and many of the houses he had inherited. Other stately homes all over the country were suffering from the same problems. Many farmers had gone through a lean time with poor harvests. They had difficulty paying rents. Many landowners sold paintings and possessions to help maintain the estate. Some sold libraries and furnishings. ECP seems to have sold what he could.

After the sale of so much of his land and so many of his houses in 1919, his Inland Revenue Tax assessment of 1920[3] lists only 36 cottages[4] remaining in his possession. He still owned Glen Hall, Stretton Hall and the various lodges there but rent receipts were not sufficient to maintain a rich way of life. He came with an army pension and little other income. He sold woods in 1929. Tommy Clark gives his perception of the details and the reasons: *By this time he was beginning to experience financial difficulties. Before he left Stretton Hall he sold all the trees (oaks and elms etc) in the woodland/copse areas, stretching from Stretton Hall to Crick's Retreat. The tree trunks were taken away by a horse-drawn trailer.*[5] This obviously did not bring in enough money and other sources of income had dried up. There was no money to spare in the Packe household, though they continued to live

---

[1] The rents accruing from all the houses and land he intended to sell came to £1,091 10s 9d per year. For details of rents of dwellings for sale in 1919 see chapter 5.

[2] Sir Maurice Levi (*ML*) paid £370 for *T Eason's field*.

[3] DE 1215/7

[4] These included Bott Stone House and the High Street houses built by Charles Packe, 8 in Post Office Row, the 10 cottages in Peep Row, which had not reached the auction price, plus two cottages and the lodge house at the entrance to Glen Hall, and the two Mill cottages, which had not been put up for sale.

[5] Thomas Clarke interviewed by JPh A. Aug 2003

comfortably and quietly in Stretton Hall with many elegancies and many beautiful possessions. The lavish pre-war days of Theodore Walker, who donated so generously, were over. ECP made a further attempt to raise money by holding a second auction in 1932 to sell the houses which had not been sold in 1919.[1]

In some ways, he was probably more visible and made more village appearances than his predecessors. As a retired major, he was a gentleman of leisure and therefore more available than his great uncle CWP, the Member of Parliament with great houses in London and Dorset, or his uncle Charles who mixed only reluctantly with the villagers, or his absentee landlord father the vicar, working in Essex. He did not have the same control as they had over school and church affairs now that both institutions had been effectively taken over by higher authorities. (He no longer had the advowson[2] of the church, and the school was state controlled.) As his daughter, Margaret Packe, said: *he was just a JP and a deputy Lieutenant but was never a swank. He was an important figure-head in the Leicester Boy Scouts, involved in the Leicestershire County Cricket Club and he was a magistrate.* [3]

He carried out the customary village duties. *The hunt met in Glen. He didn't ride but was always there with the stirrup cup.*[4]

The hunt meet outside The Greyhound [5]

The class system had not died with the Great War, but had merely been weakened. The deference to the inhabitants of 'the Big House' remained, but the wealth that supported it had gone. (Even as late as 1954, Glen was *positively feudal*, according

[1] See chapter 5
[2] *advowson*: the right of appointing the vicar, see Chapter 4.
[3] Margaret Packe
[4] Lilian Haines.
[5] picture courtesy of Fraser Gilbert.

to Mrs Fox who bought Glen Hall from ECP.[1]) There were strong bonds of duty, loyalty and affection between landlords and villagers. It is interesting to note, when listening to people talking about their memories, how often it appears that workers like the Haines, and the Langleys before them, stayed with the Packe family, even when better paid jobs were being offered to them elsewhere. The retainers worked long hours for low pay, but were repaid for their loyalty with rent-free houses and other 'perks.' *My parents got so little as payment. (I know because we cashed the cheque at Warner's.) Vegetables and wood from the spinney were free of course. We had potatoes and apples in the gorgeous loft, kept in straw: they lasted all year.*[2] Such conditions would now be unthinkable but survivors of a war, facing dangers of unemployment, were probably very content to be able to provide their family with enough to eat!

The Second World War Years

The 1939-46 war brought cares of a different sort. Younger men like ECP's sons went to war and were killed or injured. (His eldest son, Charles, was killed and is named on the war memorial plaque. His son Michael served throughout the war and was among those evacuated at Dunkirk, fought in Italy and was a survivor of Arnhem.[3]) Col Packe was beyond war service but 'did his bit' for the war effort by helping to form the Home Guard in the village.

One villager, Ray Pickard, remembers that the Home Guard practised with broom handles before they had guns and that they never had ammunition, as far as he knew. The story goes that someone who was driving along Station Road one night was stopped by the Home Guard. He wound down his window and the guard poked his gun through. 'Don't point that gun at me, young man', said the driver. The guard replied, 'It's all right, sir, it isn't loaded.' Another of his memories is of how 'the Colonel' helped the schoolboys learn to use the phone: *There were very few telephones in the village and so when a phone was installed in the Air Raid Wardens' office someone, possibly Col Packe, came up with the idea of giving children from the school the opportunity of using the telephone – most of us never having seen or used one in our short lives. We were coached one morning on what to say and then in the afternoon we were walked along to the ARW office (in the tack room adjoining the stables in the grounds of Ruperts Rest) and, standing in a queue, we were each in turn handed the telephone. Col. Packe was on the other end of the line up at the hall. The conversation went: Child: Good afternoon, Sir. How are you? Col Packe: I am well, thank you. Goodbye. Child: Goodbye.*[4]

---

[1] Mrs Fox, in conversation in 1980: *We only mixed with the people in the other big houses. The villagers were the hoi polloi who worked for us!* She was speaking of the past in a humorous and self deprecating manner, but there was an element of truth in what she said.

[2] Lilian Haines

[3] His novel *Winged Stallion* tells the story of the formation of the First Airborne Division.

[4] Ray Pickard interviewed by Judy Phythian Adams Sept 2002

Great Glen had no direct attacks during the war but it had its 'Dad's Army' and an Auxiliary Fire Service with a squad of eight and two message boys. Wally Allen tells the story of the night Stackley House was hit by an incendiary bomb, dropped from a damaged German plane returning from an attack on Leicester. This caused a huge fire. Wally Allen describes the look-out system and the excitement: *The ARP used to be in Main Street, next to Rupert's Rest and they had the warning. A chap called Dennis Easom, who was in the ARP, got on his bike, took a stirrup pump and went up to report that there was a hedge on fire. But when he got there it were the house that was on fire. He had to come all the way back again on his bike to tell them at the pub, the fire service. Jack Ward, the local butcher at that time, he comes dashing up, ever such a strong chap, he got everything all hitched up ready to be off when all the rest come, and they went up.*

The fire in the linen cupboard had taken hold and other voluntary fire groups from various outlying villages had also arrived. They all got the fire hoses working but initially, with groups at different sides of the house, they were all mis-aiming and the water was going right over the house and landing on the firemen on the opposite sides. They eventually got things working properly. The Misses Frisby had not wanted these amateurs and had tried to send them away because they were wanting the proper thing [a proper red professional fire engine]. But Dad's Army had come to the rescue! *The damage caused to the house was mainly in the servants' quarters...and they did damage the billiard table.*[1]

The other impact on the village was the arrival of evacuees. Evacuees had to be provided for and many, of course, had to be accommodated in the big houses. Miss Aston, who was in service from about 1936 at Dr Jamie's house,[2] throws light on the process of billeting the evacuees: *Dr Jamie used to go to Scotland for holidays and he didn't like the house left empty so one of us had to stay and we were left in charge and when the war started he went up to Scotland and Mrs Probin who lived on London Road came round and made us take four evacuees. We had to have them. He* [Dr Jamie] *was given twelve shillings for looking after them.* Taking evacuees was not a completely voluntary or philanthropic action. Twelve shillings would have been a lot of money for some of the poorer families but it seems that they offered to share their limited accommodation out of a real spirit of generosity and patriotism. Tommy Clark remembers: *When the evacuees from Canonbury Road School, Islington, arrived at the village hall, one of my sisters brought three of them, brothers and a sister, back to our house.*[3] *The girl later went to Stretton Hall but I think the boys soon went back to London.*[4]
In the same way, Col Packe went to collect his group (which included their teacher)

---

[1] Walter Allen interviewed by J P-A Oct 2002
[2] Haymes's house opposite the church on Church Road (see picture in Chapter 3 section 1)
[3] This was a very small cottage, see Chap 5 Plot 21.
[4] Tommy Clark interviewed by J PhA Aug 2002

and he, too, chose to have brothers with sisters, as he felt they would be happier not to be separated. As Margaret Packe put it: *We had eight evacuees, four boys, handpicked off the London bus by Dad. He could tell the type of boy he selected by his looks but there was one condition: each lad had to have a younger sister to protect and comfort if homesickness prevailed. (It never did!) We also had a lady teacher from the same school – Mrs Bonner, who was first rate and a help to Dad when I went to Lowesby (as a VAD[1]). I have kept in touch with one of the boys and we communicate with long letters at Christmas. He did very well and became a head teacher at a school in Reading.* Some Londoners kept up their Christmas correspondence with the Packes for many years and had happy memories of their time in Great Glen, despite the traumatic separation from their families.

Dr Jamie, a bachelor at the time, was generous to his evacuees and their parents, much to the dismay of his servants! Miss Aston remembers: *Dr Jamie treated them like his own family. Of course they all had two parents and at the weekends they came down and in his kindness he invited them all to meals. I had to put my foot down! When evacuees were here the parents came every weekend and it got too much: eight parents of four boys. They used the guest rooms, so we asked them to come just for the day once a month.* She was proud of the way Dr Jamie's household managed the children: *We got four boys, 'only' children* [having no brothers or sisters] *very spoilt, but we worked* [things] *out. We were very good on discipline. I remember them coming down with armfuls of daffs from the Hall, as a present for us. And we said, 'You can't do that!' and they said: There was no notice saying 'Don't pick'! They were about ten and stayed all through the war and a couple still write. They say, 'We discipline our children just like you used to!'*

She remembers the hard work involved when visitors arrived, expecting pre-war service: *At Christmas Mrs Frizzell and another sister of Dr Jamie's used to come and stay and that meant a fire in every bedroom. I don't know how we did it. They rang for tea in the morning.* Food rationing meant that meals were a problem, but Dr Jamie seems to have entertained quite well, thanks to competent servants and the money to pay for outside occasional help. There were also ways and means of acquiring unrationed food! Miss Aston speaks darkly of 'the Black Market' as well as of more legitimate ways of managing affairs: *I made pigeon pudding during the war and when he bought a cow I had to learn to milk it and make butter.*

On being shown KPR's 1822 menu book, Miss Aston remembered what it was like for her to cook for Dr Jamie and his guests before the war: *The most we had would be eight. County people from the various halls and Specialists down from London. They ate at 7 or 8 o'clock and it went on till 11pm. The ladies went into the drawing room for tea, coffee and petit fours. The local women loved to help with the washing up because they went home with lots of food. Savoury, a choice of*

---

[1] VAD, Voluntary Aid Detachment

soups then meat course with choice of meats, then fish course, then sweet course, then there would be a dessert and you'd finish up with walnuts or cheese sticks. Sweet is a pudding but dessert is apples, pears, fruit in a big display piled up on table. Six different knives and forks in order [for each place setting] *and we always had finger bowls of warm water with a little flower in the glass. My sister did that and made napkins in shapes. We ate separately in the kitchen but had the same food and Dr Jamie invited our relatives from Birmingham. He was very good.*

ECP was one of the select visitors to Dr Jamie's house in Miss Aston's time: *Col Packe was a gentleman. I can still see him with his walking stick. He spoke to everyone. We used to entertain them all, all the local gentry.. I used to serve eight course meals in the dining room and my sister used to wait at table and the village women used to come and help do the washing up.* She liked the colonel's unpretentious and informal manners: *Col Packe more or less adopted me and my sister. We were more like 'family'. They came through the kitchen. They used to put their finger in to taste and I'd say: Now take your finger out of that!* (Margaret Packe did not go with her father on these occasions: *I was very young when Dr Jamie lived there and as far as I know I never saw him. He was never more than a name to me. He was always spoken of as being very old and very rich. He was both a respected Leicester heart specialist and an ex-regular soldier so to some he was known as Dr or Col Jamie but to us, just John.)*

Col Packe's situation was not so comfortable as Dr Jamie's: he had no living-in help. His housekeeper, Mrs Haines, lived at the bottom of the drive, a long way when you have to trundle home a huge churn of water and then cook for your own family! Margaret Packe thinks her family did not get as embroiled as Dr Jamie did with his evacuees' families. *We didn't get too involved with the parents, as Dr Jamie did. Ours came down at weekends to see the children and joined Dad for meals and usually brought him gifts. One father liked a day's fishing in the lake.*

It was Mrs Haines who gave the kind, motherly treatment to Margaret Packe and the evacuees and others in need. Her daughter Lilian remembers her bringing in to the house the children of people who came to park in the hall drive, when they came to shelter from the bombs that were to be dropped on Leicester

Soldiers were billeted at the hall: *There was a series of regimental detachments billeted in the village - in the outbuildings of our hall. We had the best part of a regiment of soldiers billeted in the stables and numerous outhouses in the yard with sleeping accommodation in some upper rooms. It must have been very uncomfortable and they disappeared during the day to some centre in the village.*[1] Margaret herself was not one who attended the dances at the NAAFI or the hall in Orchard Lane, though they must have brought a lot of fun and excitement to the

[1] Margaret Packe.

other girls in the village! By 1940 she was in the services herself, and by a strange irony of history, working at Lowesby Hall as a VAD[1] and scrubbing the kitchen table where so many meals had been prepared for Kitty Packe Reading when she entertained people to dinner a century before.

***After the War*: 'You've never had it so good.'**

Men, like my own father, who had come from a poverty stricken childhood in 1900 and fought for their country in the Great War in 1914, felt that after the Second World War, life had improved. They found a better world and a fairer society, with the benefits of free education for their children, good health care, an adequate diet and, eventually, the security of a pension. Men like him never ceased to count their blessings. They were tolerant and understanding of money shortage and appreciative of gentlemanly behaviour and attitudes, like those of Col Packe's.

The village had changed considerably by the time ECP moved to Dell House in 1953. The once important framework knitting industry had collapsed. The factories had gone. Some had been converted into ordinary houses. *There was a glove factory in Allen's yard, High Street. It is now part of Suttons' house* [8, High Street].[2] Another factory became the school dinner centre. And another on Church Lane, near the old Fox and Goose, was destroyed. Few were left who even remember the way the work was done. Fraser Gilbert remembers Aggie Draper, one of the last to do so: *Aggie Draper, who died last year, in 2003, aged 90, remembered sitting and watching the man at his framework knitting loom and she could do all the actions with her feet and hands going bang shuttle phush phush. The factory was where the bus stop pull-in is now, by Thorpe's.*[3]

Women like Miss Aston, who had worked in service from when she was 15, discovered that conditions were better in public service and she, too, went to work away from Glen, in school kitchens in the big city (Leicester).

The smithy, which had been so important when horses were the main source of transport, no longer existed. The horse shoeing ended when machinery took over from working horses:

When I was a girl we lived at Kilby and my father used to go to Melton Market and he would give me five shillings to go to Glen and get the horses shod with the Allens in High St. I was born in 1927 and must have been about eleven then.[4]

---

[1] VAD: Voluntary Aid Detachment

[2] Fraser Gilbert

[3] Fraser Gilbert 2004

[4] Sheila Ball

Les Allen in the Smithy.The Allen's house behind the smithy.

The village thrived, despite the loss of its main industries. There was a busy row of shops on the main London Road.

The photo[1] shows The Old Greyhound, Warners house, W B Warner shop, provisions and groceries and spirits established c.1904. The Post Office and telephone exchange. Shipp and Sons Family Drapers. T Wood,Teas, Agent for Knighton laundry.

One was an outfitters, tailors, called Peter Shipp and Sons. They sold a wide variety of things carpets, hardware etc. Most of the villagers bought their things 'on tick' from him and Mr Shipp would go round the village each week to collect their payments. Mr Shipp continued to supply goods even after he relinquished the shop.[2]

[1] From a folder of photos of Great Glen in the Record Office
[2] Tommy Clark interviewed by J P-A 2002

The Victory Café is on the left of The Greyhound, Warner's house to the right of it, beside the grocers and the Antiques shop.

On seeing these pictures of the village shops in the 1960s, Margaret Packe commented: *I was surprised to notice, in your picture, in its old position, what used to be the Peberdy's Victory Cafe, no more than a shack which, as it was, could never have lasted till now, but it was a place where my brother Michael and I could spend our meagre pocket money on sweeties or, if in luck, a small ice cream. Bully for them for keeping open on Sundays!*[1]

[1] Margaret Packe Sept 2003

The village had changed. New wealth came in; new estates of houses were built: old buildings were pulled down. The old row of shops on the London Road has been replaced with a new terrace of houses facing the memorial green.

Valley House Mews.
Built early 70s

The shops moved away from the old turnpike road.

London Road 1906[1]

[1] photo courtesy of Fraser Gilbert

The turnpike road was finally bypassed.

London Road 2004

The shopping centre 'migrated' from the London Road to the newer part of the village, at the junction of Main Street, Stretton Road and Oaks Road, where the new post office was built.

Col Packe decided it was time for him to move out of the hall and he, too, migrated away from the London Road and up the hill to Dell House in 1953.

FACTFILE
I like to understand history through figures and percentages of these figures, through knowing the price of coal and the price of corn and the price of a loaf on the day the Bastille fell. I like to be free, so far as I can, from the tyranny of interpretation. Hilary Mantel, *The Clean Slate*

The Stretton Estates map. Houses owned by Sir George Robinson in 1835.

25 Oldacres/Lewin (Glen Farm, Orchard Lane)
29 Wm Burton, Homestead and hovel (The Nook)
31 Oldacres, House in two tenements (1, The Nook)
33 Thos Thompson, (Church Lane, opposite the Fox and Goose)
35, 36 Mr Cooper (site of the 1846 school), and Three cottages
37 John Glover and later Widow Glover (Main Street)
38 Wm Storer, cottage (Main Street) set in Allotments (39)

1837 VALUATIONS (Selected items). Quarter Sessions Records 27/2/193

Gross Estimated Rental had come to be established in the mid-nineteenth century as the rent per year at which the property could be expected to be let. **Rateable Value** was worked out by deducting from the GER a sum representing the annual cost of repairs…necessary to maintain the property in a state which would warrant such a rent.[1] The separation of houses above/ below £10 annual rent gives an indication of voting entitlement. A large difference between the house rental and the GER/RV indicates extensive land attached to the house.

Occupier	Owner	Description/ *present name where known*	Under £10 pa	Over £10	GER pa £. s.	RV £. s.
Wm Bosworth	Bosworth	*3, The Nook*		20	26 18	20
George Briggs	Woodruffe	*Ruperts Rest*		15	127 14	117 15
Rev F.Corrance	Corrance	*The vicarage*		25	38 12	33 10
George Cooper	Cooper	*The Yews*		32	375	358 5
Harriet Cooper	Cooper	*Sycamores*		16	104 10	97 10
Benjmn Cooper	Sir George R	(36)	9		100	94 15
Oldacres	Sir Geo R	*1, The Nook*		16	246	232
Wm Clements	Sir George R	*? Glen farm?*		14	244	229
Wm Cooper	Lowdham	land & house	10	20	177	168
Robert Haymes	Haymes, Esq	*Glen House,*		45	264	247
Wm Horton	Horton	*White House*		20	50 15	43 15
Thos Hobson	Hobson	*The Mount*		14	98	91
Wm Harrold	Harrold	house		16	16	12
Wm Norman	Day	*The Greyhound*		30	60	50
Green Hodgkin	Beardsley	*The Crown*		30	30	20
Thos Gilbert	John Gilbert	*Fox and Goose*		12	12	8
Thos Batchelor	John Batchelor	*Royal Oak*	5		5	4
C W Packe Esq	C W Packe Esq	*Glen Hall*		55	85	75
Wm Oswin	Sir Hry Halford	*The mill*		30	30	16
Martha Newton	Frances Burton	cottages	2		2 12	1 10
Alice Easom	Sir G Robinson	cottages	4		8	7
Wm Edgley	Sir George R	land & house	5		10 10	9
Thos Thompson	Sir G Robinson	Church Lane			2 12	1 10
Sam Sturgess	Sir Hry Halford	*Millerdale*	3		3	2
Job Sturgess	Sir Hry Halford	*Millerdale*	3		3	2
Wm Dencher	Robert Haymes	*Peep Row*	2		2 12	1 10
Edward Foster	Robert Haymes	*Peep Row*	2			
Laurence Grain	Robert Haymes	*Peep Row*	2			
Samuel Burdett	Robert Haymes	*Peep Row*	2			
John Roe	Robert Haymes	*Peep Row*	2			
John Clarke	Robert Haymes	*Peep Row*	2			
Robt Dickman	Robert Haymes	*Peep Row*	2			
Wm Bird	Robert Haymes	*Peep Row*	2			
Wm Carver	Robert Haymes	*Peep Row*	2			

[1] K D M Snell; *Settlement, Poor Law and the Rural Historian; new approaches and opportunities. Rural History: Economy, Society, Culture,* 3:2 (1992), pp. 145-172.

1878 Valuation DE 849/34 Houses mentioned in the text.

No.	Owner	Occupier	Property/*present name where known*	GER p a £. s.	RV £. s.
1	Wm Allen	John Sykes	Bakehouse *(Bassetts)*	20	16
6	Jos EnochArmitage	Thomas Crick	*White House* and grounds	35	28
8	J B Burdett	James Flint	*Fox and Goose*	18	14 10
11	Elias Bland	Thos Crick	*Royal Oak pub*	19 10	15 10
38	Sam Beadman	Wm Chisholm	*The Crown*	24	19
168	Catherine Norman	Richard Roberts	*The Greyhound*	16	13 10
10	Frances Burton	Aug Hunt Esq	House and grounds	15	12
12	GV Braithwaite	GV Braithwaite	*Stackley House*	71	56
23	John Bachelor	Charles Packe	House and land	29 5	24 10
33	W H Booker	Benjamin Cooper	House and grounds	25	20
34	Benjamin Cooper	Benjamin Cooper	*The Sycamores*	25	20
35	George Cox	George Cox	*The Oaks and grounds*	58	51
40	Wm Clements	Charles Packe	*North House and land*	733 10	659
48	Thomas Crick	Thomas Crick	*Ruperts Rest*	37 10	30
93	Wm Elson	Morley Lewin	House	15	12
114	Jos Freeman	Charles Packe	*House and Water mill*	70	59
118	Frank S Hodgkin	Charles Packe	*1, The Nook?* and land	270	241
127	Harriet Clowes	Sir H Halford	*17 London Road*	3 15	3
128	Wm Thompson	Sir H Halford	*19 London Road*	4 10	3
147	Morley H Lewin	Charles Packe	*Glen Farm Orchard Lane*	139 10	125
155	Joseph Lovett	Charles Packe	*Trent House and land*	46 5	40
161	Murietta Christobal	M Christobal	*Glen House and grounds*	100	80
174	Hon H O'Brien	Charles Packe	*Glen Hall and grounds*	100	80
208	Henry Langley	Charles Packe	Cottage	5	4
211	Wm Fancourt	Charles Packe	*Schoolhouse*	4 10	3 10
212	Elizabeth Hall	Charles Packe	*Schoolhouse*	2 10	2
213	Ann Easom	Charles Packe	cottage	3	2 10
214	Wm Neale	Charles Packe	cottage	3	2 10
215	George Coleman	Charles Packe	cottage	3	2 10
216	George Coulson	Charles Packe	cottage	3	2 10
217	Widow Newton	Charles Packe	cottage	3	2 10
218	Thos Grant	Charles Packe	cottage	3	2 10
219	John Grain	Charles Packe	cottage	3	2 10
220	Wm Rowe	Charles Packe	cottage	3	2 10
221	Wm Barnes	Charles Packe	cottage	3	2 10
222	Wm Achurch	Charles Packe	cottage	3	2 10
223	Chas Overton	Charles Packe	cottage	3	3 15
224	John Hodgkin	Charles Packe	cottage	3	2 10
225	George Grain	Charles Packe	cottage	3 15	3
226	James Morris	Charles Packe	cottage	3 15	3 10

1878 Valuation contd

227	Thos Capell	Charles Packe	Bott Stone cottage	3 15	3
228	Wm Grain	Charles Packe	High Street	3	3 15
229	void	Charles Packe	cottage	1 5	1
230	Isaac Clarke	Charles Packe	cottage	2 10	2
231	Isaac Grain	Charles Packe	*Peep Row (in 1881)*	5	4
232	John Pywell	Charles Packe	*Peep Row (in 1881)*	5	4
233	Isaac Muddimer	Charles Packe	*Peep Row (in 1881)*	5	4
234	Wm Peberdy	Charles Packe	*Peep Row (in 1881)*	5 10	4 10
235	George Hubbard	Charles Packe	*Peep Row (in 1881)*	5 10	4 10
236	John Wise	Charles Packe	cottage	4 10	3 10
237	Enos Atkinson	Charles Packe	cottage	4 10	3 10
238	Wm Bromage	Charles Packe	*Post Office Row*	5 10	4 10
239	Samuel Crick	Charles Packe	*Post Office Row*	5 10	4 10
240	Jonathan Rowe	Charles Packe	*Post Office Row*	5 10	4 10
241	Mary Elson	Charles Packe	*Post Office Row*	5 10	4 10
242	Daniel Allen	Charles Packe	*Post Office Row*	5 10	4 10
243	Thos Coulson	Charles Packe	*Post Office Row*	5 10	4 10
244	James Allen	Charles Packe	*Post Office Row*	5 10	4 10
245	John Achurch	Charles Packe	*Post Office Row*	5 10	4 10
246	Frank Simpson	Rev Haymes	*Haymes house*	100	80

1910 Valuation. DE2072/165. Houses mentioned in the text. Gross Annual Value

Occupier	Owner	Description/*present name where known*	GAV p a £. s.	RV £. s.
Dr Bonis	Fred Crick	*The White House*	40	32
Florence Clayton	Braithwaite	*Stackley House*	130	104
Arthur Yates	Yates	house	12 14	10 3
Hannah Brown	Hannah Brown	*The Yews*	90	72
Robert Kaye	Robert Kaye	*Manor House*	220	176
Robert Rowley	Robert Rowley	*Glen House (Haymes')*	130	104
Chas Sprigge	Sprigge	*Sycamores*	45	36
Mrs Wand	Ward & Warner	*(Valley Mews site)*	18 10	14 8
Robie R Goddard	Goddard	*Ruperts Rest*	45	36
Wm Cobley	J. Muddimer	*Old Post Office*	8 5	6 12
Rachael Campton	Muddimer	*Old Post Office*	8 10	6 16
Arthur Whittle	Clara Pochin	house	55	44
Rev John Orr		*Vicarage*	30 12	24 10
Joseph Cross	Joseph Cross	*Glen House*	120	96
Theresa Fewkes	Fewkes	*Chesterfield House*	22	17 12
Hubert Davis	Miss Sykes	*Bakehouse The Nook*	20	16
Ralph Aspinall	Aspinall	*The Mount*	60	48
J Upton Randall	George Sprigge	house	20	16
Harry Cramp	ECP	*Glen Farm Orchard Lane*	12 10	10
Henry Lewin	ECP	*Trent House*	20	16
Theodore Walker	ECP	*The Hall*	146	116 16
John Bachelor	ECP	house	13 17	11 2
Wm Clements	ECP	*North House*	17	13 12
Wm Elson	ECP	House and shop	18 15	15
Charles W Freer	ECP	cottage	18	14 8
Thos Capell	ECP	*Bott Stone cottage*	5	4
Louis Lassiter	ECP	cottage	3 5	2 12
Thos Grant	ECP	*Peep Row*	5 5	4 4
John Jarvis	ECP	cottage	5 5	4 4
Daniel Nosely	ECP	*Peep Row*	2 10	2
Kate Achurch	ECP	*Peep Row*	4	3 4
Ann Peberdy	ECP	*Peep Row*	2 10	2
Wm Barnes	ECP	*Peep Row*	5	4
Fredk Coltman	ECP	*Peep Row*	5	4
Grant/Gould	ECP	*Peep Row*	5	4
George Treslove	ECP	*Post Office Row*	5	4
James Allen	ECP	*Post Office Row*	5	4
Wm Freestone	ECP	*Post Office Row*	5	4
Rachel Harris	ECP	*Post Office Row*	5	4
Elizabeth Bland	ECP	*Post Office Row*	5	4
Green Achurch	ECP	*Post Office Row*	5	4
John Gamble	ECP	*Post Office Row*	5	4
Wm Neale	ECP	*Post Office Row*	5	4
Harriet Capell	ECP	cottage	7 16	6 5
John Achurch	ECP	cottage	6 10	5 4
Ernest Mason	ECP	*High St*	6 10	5 4
Ann Clarke	ECP	*High St*	4	3 4
Ernest Bland	ECP	*High St*	6 10	5 4

1910 Valuation contd.

Occupier	**Owner**	**Description/*present name where known***	**GAV p a £. s.**	**RV £. s.**
Wm Pywell	ECP	*High St*	9 15	7 16
Laura Davis	ECP	*Schoolhouse*	5	4
Wm H Fancourt	ECP	*School house*	9 5	7 16
Arthur B Clarke	ECP	*17 London Road*	5 10	4 8
Alfred Clowes	ECP	*19 London Road*	5 10	4 8
Joseph Henson	ECP	cottage	4	3 4
John Peake	ECP	cottage	7 16	6 5
Malvina Sprigges	ECP	cottage	8	6 8
Harry Hayward	ECP	cottage	10	8
George Sheppard	ECP	cottage	5	4

DIRECTORIES

1846 WHITE'S DIRECTORY. Gentry are listed (in alphabetical order): George Cooper, Rev Francis Corrance, the vicarage, Robert Haymes Esq., Watson Manby Esq., surgeon.

GLENN MAGNA, or *Great Glenn*, is a large and well-built village, situated in a pleasant valley, on the Market Harborough road, 6 miles S.E. by S. of Leicester. Many of its inhabitants are framework knitters, and its *township* contains 795 inhabitants, and 2011 acres of land, chiefly in pasturage; but its *parish*, which was enclosed in 1759, comprises also Stretton Magna chapelry.

Allen Daniel, blacksmith
Bailey John Peach, manufacturer, *Stackley Lodge* (and Leicester)
Batchelor Thomas, bricklayer
Brake Mrs. Phillis|| Burton Mrs. F.
Burdett Edw. hosiery agent
Clement Sarah, postmistress
Cooper George, Esq.
Corrance Rev. Frs. Thos. LL.B. vicar
Corrance Rev. Hy. Fras. B.A. curate
Edgley Wm. boarding academy
Gilbert Thos. vict. Fox and Goose
Grain Wm. parish clerk
Hall John, vict. Crown
Harrold Wm. beerhouse keeper
Haymes Robert, Esquire
Holyoak Thomas, tailor
Manby Watson, surgeon
Newton Martha, schoolmistress
Nichols Thomas, shopkeeper
Norfolk John, shoemaker
Norman Wm. vict. Greyhound
Packe Chas. Wm. Esq. M.P., Manor House (and *Prestwold Hall*)
Wright Wm. wheelwright, &c

Bakers.
Hill Wm.
Horton Wm. (& miller)
Weston Edward

Butchers.
Green Achurch
Lewin James

FARMERS *And Graziers.* (* *are Owners.*)
*Cooper Benj.
*Cooper John
*Franks Thos.
Gilbert William, *Stackley*
*Hobson Thos., *Mount pleasant*
Horton Wm. (& builder)
Lewin James
Oldacres Wm.
Timson Saml. (& maltster)

CARRIER, Dinah Glover, to Leicester, M. W. and Sat.

POST, from Leicester, daily, 8 mg; returns 8 night

Trades are listed:
Mrs Sarah Clements, farmer and post office, Wm Edgley, boarding and day school, George Elson, carpenter and shopkeeper, John Gilbert, wheelwright, Thos Gilbert, landlord of the Fox and Goose, Wm Norman, landlord The Old Greyhound , John Norman Hall, landlord The Crown, Holyoak tailor, James Lewin butcher and grazier

HARRODS DIRECTORY 1870.
The living is a vicarage annual value £235 in the gift of Mrs Packe Reading held by the rev Henry Luke Dodds. Chief owners Mrs Packe Reading, lady of manor, Arthur Haymes Esq and H F Coleman Esq. The gentry include: Miss Frances Burton, Thos Crick, Dodds, Edgley, Fewkes, Haymes, Hill, Mr Wm Horton, Miss Eliz Roby.
C of E schools for boys and girls. E Paulson schoolmaster Mrs Mumford mistress. The Wesleyans have a small chapel**Trades** John Fewkes surgeon

Mrs Rebecca Gilbert, The Fox and Goose
Mrs Sarah Gilbert, The Crown Inn
Mrs Jane Pick, The Old Greyhound
Elias Bland, The Royal Oak.
John Grain, manager Gt Glenn Industrial Provident Stores
John Why, shopkeeper
Farmers and graziers: John Beadman, Wm Beardsley, Mrs Sarah Clements, Wm Clements, Benjamin Cooper, Thos Hobson (Mt Pleasant), Wm Horton, Wm Knight, James Lewin, Wm Ragg (butcher), George Coleman, Morley Hodges Lewin, Fredk Ragg, farm bailiff.
Bakers: Freeman, the miller, Wm Harrold, Wm Hill.
Boot and shoe makers: John Easom, Wm King, James Norfolk, Matthew Pywell.
Carrier Edward Bindley. Carrier goes to Leics Weds and Saturdays
Submistress is Mrs Mary Elson.

KELLY'S DIRECTORY 1932
Chief landowners Col E Packe, Sir Maurice Levy, RW Kaye, W H Heard, G Sprigge, R Rowley. The village is lighted by gas supplied by the Leicester Corporation. The church has six bells dating from 1625 to 1785 retuned and rehung in 1898, two being recast in memory of Charles Packe. In 1920 Robert Rowley Esq JP presented a tablet bearing the names of the men of the parish who fell in the Great War 1914-18. A village hall was erected with a legacy bequeathed by Charles Packe
Postal Telegraph office at GG station. Open on Sundays from 9 to 10-30 am
Carrier Albert Gibson
Rev Anderson Rupert's Rest
Vicar Barclay The vicarage
Misses Edith and Jessie Frisby, Stackley House
Robert Kaye, The Manor
Harold Moore, The Firs [now Chesterfield House]
E C Packe, The Hall
Robert Rowley, Glen House
George Sprigge, The Sycamores
Misses Thompson, The White House
Hedley Batchelor, builder contractor
John Bodycote, boot maker
Thos Franks Gilbert, clerk to the Parish council and rate collector
Heard, farmer, The Mount
Mrs L Perberdy (sic) dress maker
Shipp and son, drapers
Victory café, A. N. Brandrick
Miss Florence Wood, confectioner

Glen Magna, a large well built village and parish 6 miles from Leicester and 9 from Market Harborough, 103 from London, containing 795 inhabitants and 2,011 acres of land. The living is a vicarage worth £217 per annum in the gift of CWP Esq MP; Rev Francis Thomas Corrance is the incumbent. The church dedicated to St Cuthbert is a neat building with a nave, chancel, aisle and a square tower containing five good toned bells.

Hagar's Commercial Directory 1849

The Church in the time of CWP and KPR

When CWP came to Great Glen the church was still in a rather dilapidated state. It had lost its spire in 1768 and when Throsby saw it in 1790 he had described it as *not well attended on the Sabbath. The walls are green from copious streams of water; and broken benches lie in all directions, richly adorned with the labour of spiders.*

Various attempts had been made since then to improve the condition. In 1837, Great Glen, as part of the archdeaconry of Leicester, had been removed from the Diocese of Lincoln and attached to Peterborough Diocese. By the time Archdeacon Bonney made his Visitation in July 1842 he was able to record that *the church tower is strong but needs a little pointing and the body of the church is in a decent state. The Chancel, repaired by Sir George Robinson, is in a fair state. The minister Frances Thomas Corrance resides in Vicarage House, which is in good Order. Signed J K Bonney, Archdeacon.*[1] White's Directory of 1846 mentions that the Rev F T Corrance *has a good residence near the church.* CWP certainly found no reason to contribute to the cost of improving the church fabric, when requested to do so by the vicar Dodds in 1862.[2]

---

[1] DE 2933/108/3 Archdeacon Bonney's Visitation: *As to the parish clerk he is a very respectable man and gives great satisfaction. The church is swept every week and washed once a year.*

[2] See below p.

The advowson, or right of appointing the vicar, was one of the responsibilities of the Lord of the Manor. The Rev F T Corrance[1] had been appointed by Sir George and Lady Robinson; CWP appointed his successor, R J Mapleton, in 1851.[2] At the same time he seems to have made an agreement with a young curate, George Boyle, that he should take over the post when he came of age. This appointment was to cause CWP and his wife considerable hassle and embarrassment because George Boyle, at the last minute, declined to accept the post. He decided the vicarage was not adequate and the income was lower than he had been led to believe. He wrote to CWP on April 28 1855:
My dear Mr Packe,
It is with sincere regret that I write to you to say that in consequence of the investigation we have made into the state of things at Glenn, I fear it will be quite out of my power to be the next incumbent. My Mother and I went there yesterday and we had a builder from Leicester to give us some idea regarding the wants of the fabric. The house is a very damp one and this arises from an imperfect construction of the original building and the character of the addition made in the time of Mr Corrance. In short after every attempt to make the best of matters we found that an outlay so considerable was required that we have given up all idea of settling at Glenn. Mr Mapleton assured me in the autumn that this living has never since he had it exceeded £200 a year.[3]

KPR wrote frantic letters to him from Richmond Terrace in May 1855, explaining how embarassing it was to be so let down. She writes (with lots of underlining and double underlining): *My dear George, It is hardly possible to exaggerate the GRIEF I feel and the consternation And EMBARASSMENT of Mr Packe on reading your letter last night or rather I should say at 2 o'clock this morning.* (Her letters are very enlightening as to the life led by the Packes.) *We returned from Branksome last night at ten o clock and having set Mr Packe down at the House of Commons I proceeded home EXTREMELY TIRED and I found as usual loads of notes and cards- but being so tired I took them all up the stairs and prepared for bed and then drawing my chair to the fire, opened your mother's letter thinking I would just have a chat with her before I resigned myself to much longed for rest—imagine then my dismay! I never was so very grieved and disappointed I think in my whole life and as I gathered from her letter there was one waiting Mr Packe from you. I determined to sit up for him as I knew he would also be much vexed and indeed dear George he was so! We talked it over in all sorts of ways and heard the clock strike two and three – and I have a wretched headache today in consequence of over fatigue –*

[1] Rev F T Corrance, Sept 1814 to Jan 1851.
[2] Mapleton remained until 1855.
[3] DE1667 18 Rev George Boyle, from Church Street, Kidderminster

Because her husband has been so busy, she writes on his behalf to convey his extreme displeasure: *Mr Packe...had to receive Sir Henry* [?] *Stafford and some hosiers at ten and go to the committee of which he, Mr Packe, is chairman at 12 and will not come home till 6 or 7. He has deputed me to write to you ' in the kindest manner possible but at the same time to make you understand his disappointment* [and] *extreme perplexity at this sudden and quite unlooked for change after your having accepted the living four years ago.'* She goes on to suggest a meeting: *I really think it is impossible to settle anything without SEEING you it is so impossible to explain in writing all our great difficulties, puzzles and to concoct some remedy for it all without a personal interview with you – recollect we are not at all satisfied with the present state of affairs that we have been looking forward to you for four years.*

Stressing the necessity of talking face to face, she suggests he take a day ticket by train to sort things out better with them. He replies that he prefers to write, as it is: *easier for me to say in writing that the inadequacy of private means prevented my becoming incumbent of Glenn than to do it viva voce.* She explains their difficulty in getting on with village affairs without him: *and therefore making the best of much that is wrong, putting off setting things right especially about the schools till you should be there.* Being let down at such short notice is a great embarrassment: *Mr Packe is in a most awkward position which would not have been the case if he had known this four years ago or even two years ago but now you are expected to take possession in three weeks - when all the parish knows you are coming and the neighbouring clergy expect it also – what is Mr Packe to do? At such short notice.*

CWP himself wrote to Boyle May 19th 1855, but to no more effect. (His letter seems by contrast much more 'masculine', straightforward and unencumbered with the niceties of tact and human contact than his wife's, which always seem breathless and anxious not to offend.) He points out that George had had a chance to speak out when he stayed at the vicarage six months before: *touching objections which were equally in existence then as three weeks before you were to have taken possession.* He also reckons George was misinformed as to the annual income.

The matter ended in the appointment, in Aug 1855, of H L Dodds, a bachelor vicar born in Woodfordbridge, living with his mother, aged 72 and four servants, in the 1861 census. He remained as vicar until Aug 1886. In some ways it was out of the frying pan and into the fire for the Packes; Dodds' dedication to his job was later to become the source of much grief to each of them in turn! Kitty Packe-Reading seems to have done most of the letter writing to the vicar, on behalf of her husband. The correspondence[1] between her and Dodds is interesting (though the terrible handwriting of both correspondents makes reading it a difficult task!). Dodds

---

[1] DE1667 9 4

writes (in thick black ink) to Mr Packe on 17th March 1862 to ask for funds for church renovation and Kitty Packe Reading replies two days later rejecting the request.

Dear Mr Dodds 19th March 1862

I am sorry to say I can give you no hope whatever of Mr Packe entertaining any thoughts of 'restoring' the church at Great Glen. He is very much astonished that it should require any material repair. She goes on to suggest that repairs have in the past been no concern of either the vicar or the Manor but that there was: *a fund to repair the church and poor dear old Mr Haymes*[1] *managed it, Mr Packe believes, entirely* [on his own]. *We were residing at Glen. Of course we were too new as inhabitants there to think of interfering and he is nearly sure that the clergyman then, Mr Corrance, had no voice in the matter.*

On these grounds, CWP rejects the plea for funds: *While there is such a fund for keeping Great Glenn church in repair Mr Packe feels that he has many, very many claims on his funds for 'Works of Piety and Charity' which must take precedence of the restoration of Great Glenn church, being torn away through no fault of his own from his paternal residence while he still feels bound to attend to the poor there (plus residence in London and misery there...) You see that he cannot at all entertain the idea of appropriating any money to the church at Great Glen.*

A further letter indicates that the Packes think that Dodds could use his own money if he should feel so strongly about the matter:

24th March 1862

Dear Mr Dodds,

Mr Packe desires me to say that he cannot possibly with propriety – nor has he the least wish to interfere with you or any one in the disposal of ***your own money!*** *Still less to check any work of generosity piety and charity; so that he is not required to do that which he either can not afford or does not think necessary in comparison to other prior claims- on the contrary he thinks your intentions are most kind, and that you should take so much interest in the Church and poor dear old Glenn Magna is a great gratification to us both.* She promises she will not bring the matter to public attention until she sees his improvements put into action: *as you may change your mind when you find what the expence will be. But you have our good wishes.*

Dodds persevered and used his position as chairman of the Parish Church council to vote that Sunday collections should be devoted to a rebuilding of the church.[2] (He

---

[1] She may be referring to Robert Haymes who built Peep Row (See chapter 6 Lots 32 and 33) or to his son the Rev Haymes.

[2] As had been done in 1817 when £703 was borrowed to repair the church. It was unanimously decided to pay back the sum borrowed by a shilling levy every year on the rate. QS 92/2/65

was later severely reprimanded, by the Secretary of the Missionary Society[1] for allowing money to be collected in this way for church repairs.) He also arranged fundraising concerts in the village: *In the year 1866 we had a concert for the same purpose, when ladies and gentlemen came and sang and played on the piano and violin: the good nature of everybody made it a most pleasant entertainment, the room was choke full: the night was pitch dark and people lost their way going home. We had another Concert the next year.*[2]

By 1868 Dodds seems to have despaired of success and he announced his decision to give up the benefice. KPR, doubtless much relieved, offered the job to her nephew, the Rev W J Packe, younger brother of Charles:
From the hall, Great Glen 10th August 1868 My Dear William,
Have this day received a note from Mr Dodds announcing to me as patron that on the first of May next he intends to give up the Benefice. You are the only person to whom I should wish to offer it…a great blessing to the village and a great comfort to me [lots of crossings out] *all the various shades of low church and high of the ten clergymen with whom I have been hitherto connected I might as well ask the advice of a child as apply to Mr Dodds on any matter of L S D.*[3] *He has done much mischief to the Good Cause by his hatred to and harshness with Dissenters.*[4]
WJP replied on 11th Aug 1868 from Chelmsford, thinking the matter over. He asks questions: *In the event of my accepting the living would you mind my having the direction of the school? I am especially fond of school work.* He took advice as to the financial rewards, and arranged a visit to Glen where, he says, *I found Mr Dodds very civil, though I could quite trace the peculiarities you speak of.* William learned from Mr Miles, his adviser, that *the income is not more than £250* and he finally refused the kind offer because he felt so happy in his present post, *having spent eight years of my clerical life in this Diocese* [Chelmsford].

Dodds did not in fact leave. The bishop refused to accept his resignation, much to KPR's dismay. She wrote to William again for advice and on 29 Dec 1868 he replied warning her that Dodds' resignation would not be legal unless confirmed by the bishop. He roughs out a letter for her to send to Dodds: *I have received from the churchwardens an intimation that your resignation of the living of Glenn has been refused by the bishop. I am of course at a loss to know what motives could have induced His Lordship to take this step. I thought, as I still think, that it would have been happier for yourself as well as better for the parish that your original intention as announced should have been adhered to.*

---

[1] Dodds got his own back in his letter to Parishioners in 1876 when he wrote with heavy sarcasm of the *venerable Missionary Society*'s accusation of his *venial sin* in allowing part of the Sunday collection to be used for church restoration.
[2] DE 849 79 Dodds 1876. *Letter to his Parishioners*
[3] LSD, pounds, shillings and pence
[4] Non-conformists. The reference to Dissenters is interesting in relation to KPR's own views.

WJP sympathises with his aunt but thinks all she can now do is smooth things over. *And the result is you still have got a somewhat awkward and inefficient person as your clergyman for a time longer. Very vexatious I agree but not an unsupportable calamity.*[1] Knowing that it was necessary for her as Lady of the Manor to work with the clergy, she writes to Dodds: *I shall therefore in future look for your cooperation and assistance in such matters for the good of the poor people of Glenn.* Dodds stayed for many more years, long after KPR had died, and he finally received the money to pay for the renovation of the church from Charles Packe, who succumbed to his persistence.

Methodism in the Village

The reference to 'Dissenters' is interesting because Glen had a strong Wesleyan community and a fine new chapel built in 1827. KPR herself was somewhat hostile to the movement, if not to the individual Chapel members: *Now I can sympathise with any body in Dislike to Dissent but I have no dislike of the poor Dissenters. I would not willingly let a cottage or a Farm to a dissenter and even for an allotment I would give a preference to a Church Person, if equally moral and industrious but those already in possession I would not turn out and in all occasions of sickness or great need I would help everyone equally.* She feels they are less dangerous than agnostics or Independents: *I fear we have a due proportion of Nothingarians but the Independent chapel is at Kibworth …and I consider that we have much reason to be thankful that in Great Glen we have only Wesleyans as avowed Dissenters among the poor.* Dodds' views were stronger. He wrote an (undated) note as *INFORMATION FOR MY SUCCESSOR*: *the church is very weak in the parish. The church people have little zeal especially for missions.* And he contrasts them with the Wesleyans, led by important and influential people in the village: *The quiet but very vigorous opposition to it is led by the Haycocks and Mrs Cooper.*[2]

The Wesleyans flourished. Chapel repairs and redecorating were done free. They had a new Harmonium and in 1868 they had an offer to enlarge the vestry to make it more suitable for a day school. In 1875 they had a new pulpit and more repairs and painting inside. In 1876 they agreed to instruct an architect to draw a plan for a new front to the Chapel to be bring it ten feet further out and Mr E Haycock was thanked for his kindness in white-washing and colouring out the chapel free of expense. The congregation expanded: *The seats in the chapel being all let and others wanted it was decided that two seats be fixed under the gallery and let to supply the need.*[3] No wonder Dodds felt aggrieved!

---

[1] DE 5047 letters. Jan 1st 1869

[2] Interestingly he mentions that the Clements come to church, despite being Dissenters but the Coopers, who have so many prominent graves in the churchyard, close to the main door of the church, had certainly changed their allegiance. Their memorials are in the chapel

[3] DE 1160 (N/M/179/27)

The Church in the time of Charles and William J Packe

The building fund started by the Rev Dodds grew so slowly, despite all his money-raising activities, that the church restoration, as Dodds himself admitted,[1] *might possibly have been deferred for years if it had not been for the liberality of the patron, Mr Charles Packe.* As Lord of the Manor, Charles took on duties with regard to the church. He was chairman of the Vestry committee in 1874, and was elected churchwarden by Dodds, the vicar. He was also on the Town Lands Charity commission which included the maintenance and repair of the church.[2] Before he became involved in building and buying houses, he was inveigled into the Church Restoration project, which CWP had managed to avoid.

The great rebuilding plan then forged ahead. In 1875 the Bishop (of Peterborough) authorised the work of restoration and reconstruction. This took nearly eighteen months to complete and cost £3000. It was not done without problems. On Feb 18th 1876 Charles Packe wrote letters (from Stretton Hall) complaining about the quality of the wood being used[3] and at one point just before the reopening, Dodds complained to Packe that Wm Allen, the sexton, had wheeled away surplus soil when the heating apparatus was installed and had cut down a hedge which separated the old and new churchyards, on Packe's instructions. Charles in fact lost patience with Dodds on several occasions but finally the work was finished. The church was reopened by the bishop on 30th Nov 1876. Dodds made some detailed drawings to show the new and improved alterations to the church (and sold them for church funds).

The event was reported in 1877[4]: *Perhaps no two churches had suffered so much from various causes and more needed skilful treatment of the architects than those of Glen Magna and Gumley. The former had evidently suffered much from fire and had been so modernised that scarcely any of its original beauty remained. Some interesting features however of the Norman and of the Early English periods were discovered and have been carefully preserved. The main body of the church has been rebuilt or repaired with great care, all ancient features being conserved and an entirely new chancel with organ recess and vestry erected. These two churches will repay a visit from any of the society's members.*

Despite this happy conclusion, all did not continue smoothly. By 1878 Charles Packe had to deal with problems with Dodds in relation to the school, which also created difficulties between the two men. Problems were ended when in 1886 a new vicar, the Rev. Arthur Thellusion Oddie, succeeded Dodds. He became a close

---

[1] DE 849 79 Dodds 1876. *Letter to his Parishioners*

[2] DE503 15. Parish Council Accounts

[3] DE 1667 10

[4] *Transactions of Leics Archaelogical Soc vol V* 1877

friend of Charles and Selina and is often mentioned in letters from Charles, who later referred to him, in his will, as *my friend Arthur Thelluson Oddie.*

In 1894 the church problems concerned minor matters like heating. Charles was not personally in favour of excessive comfort and he opposed the idea of having heating installed in the church, just as he did in his own rooms.[1] When his brother William sent him the gift of a stove, which he rejected, it was to Oddie that he first planned to give it. *Feb 8 1894. Will give stove to Oddie as a present from you.* After Charles' death, church bells were installed and dedicated to Charles Packe and to Oddie. *Jan 17th 1898. Our bells are now being re hung, commenced today, will be completed in about ten days.*[2] *Jan 26th 1898. Church bells arrived. They look so nice and the inscriptions are so well done! The Tenor bell: In memoriam Caroli Packe de Stretton obiit 1896. Treble bell: Arthurio Thellusion Oddie Vicario 1897.*[3]

In 1914, long after Charles Packe had departed this life, a fire broke out in the church on Dec 30th caused by a broken or overheated stove pipe passing through the roof. (Perhaps Charles Packe would have thought it was a judgment on the luxury of stoves and heating!) Thomas Capell, the sexton, discovered the fire at 2.30 in the afternoon and called for help from various men who were nearby. The roof was saved by their prompt action under the supervision of churchwarden, Theodore Walker. *Fears that the whole roof would be destroyed were dispelled when it was realised that as the wind was from the south and as the fire was seated on the north side, near the tower, it was sheltered by the ridge of the roof. Some of the men got onto the roof while others fetched water from the vicarage tanks which fortunately were full. By the time the fire brigade arrived from Leicester, twelve minutes after they had received the telephone call, all danger was over and, due to the prompt action of the men. only about £100 of damage was caused.* Central heating was installed in 1915, a year after the fire in the church.[4]

In 1968 the Packe family relinquished all control over the church. *The Leicester Mercury*[5] reported that from March 1ST 1968 [6] *the Bishop of Leicester will appoint all future Vicars of Glen. The patronage has been handed over to him as a gift. It has been in the hands of the Packe family for the last 60 years. Col Packe, who died in 1961 appointed the Rev C Taylor, who left the parish last month. The present patrons, his son and daughter (Mr Michael St J Packe, an author living in Alderney, and Miss Margaret Olivia Packe, a lecturer at Leeds University) have relinquished the position as neither had visited the village for several years.*

---

[1] See Chap 1 Charles Packe letters to his brother WJP
[2] DE5047/144/35 letter to WJP
[3] DE 5047 154 letter from Oddie to WJP
[4] Parish church notes. I am indebted to Fred Stocks, churchwarden, for the information.
[5] Dec 1969
[6] Leicester Mercury cuttings library, George St. Leics

CHAPTER 5 THE SCHOOL

The years of Victoria's reign were years of educational ferment. It is difficult to know what percentage of the labouring classes' children attended school. Estimates suggest that it ranged from about one-third to one-half in the first few years of Victoria's reign. The most common schools were Sunday Schools where children could go if they were not working and could learn to "read" the bible. What schooling there was, was sporadic and its primary function was to fit people for their place in the social order.

Bruce Rosen, *The Victorian Web.*[1]

In the time of CWP and KPR

Before CWP built his school in 1846, there was a church school in Great Glen in 1818, run by the National School Society[2] and two Sunday schools. (St Cuthbert's Sunday school had 32 boys and 28 girls in 1833 while the Methodist Sunday school had 37 boys and 33 girls.[3]) There were other smaller 'academies' in the village. In Pigot's 1835 Directory there is a ladies boarding academy run by Phillis Brake and an academy run by William Edgley. In the 1841 census Elizabeth Brake[4] seems to be running the boarding school, with 3 children, aged 8,10 and 6. Her establishment is described as a *ladies seminary* in Hagar's Directory 1849. The 1851 census gives her occupation as schoolmistress, with her sister as housekeeper, boarding seven children aged from 7 to 12. She is still schoolmistress in directories of 1861 and 1863. The 1861 census has her in Orchard Lane, aged 57, a governess born in Dorset with a sister Grace Hodgkin and one boarder, aged 7.

Wm Edgley's school is recorded in the Post Office Directory of 1848 as a boarding and day school, but no children, apart from his own, are named in any census. The census of 1851 describes him as a married man, a schoolmaster aged 44, living near the Fox and Goose and born, like his two young children, in Glen. In 1861 he is *shopkeeper and schoolmaster* in Drake's Directory. The 1862 Education Committee of Council reported that there were three infant schools (21 children), a day school [Packe's] for 40 children and a boarding school for 15 children.[5] It is not clear which of these is Edgley's academy. By 1871 the census describes him as

---

[1] Bruce Rosen *The Victorian Web*: *Literature, History and Culture in the age of Victoria*
[2] founded in 1811 for the promotion of Christian education in schools. Its aim was to found a school in every parish in the country. It offered grants to prospective founders and was involved in the founding and funding of most C of E schools, originally known as National Schools.
[3] Information from Max Wade Matthews, *Great Glen, the story of a Leicestershire Village*
[4] Elizabeth Brake, aged 37, born in Dorset, living with her mother, Phyllis, of independent means.
[5] VCH vol V. p.106 footnote 55

aged 64, a *retired school teacher*. We do not have any information about his school but he appears to have been a comparatively wealthy and respected man.
CW Packe built his day school, for 30 boys and 10 girls, in 1846, when he bought Stretton Hall and became Lord of the Manor. He provided a pair of houses opposite the school for the teachers. The first teacher at CWP's school was Martha Newton, named as a schoolmistress (aged 35) in the 1841 census and listed in the 1837 Valuation as living in a cottage rated as £2 per annum, rented from Frances Burton, possibly at one end of the site later used for the school.[1] She probably lived there until the schoolteacher's house was built in 1846. No schoolmaster is recorded at this point. White's directory of 1846 lists her as schoolmistress, still with no schoolmaster. Hagar's Directory of 1849 specifies that she is the *Free School* mistress. In the 1851 census she is described as a widowed schoolmistress, aged 44, with a neighbour, the schoolmaster, Thomas Turlington, a married man aged 35. He is named as teacher in Melville's Directory of 1854 but by 1861 there is no mention of him. In Drake's Directory of 1861, his place is taken by James Cock, a young man of 24, born in Chepstow, with a wife, Rebecca, born in Foxton and a 15 year old brother, born in Somerset, all teaching in the school.

It is a pity that we have no preserved log book of the school, such as the one found in the neighbouring village of Oadby.[2] From that we could have learned the day to day attendance at school, the reasons for absence and lateness, the state of the buildings, the success or otherwise of lessons, the role of the pupil teachers, the salary (£60 per year for the qualified mistress in 1872) and the reports made by the Inspectors. We have no such early records for the Glen school. We do not know if CWP had any teething troubles with the school, but in 1869, when Kitty Packe Reading had succeeded her husband, we have her correspondence with the teacher. While this does not give us all the information we would have liked, it does give a very detailed picture of one episode in particular, when she had to sort out a dispute between the headmaster's widow, Mrs Mumford, and the vicar, Mr Dodds. She was to have a difficult time with the ever-problematic Mr Dodds over the running of the school, negotiating between him and Mrs Mumford, tactfully keeping them apart and Dodds out of the school. It is interesting to see her combination of tact and respect for the vicar's position as churchman and frustration with his interference in the management of her school.

The terrible handwriting of all three of the people concerned makes this an arduous task![3] The letter from Mrs Mumford to Kitty Packe Reading is very difficult to transcribe! It begins with a report on the recent improvements to the school then goes on to complain about the behaviour of the vicar, H L Dodds:

---

[1] Cottages on plot 36 on the 1835 Stretton Estate map. See Factfile in Chapter 3.
[2] Oadby Board School log book edited by Pauline Buttery 1979.
[3] DE 1667/22/1-12 Gt Glen school episode correspondence 1869

Honble Madam
I must now thank you for allowing the shrubs to be partially cut down at the front of the school building as it is a great improvement as its so much more light of sun both to the school and houses. I hope you will like the change very much when you see it. Henry Langley came to shew the man [Stan Vann?] *where to cut them.*
I am told that Mr Dodds is now [about?] *to build a new church he has had £500 towards it and wants to begin in the summer.* Then she comes to the heart of the problems and pours it out at great length:
Last Sunday I got the school ready and the children were assembled and sat waiting for Mr Dodds to come and open schools with prayers but about 10 or 15 minutes passed Mrs Benson (?) brought a note in to me to read...saying it had come from Mr Dodds. It said he had not received permission to enter school buildings and requested us to take the schools to church. We were a little perplexed at first, but after consulting together a minute or so concluded that he had not permission to make use of Your teachers and to call them hither and thither as his fancy might be so we got Matthew Pywell to go to say to him that the schools were waiting for him to read and that neither Mr Poulson nor Mrs Mumford were willing take the school up to the church. But he did not come so we commenced without prayers and told them to go to church at the proper time...in the afternoon, which they did. We shall be glad to know your wish respecting it before another Sunday as it seems a pity to be at the trouble of preparing the room for the Sunday and light the fires if they are not to be used. Having had practical experience of Mr Dodds...the less I have to do with Mr Dodds the better. (The writing gets even worse as the letter goes on!)

Mrs Packe Reading has to act much as a Board of Governors would do now. Problems had arisen over Mr Mumford's death, which had coincided with some festivities arranged by Mr Dodds for the Sunday school children and KPR had asked the vicar to respect Mumford's memory by not using the schoolroom. Mrs Mumford had been most displeased by Dodds' decision to do so and, in support of her teachers, KPR writes, from Branksome Towers, to ask Mr Dodds, very formally, to discontinue his visits to her day schools: *Mrs Packe Reading Feb 26th presents her compliments to Mr Dodds and begs to repeat her wish and determination to allow no-one to visit either her Boys or Girls school for the present. She is resolved that her School Master and school mistress shall have the entire management of her day schools without any interference, or anyone other than herself to visit the school and confer with them and in this she wishes to give no offence to Mr Dodds but he is NO exception to the general order of exclusion. Mr Dodds must be perfectly aware that Mrs Packe Reading never prohibited his using her schoolroom for the teaching of his Sunday school. She only requested him as a favour to abstain from using it during the dangerous illness of their much esteemed school master and also entirely prohibited the use of her school rooms for the gay and noisy festivities of the feast week.*

On March 1st he replies, explaining that he had mislaid her note: *My Dear Mrs Packe* (Is this an oversight or a deliberately insulting negligence about giving her full title of Packe-Reading?). He says it was difficult for him to alter arrangements made for the usual village festivities at short notice. *My defence is this: I gave my invitation to the Feast before poor Mumford was taken ill. He was taken suddenly ill, died (requiescat) and was buried before the Feast time came.There was no impropriety in keeping of our annual Festival, which did not admit of being put off, after the poor man's funeral, after also every member had withdrawn from the vicarage in a place far removed from the house which he had inhabited.*

His reasoning for not mourning the late headmaster more elaborately seems quite convincing, though it must have seemed heartless to the recently bereaved widow: *Mumford had but lately come among us, we could not be expected to feel more than what we did feel, good will and pity for him—a sensible sorrow for his loss would not have been natural and* [would] *have done more harm than good if I had disappointed the children of a holiday that they had long looked forward to – that would not have tended to endear Mumford's memory to them, but probably much the reverse.* All this sounds very reasonable, but he does end with what sounds like an attack on Mr Mumford by contrasting him with the new head : *The new man* [Mr Paulson] *seems to have no liking for strife and division and I expect that he and I will work harmoniously together.* Matters seem not to have improved, however, and on March 5th 1869 Mrs Mumford wrote, *From Girls School House*
Honorable Madam
Mr Dodds still comes regularly to school. I have said nothing to him as I do not think he would take any notice...I will do so if you wish it as I do not feel quite comfortable that your requests are not regarded by him in staying away. He said to my girls last Monday morning 'Don't be so fidgety. If you are I shall call Mrs Mumford to take my part'. She obviously did not like to have to support Dodds in keeping discipline for him! She also thought his catechising style was too far above the heads of the children: *I contend that his questioning is too high for the children and that lessons from him in person would be of more real service to them but it must be your wish.* Bible story lessons might have been more welcome.

She goes on to give general news of the school and illnesses: *Benny [?] Johnson has been very badly but is now better again. Some children have been laid up with coughs and influenza and sore throat and a good many are poorly this week too. I too was at the beginning of the week or I should have written sooner to you.* And then gives another report of Dodds' behaviour: *Mr Dodds never came into my schoolroom at all on Sunday but kept in Mr Poulson's. I think he seems rather queer [quiet?] with me. Mr Poulson said he seemed very strange and asked me if he always flew about in that way. He says he was very strange with the little boys he was teaching and [warned?] them they should not have a laughing lesson [?] on Sunday.* It is clear that she is worried by the vicar's strangeness:
Honble Madam

I sometimes feel rather sorry for him as I do fear he is not quite right at times, Yours obediently LH Mumford.

Kitty Packe Reading took action immediately and wrote to the vicar from Branksome Towers on Mar 6th 1869: *Sir, I am more astonished that I can express by finding from a letter received today from my schoolmistress that you still continue your visits to my Girls' School. I beg once more to expressly forbid your entering my Girls school in Great Glen during the week on any pretence whatsoever and warn you that I shall consider your visits there in future to be trespass on my Property.* She sends a copy to the schoolmistress the same day with a covering letter: *Mrs Mumford... meanwhile be careful of what you say to or of Mr Dodds to anyone but myself. Prevent Mr Dodds from visiting (no matter what he says). Perhaps your best plan will be to keep both the schoolroom doors locked and if he should come, go round the back and meet him in the front of the house and tell him at once that you are not to admit him on pain of my displeasure. I wish to shield you from giving him offence in every way that I can but I will be obeyed in this matter.*

By 1870 things seem to have quietened down. In January the schoolmaster mentions no difficulties in his letter to Kitty Packe Reading: *With respect to the school, we are going on much the same, with the exception of severe coughs among us. The number of boys last week was 42 and I have about the same today, Edmund Paulson.*[1] Kitty Packe Reading died later in the year, leaving an apparently smooth running village school for her nephew Charles Packe.

The school stood in the centre of this picture, between Peep Row and 41 Main Street.

[1] DE 5047/5

The school in the time of Charles Packe

Charles Packe's arrival in Glen coincided with the 1870 Education Act, which revolutionised the provision of elementary schooling (provided then by Voluntary Societies). The act contained proposals for School Boards, elected by ratepayers, to be set up to govern the schools. The debate as to whether Glen school should keep its Church of England voluntary status or change to accepting a school board continued throughout Charles Packe's time. The final decision was not made until after his death. The first problems for Charles were of a domestic nature, a continuation of the problems faced by his aunt, KPR.

When Charles Packe arrived in Glen he appointed Wm Henry Fancourt as head[1] and no problems with Dodds erupted over the school for several years. The Restoration of the church doubtless took much of his energies until 1876 but when the church was finally completed, the two men came into conflict once more. Owning a Church of England school with obligations to allow the vicar to run religious lessons was fraught with difficulties! In 1878 Charles was obliged to write to Dodds about failing in his duty to give the required religious instruction for the children.[2]

Stretton Hall Jan 17 1878

Sir, you best know how your conscience excuses you, for shirking your duty. I can only think that you have been all along seeking an excuse for escaping what you found irksome. Recollect that this is not the first time you have renounced teaching in the school though then for a totally different reason. It is idle to talk of being 'gagged'. You were at first placed on the school management and I am sure were treated with every consideration but you retired because you would not condescend to be elected. Even if you had been aggrieved personally it does not seem either Christian or logical to make the innocent children suffer for it, and I suppose you consider that your instruction does them some good.You can scarcely expect me to interfere on your behalf when not only do you entirely disregard my opinion (which you have a right to do) but you scarcely ever write me a letter without insinuating against me charges which you have no right to make.

Problems with Dodds ended in 1886 and Charles was free to put his mind to other issues. From 1879 the Wesleyan chapel Sunday school had been flourishing and a new schoolroom erected but the Packe day school was suffering from lack of funds.

---

[1] Wm Fancourt born in 1847 married in 1883 a local girl, Mary Thompson. In 1904 their daughter Grace was appointed pupil teacher. Martha Newton, called Widow Newton, seems to have been pensioned off into a cottage owned by Packe RV £3 in 1878.

[2] Schools controlled by the Church of England, as Glen's was, were limited to the bible and a non- denominational catechism for their religious teaching.

In 1888 Charles mentions a visit of the school inspector. These visits were like those described by Matthew Arnold[1] when he was a school inspector working under the 'payment by results' rule. Government school subsidies had been partly tied to test-results and teachers were judged by how many of their pupils could recite the Lords Prayer! Arnold expressed his doubts about the system in 1869 but the system was not actually abolished until 1897. When Glen school was visited by the inspector in Feb 1888. The visit seems to have gone rather well. (Though Charles speaks only in vague terms and does not give us details like the ones in Oadby's log books where in the same year, we read: *Infants school. The children are in good order and their general proficiency is creditable to Mrs Todd. The older infants should however have rather clearer ideas of number. Pupil teacher M Weston...has passed an unsatisfactory examination. Should she... fail to the same extent next year the Grant will have to be reduced under article 115 (ii).* [2] Charles gives no such details and merely writes: *Our school Inspection has been today and I think on the whole satisfactory. The Inspector has a good opinion of me because I am looking to the education of the children and not to the amount of grant.* [3]

Money, however, became an increasingly important issue. It was not an easy time, as the school was not doing well. The inspector's report of Feb 3rd 1894 was not a favourable one and Charles became increasingly critical of education; *The world is singularly deficient in accuracy and justice. The school teaching does not inculcate them.*[4] It is not clear whether he is speaking in general terms or whether he is speaking from experience in Glen! But he is certainly showing no enthusiasm for schools! He continued to take an interest in general educational matters and occasionally expresses an opinion which strikes us as sensible as well as far sighted: *I have written a letter to the education dept urging the teaching of the Metrical System within schools, which I hope will have some effect.* He does not say whether he tried this idea out on the headmaster in Glen, nor what response he had. He probably had little day to day influence on the school at this point and seems to have been more interested in shedding the burden of the school management and its financial difficulties.

In 1892 there had been discussions about the possibility of obtaining school board status, with the school expenses chargeable on the rates instead of the subscription basis which existed at the time. Charles Packe, as treasurer, would have been responsible for the collection of these subscriptions and he quite naturally decided that the School Board option would be the best solution. The chairman, George

---

[1] Matthew Arnold, the son of Thomas Arnold, the headmaster of Rugby, was a school inspector from 1851 to 1883 and wrote about the evils of the 'Payment by Results' system for teachers and schools.

[2] *Oadby Board School* edited by Pauline Buttery 1979

[3] DE5047 144 Letter to WJP

[4] *ibid* Feb 13th 1894

Brown, later wrote a letter to WJP in 1897, outlining the 1894 position.[1] *About 3 years ago a parish meeting was called in reference to school matters when Mr Packe tendered his resignation as treasurer as he had a deficit balance of about £20 or £25 and he felt the best course would be to have a Board School, then all would be obliged to contribute according to rental.*

This was going to mean a rise in rates and it is pleasing to note that Charles Packe intended to carry the extra burden for his own tenants, by paying one half of the School Board Rate that each of his tenants had to pay. Mr Brown and the committee had however prevailed upon Charles to wait to see if the situation could be resolved by making another appeal for funds rather than taking such drastic action. *I moved a resolution that if Mr P. (sic) would kindly reconsider the matter and wished to withdraw his resignation, that a deputation be appointed to see if we could not raise sufficient to avert the necessity of having a School Board. I felt many were not subscribing simply because they had never been asked. The resolution was carried unanimously and many in the meeting volunteered annual subscriptions…if we could not raise a small amount by voluntary effort we should have to raise a very large sum by a School Board Rate. We were well received and got the necessary sum, so averting the lavish expenditure of a board.*

There was a real fear that a rise in rates would affect the village adversely. Charles had been persuaded in 1894 to continue as treasurer and he continued to pay out money for school maintenance. In October he paid for the school's pit closets to be converted to earth closets (emptied weekly by John Batchelor's workmen at a rate of two shillings per visit). Three years later, Charles died, leaving the problems of the school and the debate about School Board status to his brother William, who then handed over the school to the Board of School Managers.

The school in the time of Wm James Packe

It was not until 1899 and the establishment of the National Board of Education that free public education was available to all children in England. and it was not until 1902, after Victoria's death, that public secondary education was available. In that same year, the school boards were abolished and the responsibility for education was placed in the hands of local government.[2]

One of the first problems WJP had to face in Glen when he succeeded to the estate in 1897 was that of the school's financial situation. The school was still run on a subscription basis and he had apparently donated £5 for the school, no doubt thinking he was being generous. He received a reply from George Brown, who

---

[1] George Brown, TheYews, letter to WKP 1897 DE5047 149 *I wish if you will allow me to explain as fully as I can how matters have been going.*

[2] Dr Bruce Rosen, *op cit*

lived in The Yews, thanking him for a cheque, passed on to him by the vicar, Mr Oddie, but requesting that the amount be increased to £20 as the situation of the schools was in a parlous state.[1]

Dear Sir

Mr Oddie handed to me your cheque £5 for the Glenn schools for which we are much obliged. Mr O. read me that portion of your letter holding out the hope of a further donation at another time. I hope you will see your way to make it up to £20, the amount the late Mr [Charles] *Packe gave, for we are much in arrears and if there is any falling of subscriptions the schools must either be closed or a Board school established.*

The School Board issue was coming to a head, and there was a lot of hostility to the prospect of higher rates, for landowners as well as householders, to pay for it. *The largest ratepayer in the parish has frequently expressed his determination to give up all his land if he has to pay a Board School rate. Of course someone else would doubtless take the land, but it is very clear to see in the present depressed state of agriculture that if we got a SB (sic) Rate say 1/6 in the £ it would be a burden of about 1/- to 4/6d per acre and land has to pay that rate in full the same as houses. I think your agent would tell you one of the first enquiries a farmer makes now when taking land is Have you a School Board rate?*

I should individually be very sorry to see the necessity of a SB. I believe all sections of the community are quite satisfied with the manner in which our schools are conducted. We get good reports and good grants which would not be the case if not well conducted.

In 1896 Wm James Packe handed over the school to the managers on a ten year lease.[2] It remained a Church of England school and catered for the poor children of Glen and Stretton. In 1897 it came under the control of the Leicester Associated Board of Education, under the Voluntary Schools Act. In 1904 it was the managers who dealt with the crisis of Oct 26th when a group of parents demanded that their children should be removed from religious instruction and be provided with secular instruction instead.[3] The Foundation Managers then agreed that Religious Instruction should be confined to lessons from the bible on four days of the week and that teaching of the church catechism should only be given on Friday mornings, when religious teaching by some qualified teacher selected by the parents should be allowed in a separate room.

---

[1] Feb 1897

[2] The Foundation managers included Arthur Oddie (vicar, Chairman), Theodore Walker, Robert Rowley, W Penn Lewis, Clement Stretton, Haycock and W Allen

[3] Many of the parents signing the petition were members of the Methodist church. The signatories were: Hill, Peberdy, Brandrick, Greenbank, Lovell, Loas, E. Easom, Woolman, Clarke, F. Walker, Harry Barnes, Franks, Slaney, H. Clarke, Emma Easom, Edwin Harris, Haycock, Cockbill, Thos Easom, Ruth Clowes, John Tilley, John Watkins, James Hunt, George Blanchard. 46 children were involved.

The School Managers Minute Book 1903–1938[1] gives us snippets of information about changes in membership in the board and about attendance at meetings. (For the 1907 February meeting one manager was in the West Indies, one away from home seriously ill, one having left the district and there was no quorum. In March 1914 Mr Rowley, the hosiery manufacturer who had been on the board from the beginning, resigned, owing to advanced years and pressure of other engagements. His place was taken by Theodore Walker's son, Ralph, who subsequently resigned in July 1917 for war service.)

The Managers considered such matters as:
payment:
1903: *In the future the woman who cleans the school to be paid at the rate of 1/6d per week.*
July 1909: *Fires to be lit at 7am and checked before the caretaker leaves, Caretaker applied for increase of remuneration from 9d per week and 9d for fire lighting to 1/- for each.*
staff salaries:
1903: The master's salary to be £124 or £125.16 shillings a year.
1904: Increase of salary for Miss K Iliffe, based on her having passed the King's scholarship exam and for Mrs Fancourt, having always given satisfaction, as a long service increase.
1907: *increase of Mr Fancourt's salary to £130 per year.*
equipment :
1903: *New stove and better lighting. Rev W J Packe, the owner, to carry out.*
repairs to buildings and structures:
1903: *Playground causeways and closets.*
1907: *repairs to floor, windows, hat pegs, lavatory basins, missing plugs and chains.*
Small repairs to be attended to by Allen the Blacksmith.
This work continued, in the Managers' safe hands, after WJP's death in 1908.

The school in the time of EC Packe

In 1910 the school had 108 pupils of all ages.[2] By the time the young Lt/Col moved to Glen he was not overburdened with the problems of the school, as it was now governed by a school board. We learn about the school in the time of ECP mainly from the school Minute books and from living memories, rather than from Packe letters and documents. But there is one interesting little bundle of letters

---

[1] DE 849/52
[2] By 1933 the senior pupils went to Oadby and only 70 children remained in Glen school. In 1947 the school acquired 'controlled status' and by 1957 there were 128 juniors and infants.

from the colonel where he gives a useful summary of the school history: *In or about 1840 CW Packe, MP, built the school on his own land, appointed the school master, chose the subjects to be taught, lay down the conditions of attendance and ran it as a private concern. The school building has the Packe crest carved in stone in front of it. On the death of CWP on 27th Oct 1867* [NB He gives no credit to Kitty Packe Reading] *his nephew Charles Packe of Stretton Hall inherited and carried on the school in much the same way, but in a lessening degree as Public Education began to come into force in 1870. On the death (childless) of Charles Packe on 16 July 1896, his brother the Rev W J Packe, Vicar of Feering Essex (my father) inherited the estates including the school. He never lived in Leics and on 31 Jan 1903 he let the school to the Foundation Managers who had then been appointed on a ten year lease at an annual rental of £20 on condition that the school remained a Church of England school. On my father's death on 18 Sept 1909, I inherited the Stretton and Glen Estates which were then entailed. Instead of renewing the lease of the school on the expiration of the ten years, I was induced on patriotic grounds to forego the rental and on 14 May 1914 I conveyed the school under the Authority of School Sites Acts to the then vicar and churchwardens (now all dead) on condition that the school remained in private hands as a C of E school.*[1] *Under this deed we retained our right to select our own school master and for the vicar to give religious instruction. I do not think that the importance of these privileges can be over estimated. Incidentally to my mind the school at present constituted represents one of the few remaining safeguards against Socialism, Bolshevism, in the village.*[2]

The inspector's reports were usually handed to Mr Packe but practical matters were handled by the vicar, churchwardens and Foundation managers. It was they who dealt with matters of **appointment of staff**. (In July 1910, they appointed Miss Lilian Hooper as teacher and in Aug 1910 Miss Mildred Fancourt, daughter of the former head teacher Wm Fancourt, was installed while Miss Hooper was away ill). They saw to the **repairs.** (Feb 10th 1912, it is noted that *the Stove is broken and smokes very badly. Window frames and lavatory pipes need attention* and in April 1913 1/7d has to be paid *for laying hedge and piece of lath to keep lambs out of the playground.)* They ordered **new equipment**: *Aug 6th Harmonium out of order entirely worn out and new one should be provided. Nov:Proposed by Mr Walker a new one at 50 shillings.* They dealt with the **finances.**

It is often Theodore Walker, ECP's tenant at Glen Hall, who is a prime mover in school improvements. It is usually he who proposes that money be spent! And he, along with other rich industrialists, is often recorded as making donations. Jan 1912 *Mr Walker asked permission to dig up a portion of the playground and make*

---

[1] DE 1667/ 23 pencilled notes written by ECP 1934

[2] Written in 1934 this shows the current fear of Russia and Communism.

a garden for the boys.[1] June 1914 *Mr Walker proposed acceptance of architects' plans to alter the school.* 1915 *Mr Walker was thanked for the improvement he had made to the levelling of the school yard.* Mr Kaye promised £25 towards the cost and Mr Walker also kindly promised a similar amount. In Dec 21 1918 thanks were given to *Messrs Kaye and Walker, who gave £3 each in addition to their usual subscription of 2 guineas.*

In 1914 the war started, and young men who had been attending the school a few years previously went off to fight. In Dec 1917 the managers decided to give the school a half holiday on Jan 23rd *when the tablet in the church on which the names of soldiers from this parish who have fallen or may fall in this war are to be inscribed or engraved.* And in Aug 24th it was proposed: *That the Education Authority should increase the wages of Mrs Gould*[2] *owing to war prices and increase of the cost of firewood.* In July 1919, after the war, a new headmaster arrived. And in April 1926 we read of the beginnings of free school meals, with the provision of midday soup for the children who came all the way from Great Stretton. (It was a 'Bring Your Own Mugs' system.)

One continuing problem seems to have been shortage of money for running the school and ECP comments, rather drily perhaps, that although the school is a church school: *we have no power to include the school in the Free Will Offering*[3] *scheme for three reasons.* One of these reasons is that: a*t least two of the school Managers are Wesleyans!!* It is clear that Col Packe did not wish to take on the responsibility for running the school and had only taken on the job as a school manager and then treasurer when a vacancy needed to be filled: *As regards myself except for being a nominal Administrative Trustee with four others. I held no official position in the school until a few years ago, in Barclay's time, when he asked me to be a school manager. Later still, in 1931 after Jack Brown (the late treasurer) died, Barclay asked me to take on the Treasurership as he could not find anyone else to do it.* School finances were in a poor state: *I found the finances in an awful state with a balance of only £1 1s 11d and arrears of liabilities. Ever since then I have been working them up and now we have a balance of £17 0s 0d.* It was not a role he relished. *Interest in the school seems rather to have died down. We no longer hold the regular quarterly meeting.* A pencilled draft of a letter dated 7th March 1934, from Col Packe at Glen Hall to the managers, complains that a Mr Campbell had written to him, forwarding his subscription, on March 3rd *as if I was responsible for the admin and finance of the school. This however is not the case. You are entirely responsible for both and for the method to be adopted.*

---

[1] The garden in the school grounds seems to have been a great success. In April 19 1913 the head omitted to call register because of a gardening lesson which must have caused great excitement and a certain disruption to the normal routine!

[2] Mrs Gould was appointed as caretaker in Jan 1917 and remained in post until she resigned in 1921.

[3] Church collection scheme

Some villagers remember the school. Tommy Clark, Fraser Gilbert and Joe Goddard remember attending the village school in ECP's time but it is clear that the colonel did not play a big part in school life. He did not have the financial resources of his predecessors and could not afford to match their generous gifts: *I don't remember Col Packe financing any Christmas parties but I was given a Sunday School bible by Mr Theodore Walker. All the children who attended Sunday School got one when they reached 14. I gave my copy to my son. The pages of the bible were 'tissue paper thin' and each page was edged in black.*[1]

The former pupils' most vivid memories are of the school buildings, the gardening, the dinners and the headmasters: *The school had two rooms but one was divided by a wooden screen which thus made three classrooms. The village pump was just outside the school railings, to the side of the school.*[2]

Back in the fifties there was a school garden. We had two boys to a plot and they were judged who had the best vegetables. From the door on the right we went up past the girls' cloakroom and up the stairs to an attic room where there were two dozen spades and two dozen hoes and two dozen forks etc, our gardening tools. [3]

In about 1919 the Headmaster, Mr Billy Spence lived opposite what is now the Post Office, down the slope in what is now Mr Walters' house. [4]

[1] Tommy Clarke
[2] Tommy Clarke
[3] Fraser Gilbert. See Theodore Walker's 1912 gardening scheme for the school.
[4] Tommy Clarke

For the next generation[1] in 1929 or 30 the headmaster was 'Billie Bostock', who lived in 11, St Thomas's Road. *Billie Bostock the headmaster used to sit at his desk under this window. He didn't have a private room but sat in the classroom with the phone on the desk. The door on the left was never used. The main door led into the big classroom but the children went in round the back.*

Mr Bostock, the headmaster, is shown here beside Mrs Kaye, in her public role of important local lady, speaking to the Queen of the May, Betty (?) Bland. Mr Sims, the teacher, 1953 and Wally Allen, (aged 7 in 1935) is at the front, right.

Former schoolchildren, who walked in procession from the school to the dinner centre, have fond memories of school dinners.

The school dinner centre was in the old glove factory/band hut: I went to the dinner centre. It was right on the corner of Bindleys lane, where Brookside old peoples home is now. Right onto the road.[2]

[1] Fraser Gilbert, who is Tommy Clark's nephew
[2] Lilian Haines

Lilian Haines remembers: *Mrs Riley and Mrs Brown cooked the dinners etc.*

Wonderful food Mrs Riley was a wonderful cook. That's Betty Freakes: she came after Mrs Riley. And that's Mrs Hubbard.

Col Packe's description of Great Glen in 1946 is interesting. He describes the village as small and poor: *Great Glen is a small parish of 800 (900?) people, mostly poor, and the school managers are quite unable to find the funds necessary to meet the heavy demands of the LEA for repairs to the playground and buildings etc. They will certainly not be able to find the fabulous sums for alterations and improvements which will be required under the new Education Act. They therefore want to surrender the voluntary status of the school and hand it over as it stands to the LEA to become a council school.*[1]

He was at this point trying to ascertain whether, as original owner of the school buildings, he could be entitled, under the 1944 Education Act, to some recompense when the state took it over. The Minister of Education *regretted that this would not be possible* and explained the difference between council schools and controlled voluntary schools in a letter to the managers:

Gentlemen,
With ref to your letter dated 27 April 1946 I am directed by the Minister of Education to state that, as a result of local inquiries which she has caused to be made, she now understands that it is not proposed by the managers of the above

---

[1] pencilled note from ECP to Pilditch, solicitor 27 Jan 1946

named school that it should become a Council School, but that its status will be that of a controlled voluntary school.

Under the provisions of the Education Act 1944, all the costs of maintenance of a controlled school are to be borne by the Local Education Authority and accordingly lack of Managers' Funds will not create any difficulty. Moreover the use of the premises of a controlled school out of school hours will normally be left to the Managers of the school. I am to add that the Minister does not consider that any question of compensation to Lt Col Packe arises.[1]

Lt Col Packe must have been disappointed. The LEA took over and subsequently decided a new school building was necessary. The existing school building became unviable and ECP saw its decline but not its final end. The *Leicester Mercury* reported on April 10th 1968: *A service to mark the closing down of Great Glen school was held on Thursday of last week in the Parochial Hall.* But by this time the colonel had died; he did not live to see the replacement school built in the new housing estate near Hill Top. He was not here when the old school building was threatened with demolition, nor to participate in the debate over whether the old building should be re-used or demolished.

The school was demolished, despite strong opposition from villagers, in 1968. Col Packe's remaining son, who no longer lived in Glen, was consulted as to what should happen to the site afterwards. The *Leicester Mercury* reported[2] a meeting of the Parish Council to consider the planning application presented by Mr Michael St J Packe, owner of the old school buildings, for redevelopment. *Mr Packe, an author living in Alderney,* told the council that he would like the building *to be used in any way acceptable to them, either commercial development, possibly offices or garages or he is not averse to the property being completely destroyed.*

Former students at the school speak sadly of the loss of the old building, even though Glen now has a *'spanking new school (St Cuthbert's Primary school) up on the hill'*[3]

---

[1] May 15th 1946 Copy of letter from Min. of Ed. Legal Branch DE 1667 23
[2] Leics Mercury Dec 4 1969 DECIDING FUTURE OF OLD SCHOOL
[3] Margaret Packe.

The old school buildings were completely destroyed. ECP died before the school built by his ancestors, was destroyed. He was spared the sight of the destruction of CWP's substantial building.[1]

Mercury school demolished

[1] Photo courtesy of the *Leics Mercury*

CHAPTER 6 THE SALE OF PACKE HOUSES

The houses that were offered for sale[1] by ECP in 1919 and 1932 have interesting histories. Some were here when CWP came to the village, some were bought or built by him in 1846 and some were bought or built later by his nephew Charles in the 1870s. They were inhabited by people of varying degrees of wealth and poverty and a study of their tenants gives a good idea of the different strata of society in the time of the Packes. Almost all of the houses are still standing, now mainly owner-occupied, and in considerably better shape than they were when they were auctioned in 1919 and 1932, and much increased in value. The little cottages have been smartened up and given modern facilities. Houses that could barely be given away in 1919 are now highly desirable bijou residences. The larger houses, too, have been improved, though perhaps not so dramatically. The two halls have had more varied fortunes.

After the 1919 sale ECP still owned property, including both Stretton Hall and Glen Hall but by 1930 he felt obliged to sell one of the halls and in 1932 he tried again to sell houses which had not reached their selling price in 1919. He then put up for sale the mill, Glen Hall and its lodge house.

Sale document map 1919. On the attached map each plot is coloured and numbered for ease of reference.
(The River Sence is, rather confusingly, coloured yellow.)

[1] DE 688/66-70 and DE 3060/41 and (a very fragile copy) DE849/66-70.

The *Summary of Holdings as Let* gives a description of the property, the names of the tenants and the rental per year paid by them. The sale document includes photographs of four of the houses to be sold (Lots 3, 5, 6 and 12). On a copy formerly belonging to Stuart Norman the prices reached are recorded in pencil.

Lot	Description	Tenant	Rental per year £ s d	Price Reached
3 4	Brook House,Joiners workshop store garden (pink) and grass (yellow)	Wm Elson	25	£640
5	Shop/slaughter house (grey)	Lewin	75 17	£110
5	uncultivated garden	Miss Fewkes	1 0	
6	Detached house, contractors yard (pink)	Mr Batchelor	37 10	£850
9	Pair of brick/slated cottages (blue)	Wm Fancourt Laura Davis	7 16 5 15	Sold privately
10	Ditto (purple) Post Office	Rachel Campton and Wm Cobley	10 8 0 8 18 0	Sir M L £475
11	Dairy farm with land (grey)	Elizabeth Cramp	158 0 0	Sold privately
12	Dairy farm (blue) North House	Wm Heard		Sold privately
21	Pair of brick/slated cottages with gardens (yellow) adjoining Glenn Hall	Ruth Clowes Arthur Clarke	10 8 0	£260
31	terrace of 8 brick/slated cottages with gardens [Post Office Row]	six at £5 4s 0d two at £7 16s	5 4 0 7 16 0	*£875*
32	Five cottages (purple) *known as Packe's Row*	each at £5 4s	5 4 0	no bid
33	Four brick tiled and slated cottages (blue) *known as Packe's Row*	each at £5 4s	5 4 0	no bid
34	Cottage (yellow) buildings, pasture Cow shed *adjacent to Packe's Row* garden plot and waste	Barnes Achurch	9 0 1 0	
35	terrace of three gabled cottages (purple)	Achurch, Mason Bland	6 10 0 6 10 0 6 10 0	*no bid*
36	A pair of Capital Cottages (pink)	Jos Henson Emma Pywell	9 15 0 9 15 0	*no bid*
39	3 brick/slated cottages (pink)	Thomas Capell Isabella Peers Thomas Capell	3 18 0 5 4 0 4 4 0	*withdrawn*
41	Detached brick/slated cottage with 4 rooms and garden (blue)	Mrs Capell (aged 85) for the period of her lifetime	2 shillings per week	

Many of these houses and tenants have already been named in sections which looked at other aspects of the village.

Other items for sale are fields. Some, including what is now the War Memorial green, are small areas to be sold as building land.

Lot	**Description**	**Tenant**	**Rental per year** **£**	**s**	**d**	**Price Reached**
1	Field (green) [north of TheYews]	Ellis Johnson	7			*£140*
2	Garden [by river} bldg plot (blue)	John Bodycote		15	3	*£50*
4	grass field (yellow)					
7	Allotment gardens	various	7	16	3	*no bid*
8	Fertile land allotments	various	8	1	6	*no bid*
22	Grass enclosure/building plot	Brandrick	5			*£140*
23	Excellent building site (blue)	Henry Lewin				*given to the village*
24	Two garden plots [the old Victory Café]			1	6	*no bid*
37	Garden for capital building site (blue)	Emma Pywell Ezra Mason		1	6	*no bid*
40	Small garden (yellow) High St	Charles B Clarke		6	0	*withdrawn*
42	Garden and grass [by the ford]	Thomas Capell		5	0	*withdrawn*

We now go on to look at each house separately.

Aerial photo circa 1960 looking over The White House to The Victory Café (top left) Orchard Lane, The Old Greyhound (opposite the Memorial Green) and the shops on London Road.

Photo courtesy Jane Myatt.

LOT 3 is the first house listed in the sale document of 1919. It is described as *a commodious Joiner's Workshop, store, house, buildings and large garden.* The house has a *Tiled Entrance Hall, Sitting Room, Dining Room, Kitchen, Scullery, Larder, Coal House and 5 Bedrooms. Out offices adjacent. The workshop has a store house for paint and material, Trap House, Stable for two with 2 cow stalls, cow shed for two, Boiler and fodder house and a Pig Stye.* [1]

DWELLING HOUSE
LOT 3

The detached house (then called Brook House) with its half acre garden was sold for £640 in 1919. The rental was £25.0s.0d a year for the house, with a joiners shop, garden and a grass field (plot 4).

It is one of the houses which stood in the village when CWP came to live in Glen. In 1835 the tenant was Wm Oldacres.[2] The house is described on the schedule as being in *two tenements with two small gardens and a croft.* Oldakers (sic) had rented land from Sir George Robinson in Glen and in Stretton in 1799. He is named in the 1835 Vestry Books as a Guardian of the House of Industry (The Workhouse) and was obviously a man of substance. He appears in the 1841 census as a farmer aged 45, with an aged mother and three servants. He does not appear in the 1851 census.

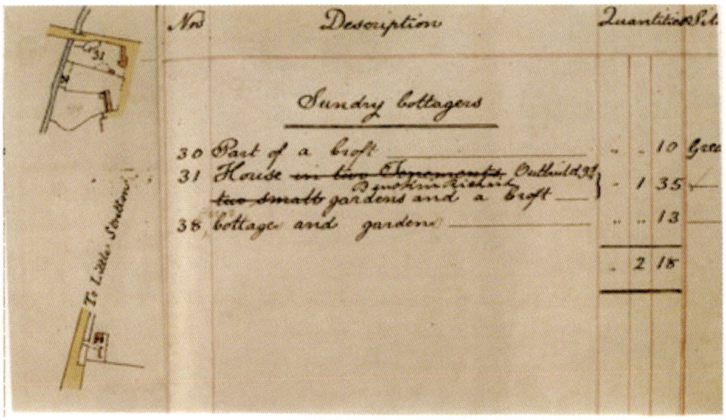

In KPR's account book of 1869 the house had apparently been converted into one detached house (<u>*in two tenements*</u> is crossed out) and the rental had been taken over by Richard Benskin,[3] whose name is inserted. The house has outbuildings, gardens and a croft.

By 1881 the house was occupied by William Elson, who lived here for many years. Born in 1840, he was the son of George and Mary Elson, who ran the village post

---

[1] Picture from DE 688/66 Sale document 1919

[2] Stretton estate map see Factfile chapter 3

[3] Richard Benskin was aged 50, in 1871, farming 167 acres and employing two men and two boys. He rented and farmed land near Stretton Hall and his name in the census appears just before Wm Allen, the baker and Frances Burton, who both lived in The Nook.

office in Main Street in 1861. William lived with them there until he was about 20, but went on to acquire a wife (born in France) and enough money to rent a superior house in The Nook. In 1871 he was a carpenter aged 30, employing a man and boy, with his wife and two daughters. By 1881 he had four young children. His mother, Mary Elson, had continued to run the post office in Post Office Row[1] after she was widowed but by 1891 William had taken over the job of postmaster from his mother (aged 76) and he ran it from this house. He is described as carpenter and postmaster with his wife as postmistress and their daughter Laura as a clerk in the post office. Their son Louis, aged 28, is described as an imbecile. By 1901 they had given up the post office job: William is described simply as a joiner, aged 60, living here with Elizabeth his wife and daughter Julie (a bookshop assistant aged 23) and Mary Biggs, a granddaughter aged 6, born in Glen. His mentally handicapped son, Louis, was then aged 36.

In the 1909 Valuation William Elson is listed as renting the house and shop at £15 per year and he was still here (aged 78) when the house was sold by Packe in 1919. (He also rented Lot 4, the field coloured yellow on the map.)

The same house in 2003.The windows have been altered but the rest of the frontage seems little changed. The back of the house has recently been extended with a swimming pool. (An example of the changes that have come to Glen!)

[1] See Lot 31 Post office Row

LOT 5 (Trent House) described as *shop, residence and slaughter house, with 8.8 acres of land* was sold privately (for £1,100) before it came to the auction in 1919. The tenant was Henry Lewin and the rental £75.17s.0d per year.

RESIDENCE AND BUTCHER'S SHOP.
LOT 5.

Picture from the 1919 sale catalogue. The butcher's shop[1] was adjacent to the house, with the slaughter house behind it.

By 1856 William Ragg had set up shop as a butcher here. His first child was born at this address in that year. He is named in a mortgage of CWP, where the house is described as a butcher's shop *in the occupation of Wm Ragg.* He had come with his wife from Market Bosworth and seems to have been a comparative newcomer to the village as he is not in the Glen census of 1841 or 1851. In the 1861 census the Raggs had two children, Elizabeth aged 5 and James aged 11 months, both born in Glen. He had an apprentice, Jack Hill aged 18, from Oadby and a local boy, Frederick Grain, aged 16, as a servant. The family also had one servant who had been born in Market Bosworth and one, Elizabeth Wormell, aged 14, born in Glen.

They seem to have moved elsewhere by 1869 when the house was rented to Joseph Lovett. In Kitty Packe Reading's account book of 1869-70, the house, with butchers shop, yard and premises, is listed as number 28a, and the tenant is Joseph Lovett. He also rented Round Close (now the war memorial green) and the big field beside the house, which brings the total acreage to 9 acres 1 rod 25 perches. When Joseph Lovett died, in 1896, his widow, Sarah Ann Lovett, continued to live in the house with five children all born in Glen, and William Burdine, a young butcher. In Charles Packe's Estate Duty of 1896 the rent is described as payable *by Joseph Lovett's executors* and the property is valued at £66 per annum.

---

[1] There were other butchers' shops in the village. In 1849 there were two butchers listed in Hagar's Commercial Directory: James Lewin (in Orchard Lane) and Green Achurch (in Main Street). They are named in the 1841 and 1851 census.

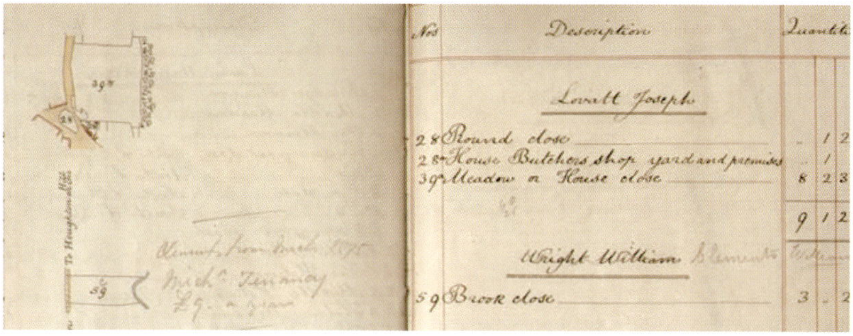

Nos | Description | Quantity

Lovett Joseph

28 Round close .. 1 2
28a House Butchers shop yard and premises .. 1
39a Meadow or House close 8 2 3
9 1 2

Wright William

59 Brook close 3 - 2

By 1901 Morley Hodges Lewin had moved with his family into this house, from Glen Farm,[1] their butcher's farmhouse in Orchard Lane. In the 1901 census he is described as a grazier aged 65. His two sons, Henry Lewin, a coal merchant and butcher (aged 30) and Morley Lewin, a butcher (aged 24) were then living with him here in Trent House. In the 1909 valuation, the land, house and buildings are recorded as rented from Capt Packe and occupied by Henry Lewin, son of Morley Hodges Lewin.

In 1903 Henry Lewin married Elizabeth Ellen Cramp of Glen Farm and they lived in Trent House. They were here in 1919, when Packe sold it, but some years later they moved back to Glen Farm, where Henry had been born. It so happened that his mother in law, Elizabeth Cramp, as sitting tenant, had bought the farmhouse, when ECP sold it in 1919, and in 1922 she gave it to Henry and her daughter, Elizabeth Ellen. So Henry and Elizabeth Lewin moved from Trent House and returned to the Orchard Lane farmhouse, which Henry's grandfather had rented from CWP in 1846. Henry remained there until his death in 1948.

Trent House, built about 1760, elegantly positioned beside The Memorial Green, next to The Crown Inn. It has Royal Insurance Co. plaques on the front wall and a huge butcher's wheel, used for hoisting and hanging carcasses, in the original butcher's shop. This part of the house still manages to retain something of its original quality as a cold store, despite modern central heating in the house!

[1] See Lot 11

LOT 6 is described in the 1919 sale document as *Detached house and garden, contractor's yard and pasture. The house has Sitting Room, Dining Room, Office, Kitchen, Back Kitchen, Cellar, Larder, Four Bedrooms and a Box Room. Wash House and out offices in the adjacent yard. The lot is sold subject to an easement for the free passage of water through the pipes laid through this plot for the benefit of adjoining cottages.*[1] *Tenant: E E Batchelor. Rental £37 10s 0d a year.*

DWELLING HOUSE.
LOT 6.

This is one of the few Packe houses no longer standing. It was in fact two dwellings, perhaps built as one house and converted into two, with one door at the side of the house.

Mr and Mrs Terry lived in that half [on the left of the picture] *and their door was round the side and back. There was a wide entrance and a five barred gate into quite a big yard with outbuildings.*

The right hand half was Batchelors. Harvey Coulson was a builder and undertaker in that house and was manager or director for Batchelor. I was friendly with Mary Coulson and often stayed with her in her nice big rooms.[2]

Today's villagers remember the house well. Mr Stan Gibson explained: *Batchelor had a builders yard there and one in Oadby and one in Fleckney. Batchelors were builders, undertakers, everything. Batchelors never lived in that house [in living memory]. Harvey Coulson did. He was the manager of that yard.*[3] Mr Tommy Clarke confirmed this: *Hedley Vere Batchelor, the builders and undertakers, had their Great Glen branch here with these cottages in the front and their workshops at the back. Mr Harvey Coulson lived in one and a Mr Albert Terry, the gardener for the Miss Frisbys at Stackley house, lived in the other.*[4]

The Bachelors had been long established as builders in the village. In 1836 a Thomas Batchelor was employed to repair the walls and windows of the village

---

[1] Tommy Clarke remembered that, in the vicinity of this house, Mr Packe *gave a tap between Bachelor's yard and the Working Men's Club.*
[2] Kate Westby, interviewed in 2002
[3] Mr Gibson interviewed in 2003
[4] Tommy Clarke, interviewed by J P-A 2002

workhouse. In the 1837 Valuation he rented a house from Mr Cooper for £3 a year. He also owned The Royal Oak, rented to his brother John in 1837 for £5 a year. In the 1841 census Thomas Batchelor was described as a builder aged 40, born in Warwickshire but married to a local girl. They had 7 children including three sons, Thomas (7), William (3) and John (2 months). He was still here in 1851, a master builder aged 51, employing three men, but by 1871 two of his sons, young John Batchelor (now 30) and William (33), had inherited the business. (By 1881 William is not mentioned.) There is a reference to John Bachelor in this house in the 1877 sale document of Post Office Row[1] which is described as: *the other part of the said Close of land fronting the Town Street of Great Glen in occupation of John Bachelor and Mrs Durrant.*[2] In the 1878 Valuation Charles Packe rented the house to John Batchelor for £29 5s a year.

John Bachelor, builder and grazier (aged 40 in the 1881 census), employed five men and two boys. In 1909 he still rented this house and land from EC Packe. In the same year, he was given the honour of having his name inscribed on the new church bell, beside that of Theodore Walker. John had two daughters and a son, Ernest Edgar, born in 1876. This son was the tenant when the house with the contractors yard was sold in 1919, for £850.

In its place there now stands a row of houses called Packe Terrace.

[1] DE 1215/6 Purchase of lands from Gilbert the innkeeper 1877.See Lot 31 Post Office Row.

[2] In the 1881 census Mrs Elizabeth Durrant is described as a widowed dressmaker aged 42 with an apprentice dressmaker and a boarder aged 11.

LOT 9 The school houses[1].

The houses are dated and initialled to show they were built in 1846 by CWP. The teachers who had lived in these houses were: Martha Newton (c.1837-1851), Thomas Turlington, (1851), James Cock (1861), James Mumford, with Mrs Mumford, and Edmund Paulson and his wife Ellen, with three young children (1869).

Pair of cottages and gardens. Tenants: William H Fancourt, paying £7 16s rent per year, and Laura Davis paying £5 15s, in 1919. Fancourt's house had three bedrooms and Laura Davis's had two. They were *Sold privately*.

Before the schoolhouses were built the schoolteacher Martha Newton is named in the 1841 census (aged 35, born in Smeeton) Various documents refer to *Widow Newton* and her dwelling may originally have been in a cottage on the opposite side of the road, near where the school was to be built. By 1846 she had probably moved into one of these specially built schoolteachers' houses. No schoolmaster is recorded in 1846.and it is not clear which of the two houses she lived in.

The first *Free Schoolmaster*, Thomas Turlington,[2] appears in Hagar's 1849 Directory with Martha Newton as *Free School mistress*, of the *Free School for Boys and Girls*. In the 1851 census Martha and Turlington, a married man of 35, with a young son (born in Great Glen), appear in adjacent houses. In Slater's 1850 Directory, Turlington appears (as *Thomas Corsett Parlington)* listed with Martha Newton, at *C W Packe's school.* The 1855 Post Office Directory records him as *Thomas Tarlington, master of St Cuthbert's school* and the mistress is named as *Martha Grain*. (These are almost certainly mistakes that have crept in. Martha was written down as *Mrs Martha Gray* in Melville's Directory of 1854 and the *Martha Grain* version probably came from the name of William Grain, the Parish clerk who appears immediately below! It is possible, of course, that she had remarried but unlikely that this should have happened twice in such a short time! It is more likely to have been a directory error.)

It is unfortunate that CWP's account book does not include the schoolhouses and that KPR's letters do not include this period of school affairs. They would have given some details for us! By 1861 both Martha and Thomas Turlington have disappeared from the census. The schoolmaster's house is inhabited by James

---

[1] See also Chapter 5 The School

[2] spelt as Tailington. His name is differently spelt in various Directories

Cock, a young schoolteacher of 24, with his wife Rebecca as schoolmistess and his 15 year old brother as pupil teacher. He had two sons christened in Glen in 1863 and 1865, but there is no mention of him in any later Glen census. James Mumford was appointed as teacher, with his wife, in 1869 but he died very soon after his appointment. Edward Paulson followed him[1] as *schoolmaster of the Church of England schools for boys and girls* with Mrs Mumford as schoolmistress. (These are names we know from Kitty Packe Reading's correspondence about the school.[2]) In the 1871 census Edward Paulson appears as a schoolmaster, aged 44, living here with a wife and three children, aged 9, 5 and 3, all born in Leicester. He left his post soon after, when Charles Packe succeeded KPR. We do not know why he went and it is not clear what happened to him, or to Mrs Mumford.

Charles Packe appointed W H Fancourt as headmaster in 1871. He does not appear in the 1871 census but by 1881 he was living in the schoolhouse, a bachelor aged 33, next door to the elementary school mistress, Sarah Ann Hall, a spinster aged 39. Fancourt married a local girl, Mary Thompson, in 1883 and remained as schoolmaster (and organist) for many years. The 1901 census lists him as William H. Fancourt, schoolmaster, a widower aged 53, with a son, William L. Fancourt, a pupil teacher aged 16, and a 12 year old daughter, Grace Fancourt, who became a pupil teacher in 1904. In 1903 W H Fancourt's teaching salary was £124 a year, raised to £130 in 1907. The gross estimated rental value of his house in 1910 was £9 15s a year. Nine years later, he was still the tenant when the house was auctioned, advertised as bringing in £7 16s in rent.[3] It was sold privately.

In 1881 the smaller of the two houses was lived in by Sarah Ann Hall, described in the census as an unmarried Elementary schoolmistress aged 39. But when the head teacher had a teaching wife, this house was let to non-teachers.

By 1891 the tenant of this house is a non-teacher, Mrs Elizabeth Annabel, who must have been in Glen for at least 6 years, as her six year old daughter Elizabeth was born here, in 1885. By 1901 the tenant was Laura Davis, described in the 1901 census as a widowed hosiery hand aged 32, with two young children, aged 4 and 2, both born in Great Glen. She remained in the house for many years and is listed as a tenant of Packe's in 1919, paying £5 15 shillings a year in rent.

---

[1] Harrods Directory 1870

[2] See Chapter 4. The school.

[3] The lower rent could be explained by a change of agreement as to the payment of rates.

LOT 10 a *Pair of cottages and gardens (coloured yellow on the map). Tenants: Rachel Campton and William Cobley.* The catalogue states that *one room is used for the purposes of the Post Office*. Rachel Campton was the sub-postmistress here from 1903 –1919.

Lot 10 The old Post Office from a photograph about 1900

The cottages have a complicated ownership history as they were built on a strip of *waste land beside the highway leading to Stretton* (ie Main Street) owned by CWP and leased in 1864 to Thomas Crick. In 1903 Frederick Crick assigned the two leasehold cottages built on this land to a Mr Muddimer. The deed refers to: *409 square yards land formerly belonging to CWP with two messuages then erected thereon with the outbuildings carriage house and premises thereto late in the*

occupation of Thomas Read and another and now in the occupation of Miss Campton, postmistress and Wm Cobley.[1]

By 1911 the houses were owned by ECP, with Rachel Campton and Wm Cobley as tenants. Rachel Campton ran the post office from this house and William Cobley lived in the neighbouring cottage. He was named in the 1871 census (aged 27) as a gardener for Thomas Crick at Rupert's Rest. For many years Cobley was a lodger in other people's houses[2] but by 1901 he had married his ex landlady, Hannah Bland and moved into the cottage here. He was a Parish councillor and in 1906 a school governor. In 1919 when the house was sold he must have been about 74. The provisional valuation was estimated at £260 for both cottages together, with gross annual rent at £16.[3] In 1919 both cottages were bought by Sir Maurice Levy for *£750.* (The figure, written in pencil in the margin, refers to the price paid for the pair.)

LOT 11 (Glen Farm, 15 Orchard Lane) is described in the 1919 sale document as a *Compact Dairy Farm coloured grey on map. Tenant: Elizabeth Cramp. Plus garden and 78.882 acres. £158 p.a. Hall, sitting room, greenhouse claimed by tenant, Dining room, Kitchen, scullery, larder, Dairy, cellar, seven bedrooms and store room. Two staircases and Usual out-offices. Farm buildings, 3 cowsheds each tying 8, Bull stall, calves house, Root house with loft over, Barn, Waggon House, Implement shed, Stable for 2, chaff house, Trap house, 4 pig styes with a boiler house and a liquid manure Tank.*

The present owner has made considerable alterations and improvements to the original house. *When I first walked into this house the water was up to here* [about two foot high], *from a blockage at the well, not from floods. The land didn't flood this high up.*[4]

Glen Farmhouse was part of the Stretton estate when it was owned by Sir George Robinson and is marked as plot 25 on the 1835 map, rented by Wm Oldacre, who

---

[1] DE 1215/6 Assignment of leasehold cottages 1903

[2] 1881 census, Wm Cobley an unmarried gardener lodged with Achurch, a Turnpike road labourer. In 1891, aged 43 and still unmarried, he lodged with Hannah (aged 24) and Mary Bland in Main St.

[3] DE1215/7 Solicitor's letter to ECP May 1911

[4] The present owner, interviewed 2003

also rented plot 31. The schedule describes it as a *house, outbuildings, yards and potatoe* (sic) *fields.* James Lewin, owner of nine dwellings and a great deal of land in Glen, took over the rental of this plot from Oldacres.

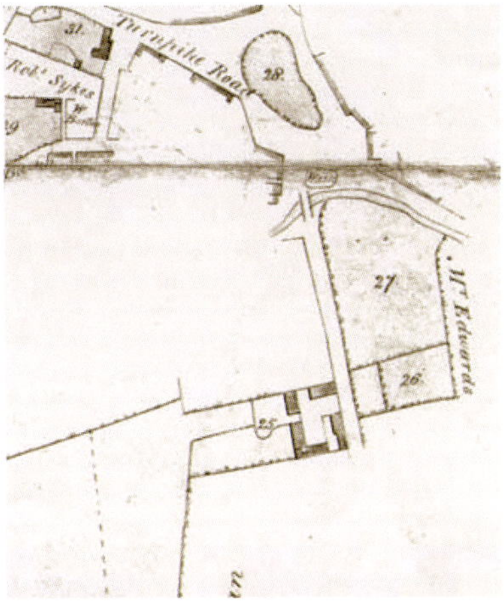

The 1835 map, showing plots 25 and 31, rented by Lewin and Oldacres.

Both James Lewin and Oldacres appear in Vestry Books in 1835 [1] as Guardians of the House of Industry (The Workhouse). Lewin is listed as an Overseer of the Poor in 1851 and 1854. In the 1841 census James Lewin, butcher and farmer, aged 35 and born in Billesdon, lived here in Orchard Lane, with his wife, Martha, and three children (Joseph, aged 8, Morley, aged 5, and William, 3), all born in Glen. In 1851, he employed four labourers and one indoor worker and lived here with his wife and son, Morley Lewin aged 16. In 1861 James Lewin is listed in various directories as a butcher and he appears in the census of that year as aged 55 living in The Lane (Orchard Lane), with sons, Joseph, aged 28 and Morley, aged 25.

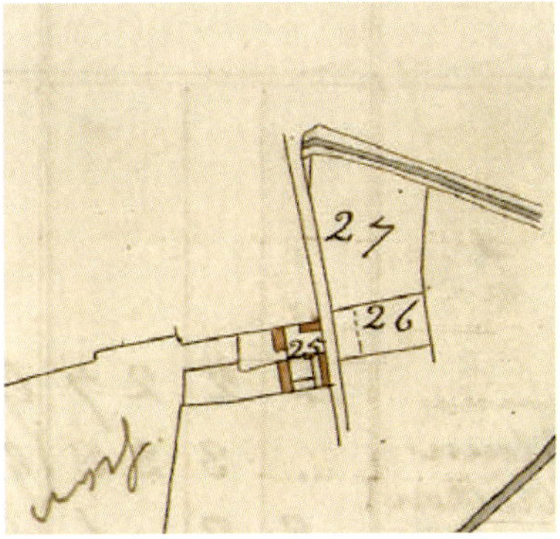

CWP's account book 1862

In 1862 both James and his son Morley appear, renting plot 25, Glen Farm, and the garden and field (plots 26 and 27) on the opposite side of Orchard Lane. In KPR's account book of 1869/1870 the name of Morley Hodges Lewin appears in place of his father, James. Morley's name also appears in the Guardians'of the Workhouse book in 1887, a fair indication of his wealth and standing in the community.

Morley Hodges Lewin, a wealthy farmer, butcher and grazier, owned two dwellings in 1878, plus a paddock with stabling, which he rented to George Wm Cooper for £20 per annum, and a drapers' shop, occupied by Samuel Shipp. He also owned a house with a gross estimated value of £15 a year, rented out to Wm Elson. He nevertheless continued to rent his own farmhouse from Charles Packe. In the 1881 census he appears, with his wife and seven children, in Glen farmhouse, as a farmer and grazier, employing five men and a boy. He is still named as butcher here (with his large family plus elderly relatives) in the 1891 census but he moved to Trent

[1] DE1667/16

House some time before 1896, when Harry Cramp is named[1] as renting Glen Farm. When Harry Cramp died, in 1912, Elizabeth Cramp, his widow, took over the tenancy. When the farm was sold by ECP in 1919, her rent was £158 a year for the house and farm. She proceeded to buy it.

Eliz Cramp, my grandmother.[2] *Her son, John Edward Cramp, my father, farmed here. They farmed a big area. The others* [her other children] *all went to Canada before the war and all came back and visited Grandma. They all lived in Orchard Lane before they went away but my grandmother was in that big house with just my father at the end. She used to wake him at 4 o'clock saying. 'It's a lovely day. Out you go!'*

Mrs [Sheila] *Allen's grandmother gave the farmhouse to her son in law, Lewin.*[3]

Elizabeth and Harry Cramp had eleven children. The eldest daughter, Elizabeth Ellen,[4] married Henry Robey Lewin, son of Morley Lewin, the butcher whose family had moved from Glen Farm to Trent House. In 1922 Elizabeth Cramp gave up the farm and the farmhouse she had recently bought and handed them over to her daughter and son in law. She moved out and then lived with various of her children and died in 1937. Her daughter and son-in-law, Elizabeth and Henry Lewin, became the owners and lived here. It is interesting to find that the Lewins had returned to their nest in Orchard Lane by marrying into the Cramp family.

From the back you can see the barn and hayloft above with the opening bricked up. There were cowsheds and the building joined onto what became the co-op farm. A square of bricks covers the old well. A cellar goes under the whole house. Air ventilation grills for the cellar can be seen in the stone base of house.

After she sold her farm, Elizabeth Cramp moved with her youngest son, another Harry, in 1925 to the butcher's shop which is now run by Wilson Ragg's family.[5]

---

[1] in the Packe Inland Revenue Tax returns

[2] Picture courtesy of Sheila Allen, granddaughter of Elizabeth Cramp.

[3] Walter Allen 2002

[4] Elizabeth Ellen Cramp, born in 1879, married Henry Lewin in 1903

[5] The Raggs of Oadby know of no family connection with the William Ragg who was the Great Glen butcher in Trent House from 1856 to 1869 (Lot 5). The coincidence of the names is intriguing!

LOT 12 North House Farm 13.273 acres.
North House included what is now Manor Farm when it was sold in 1919 to the sitting tenant, William H. Heard, who also rented nearly 300 acres in total from EC Packe, for £452 a year. The catalogue points out that the *First floor is reached by two staircases,* which fits in with an early description of the house as being *a messuage formerly in two dwellings or tenements with gardens and croft and a homestead and hovel*[1]. The 1919 catalogue indicates the size of the house: *There are four bedrooms, two store rooms whilst on the second floor there are two bedrooms.*

North House Picture from the 1919 sale catalogue.[2] The farm manager lived in the adjacent cottage, probably an older building than North House.

North House is not marked as part of the Stretton Estate in 1835 because Robinson did not own it. On the 1835 map this land is owned by *Mr Edwards.* It is not clear when CWP bought it.

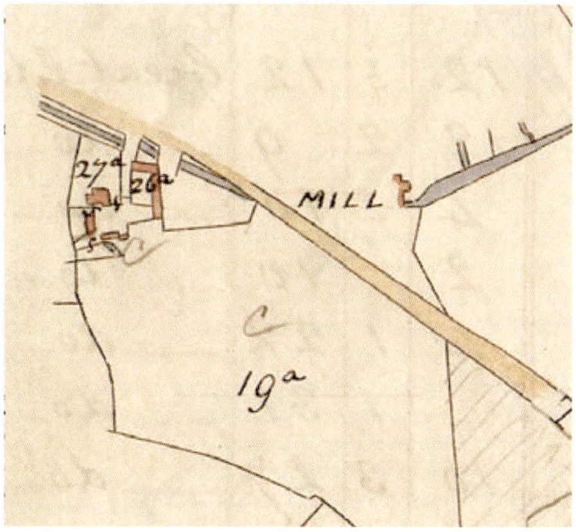

In CWP's account books the plots are numbered as 26a and 27b, indicating that they were later acquisitions.

The house and lands were rented by Sarah Clement. She rented the croft field 19a, a large ridge and furrow field on the opposite side of the road to the mill.

In 1841 Sarah Clements is named as head of the household in the census of that year. She is described as a widowed farmer/grazier, aged 31, with seven children (Elizabeth 12, Sarah 10, William 8, Mary 6, Abraham 4, Jane 2 and Thomas 1, all born in Glen). She has two male servants (to help with the farm) and one female servant (to help her with the house and children). It sounds a tough undertaking!

---

[1] Indenture list of 1849
[2] Sale document 1919 DE688/66

And to make matters worse, she was also the *postmistress,* running the post office from this house.[1] (How did she find the time and energy?) In the 1851 census she is a farmer of 125 acres employing three outdoor agricultural labourers. All the children are still living at home and she has her father, Abraham Wright, a house proprietor, aged 81, living with her. By 1861 she had relinquished the post office job. (The role of postmaster had passed to George Elson by this date.[2]) Her eldest son, William, took a greater share in the farming.[3] Thomas and Mary remained at home and the census also includes her daughter Sarah (now with a married name of Seaman) with her two young daughters. In 1871 Sarah Clements, now aged 61, is farming 345 acres, with only her 37 year old son William at home with her. They employ four men and three boys and have one young house servant.

In 1881, William, aged 47 and still unmarried, lived in the house with his now widowed sister, Sarah Seaman, and one servant. He employed eight men and three boys for his 590 acres, having inherited his mother's lands. He was still in the house in 1891, alone with one servant. By 1901 the census records his sister Sarah Seaman (aged 70) living with him and the servant. His younger brother Abraham, also a farmer (aged 64) and Mary, their sister (aged 66), live nearby, in a house (RV £15) owned by William. In 1910 William still rented North House as well as a lot of land from ECP and from other landowners and his sister Mary rented the house at the top of Orchard Lane from him. (Did she pay him the estimated gross annual value of £19 or did he let his younger sister have it free, I wonder.)

By 1919 the tenant of North House was William Heard, who also rented cottages in Post Office Row (see Lot 31).

The house can scarcely be seen today because of the trees which have grown to hide it.

North House. Photographed in 1984[4]

[1] The directories of the time gives us details: Post Office: Clements Sarah, postmistress, letters arrive from Leicester 9am depart 7pm.
[2] See Lot 31 Post Office Row
[3] In Kitty Packe Reading's 1869-70 account book the tenant changes from Sarah to her son William, Clements, who rented more than 350 acres of land from the Packes.
[4] DE 3736

LOT 12 (continued) Manor Farm, (included in the sale of the adjacent North House) *was built in about 1690. This was the farm manager's house. Simpson, a butcher, lived here. There were no doors at the front. The front door was round the back. The porch is new.*[1]

Tommy Clarke remembers his father working at the farm: *My father Arthur Clarke worked for Mr R W Kaye first at the Manor House but then at Manor Farm. The farm had a huge dairy herd...They supplied Kirby and West with milk.*[2]

Manor Farm yard buildings *about 1928.*

The doors and windows are of a similar design to those still standing in the yard of the Old Greyhound inn. The picture, dating from about 1928, shows Mr Gibson,[3] the carrier with his van in Manor Farm yard.

Mr Gibson's son, Stan, remembers the farm: *You went over the bridge to the farm into the farmyard. You can see the farm buildings here where they used to milk all the cows. They were corrugated Dutch barns.*

The ownership of the farm switched for some time between EC Packe and Robert Walter Kaye. It appears in CWP's 1862 account book. but by 1917 the farm was owned by RW Kaye, a wealthy industrialist. He and Marion his wife donated the church lychgate on Church Road as a thanksgiving for the safe return of their son

[1] Nigel Hurst, the present owner
[2] Tommy Clark interviewed by Judy Phythian Adams 2002
[3] Picture courtesy of Stan Gibson, his son.

from the 1914-18 war. They lived in Glen Manor,[1] built for Robert's father and designed by Henry Goddard.[2] Joe Goddard, the architect's grandson said: *The Kayes made shoes, had lots of money and Old Kaye thought Money talks. He wanted to have the manor at Newton but Grandfather said he couldn't, so he said, ' Well, if I can't have it you can design one for me to go up in Great Glen'. So H L Goddard designed the Glen Manor (now the school) for him, based on the Newton Harcourt manor house.*[3] Kaye sold the farm back to ECP in 1917 and in 1919 when EC Packe put it up for auction, it was sold privately to Wm Heard, the sitting tenant, who sold it back to RW Kaye in 1921! In 1948 the farmhouse, buildings and pasture land were sold to the Simpson brothers of Oadby, for £12,100. In 1956 Francis Cyril Simpson bought out his brother's share and ran the farm.[4] Dick Hull, whose family lived in the Lodge to Glen Hall around this time, remembers working in the farmyard when he was young: *I collected eggs from his haystacks in the yard. We got paid for it and enjoyed it.* Mrs Sheila Ball remembers being given milk by Mr Simpson for her prize cats.

LOT 21 (cottages on London Road) was sold in 1919 for £260. The sale catalogue describes the cottages as: *a Pair of brick and slated cottages with gardens, adjoining Glenn Hall. Sitting room, Kitchen, Pantry and two bedrooms, washhouse and closet. Rents weekly determinable by 4 weeks notice. Rental £10. 8s. 0d per annum. Tenants: Ruth Clowes Arthur B Clarke.*

Mr Thomas Clarke, grandson of Ruth Clowes, and still resident in the village, was born in the cottage on the left of the picture, in 1914. He remembers the cottages well: *This picture is modern. The house used to be thatched and covered in ivy creeper. It had different windows and no porch. Granny Clowes lived here* [in the house on the right]. *Harriet, my mother, married Arthur B Clarke, my father and they lived in the cottage on the left.*

They were owned by Sir Henry Halford in 1878. (In 1837 he had owned only the mill and its two adjacent cottages.) The tenants listed in the 1841 census are William Clowes, a wheelwright (aged 20, with Harriet his wife and a son, Joseph, aged 2) and his neighbour, Thompson. The 1851 census (which gives ages more

[1] Now the private school, at the top of London Road.
[2] Henry Goddard, from a long line of architects, lived at Newton Harcourt Manor House.
[3] Joe Goddard interviewed 2002
[4] Information courtesy of Nigel and Cheryl Hurst from their deeds dated 1996. Jayne Frances Simpson, inherited in 1973 and later sold the property in her married name of Jayne McVeagh.

accurately) describes Clowes as a wheelwright aged 33, with Harriet aged 42, and sons Joseph 12 and Alfred 2 months. The family does not appear in the 1861 census (for some reason they were not at home) and by 1871 Harriet is described as a widowed framework knitter aged 62, living here with only Alfred her younger son, aged 20. John Thompson, their neighbour, was also a framework knitter. He paid slightly more than the Clowes in rent for his cottage. (In 1878 he paid £4 10s a year in rent and Harriet Clowes paid £3 15s.)

In 1881 Alfred Clowes, described as a railway worker aged 30, had become the head of household, with his wife Ruth, a laundress and their three young children, Harriet, his mother (now 72) and a lodger. Their neighbour, John Thompson, is described as a gardener aged 30 with three children, two of whom work as hosiery hands. By 1891 Alfred had six children (Henry, 15, Harriet 12, Frederick 8, Joseph 6, Florence 3 and Cecil aged 1). Both families were still here in 1897 when Sir Henry's heir, T.Freemantle, sold the cottages to W J Packe, for £200. The deeds state that the cottages were in the occupation of Alfred Clowes and John Thompson.[1]

In 1901 Alfred Clowes lived in the right hand cottage with his wife Ruth and seven children plus a grandchild, Dorothy, aged 3. The four older children were all hosiery workers (though Florence/Flossie is only 12). Alfred's daughter Harriet (named after her grandmother) married Arthur B Clarke.

Arthur Clark and Harriet came to live in the cottage next door to her parents. They took over the tenancy from John Thompson, and produced a large family of children. Their son, Tommy Clarke, interviewed in 2002, described what life was like here in his childhood, with three brothers and five sisters. His mother and father slept in a kind of lean-to downstairs and the children slept in the two rooms upstairs (one of these was very small). The bedroom floors, made of gypsum, sloped to the middle. The wash-house was a further lean-to with a corrugated iron roof. The two cottages originally had thatched roofs. They had a communal water pump in front of the four cottages. *There were nine of us* [children] *and on a Sunday night for Monday* [washday] *we came down to the dippy hole in the brook here, by the bridge to the farm* [Manor Farm]. *We carried buckets for the washing.*

---

[1] 12D 43 129/6 Halford Deeds

We were a big family and used a lot of water. The pump might well go dry. We used that for drinking water.[1] His father paid half a crown a week [two shillings and sixpence] rent in the 1920s and remained in the cottage until he and his wife died in the 1960s. He worked for Mr Robert Kaye at the Manor House and then at Manor Farm,[2] where they had a huge dairy herd and milked two hundred cows at any one time. Robert Kaye offered to sell this cottage to Mr Arthur Clarke, together with the adjoining cottage, for £26 all told. Mr Clarke's reply was: 'I haven't got 26 shillings, never mind £26'. This was the cottage where Tommy Clarke's family volunteered to accept evacuees during the war (see Chapter 3). It was used to being a 'Full House'![3]

LOT 31 Post Office Row *Eight cottages and gardens (coloured yellow on the map). This lot is sold with the benefit of the existing Water Supply drawn from lot 6.* The whole row was sold by Packe in 1919 for £875.

...desirable additions to the [Packe estate] *property...but not a profitable investment.* (Charles Packe)

The cottages in Main Street were known as Post Office Row. The land next to them went right up to the hollow next to Dell House. The hollow had been a gravel pit.[4]

It is not easy to say when the cottages were built. The land on which they stand was Town End Close, owned by *Mr Harrison*[5] and was later bought by W J Gilbert. Ten houses were built on about three acres of *Town End Close, formerly in the occupation of Thomas Harrison afterwards of Thos Nichols since of Wm Collier*

---

[1] Tommy Clarke

[2] Lot 12 North House and Manor Farm

[3] *The two cottages beyond the two in the picture were built much later, in 1927, for Mr Kaye.* Sheila Ball who formerly lived in one of these later cottages remembered: *The drains were connected to the old cottages. In 1950 there was in the back corner of the house an outside pan lavatory and a man came round emptying it. But we had one fitted inside upstairs.*

[4] Tommy Clarke, interviewed by J PhA. 2002

[5] Thomas Harrison inherited from Matthew Harrison who is named in the Enclosure Award of 1790

then late of Wm Cooper and Henry Cooper then the said Gilbert.[1] Eight of these dwellings are the row of cottages which Charles Packe eventually decided to buy in 1876.[2] He bought all eight cottages plus Batchelor's house (see Lot 6) in 1877 for £2,000 from John Gilbert, the innkeeper of the Fox and Goose. The 1877 sale document names the occupiers as: Wm Bromwich, Samuel Crick, Jonathan Rowe, Mary Elson, Daniel Allen, Thos Coulson, James Allen and John Achurch. These names are also listed in the 1878 Valuation, as tenants of Charles Packe.

The name of Mary Elson is interesting in relation to the name 'Post Office Row'. She and her husband appear in the 1841 census, when he is described as a *carpenter.* By 1851 he is described as a *carpenter and grocer* and Mary is described as 'DD', a wife with Domestic Duties. She, like her three children, had been born in Glen. Her husband, George Elson, was born in Northants. By 1861 he is described as *carpenter and sub-postmaster* and Mary, now 46, is the *letter carrier.* Together they ran the post office, from what is now part of 41 Main Street. When her husband died she seems to have moved to this row of cottages, on the opposite side of the road. By 1871 she, a widow aged 54, had taken over the job of postmistress and she ran the post office from this row until about 1891.

In the 1891 census, Mary Elson is described as 70 (or 76, her age is very variably given!). Her neighbours include James Allen, who had lived in the row since at least 1877, and Wm Neale who had arrived by 1881. In 1891, he lived here with his wife and six children, having moved from Peep Row. The others were newer arrivals.[3] Mary remained here but her son William took over the running of the post office from his house in the Nook, in 1891, presumably when it got too much for her. By 1901 Mary had died and a newcomer, George Harrison, had taken over the post office from William.

---

[1] The other two houses are referred to as *those two messuages or tenements with the butchers shop also then sometime since erected formerly in the occupation of Thomas Bachelor and Widow Woodcock...formerly one cottage occupied by Thomas Stickles and now in the occupation of Green Achurch and George Ellson.* See Chapter 3 .

[2] See Chapter 1 part 3. Letter from Charles Packe DE 5047. *There are eight cottages...which are to be sold by auction on Sept 5th. They arle very desirable additions to the property.*

[3] Tenants in 1891: John Gamble (ag lab aged 50, born in Glen), Wm Neale (ag lab aged 49 with wife and six children, all born in Glen), Wm Clarke (a gardener aged 36, born in Waltham), Job Smith (ag lab 60), Wm Bennett (coal agent, 28) and George Freestone (ag lab aged 54).

The tenants of Post Office Row in 1901[1] and 1910[2] included Elizabeth Bland (a widow aged 40 with five sons and a daughter aged 4, all born in Glen) as well as James Allen, now 52, a woollen glove manufacturer who had been here since 1877. In 1919, when the row was sold, the residents are named as: Annie Eglesfield, John Gamble, Mrs Knowles, Elizabeth Bland, William Heard, Wm Freestone, James Allen and William Heard. Each cottage was rented at £5 4s per annum, apart from the two rented by William Heard, who paid £7 16s per year. One of these (number 28) was an end house, which usually brings more status! But why he paid more for the other I do not know. Nor do I know why he rented two cottages here, unless he was sub-letting.

One of the cottages was re-sold in 1929 by Edwin Neale. It was bought by Frederick Checkley, a licensed victualler at the Greyhound in Billesdon. The deeds refer to this cottage as *Bawtry, number 21 Post Office Row* and it is described as *having a coalhouse and piggery, garden and rights of way of use and access to the pump spring and well...and outbuildings and other appurtenances as now used and enjoyed by the owner and occupier.* In 1945 Checkley sold it to Arthur Whittle,[3] a butcher in Humberstone Rd, Leicester, for £775.

LOTS 32 AND 33 Packe's Row (the familiar name of Peep Row has now been established in common parlance, supposedly because the occupiers were known to peep out of the small leaded windows to see passers-by! The 1861 census refers to it by its pre-Packe name of *Street Row, Stretton Road* [Main Street]. The row of nine cottages was offered for sale in 1919 as two lots (coloured purple on the map).

LOT 32 *A Row of Five Cottages known as Packe's Row. Living room, Kitchen pantry and 2 bedrooms. Tenants: Wm Gould, Alice Reynolds, Richard Burdett, Harriet Neale and F. E Colptman. Out offices are at the rear.*

[1] Tenants in 1901: George Treslove (69, ag lab) and William Freestone (31, a shoemaker, who had succeeded his father as tenant), William Lovell (32, bricklayers labourer), Elizabeth Bland (a widow aged 40 with 5 sons and a daughter aged 4, all born in Glen), Green Achurch, John Gamble and William Neale

[2] In 1910 the tenants remained the same, with only one new name, that of Rachel Harris who replaced William Lovell.

[3] Arthur Whittle also bought Peep Row cottages. See Lot 32.

GREAT GLEN OS map surveyed 1883-6. Published 1907

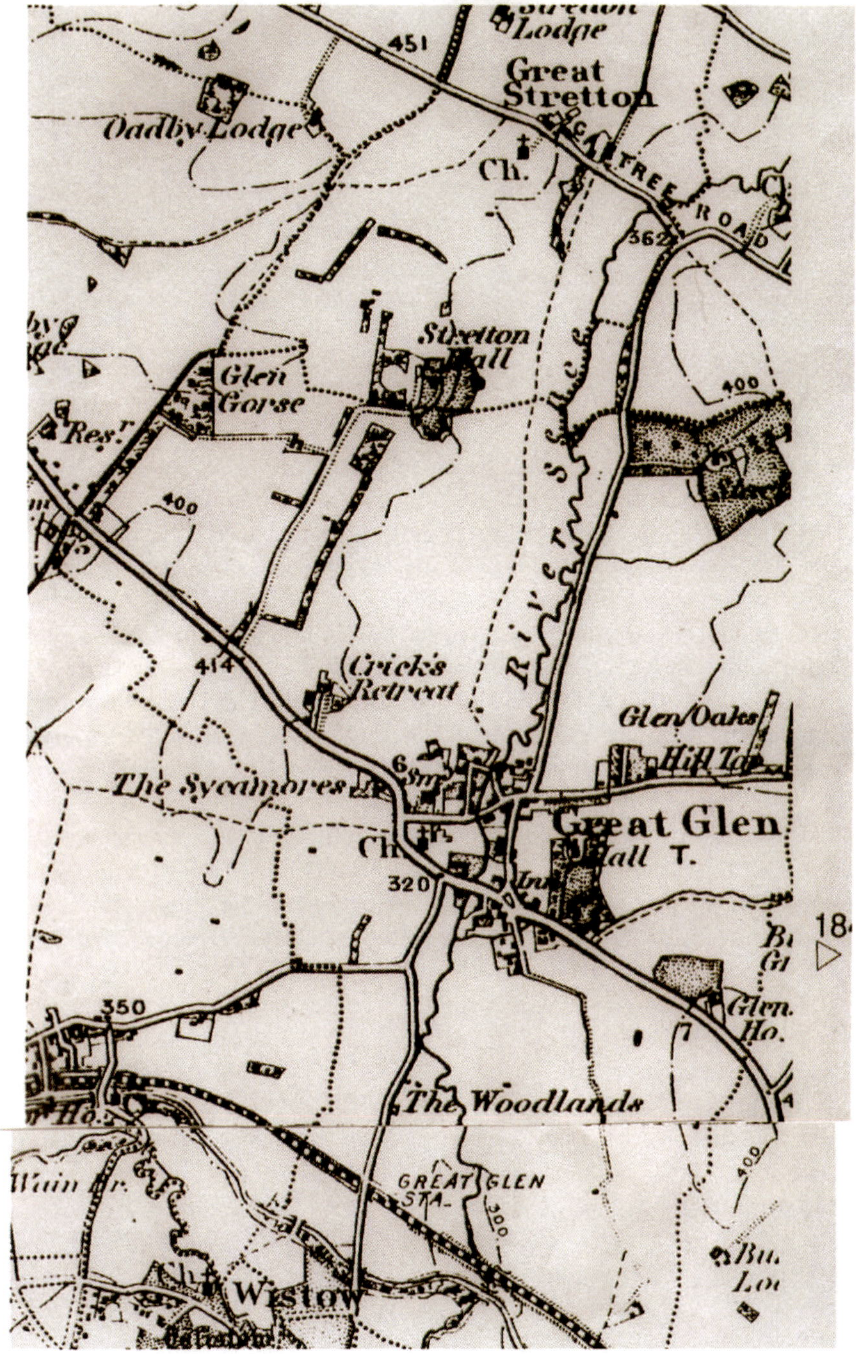

LOT 33 *Four Cottages known as Packe's Row with tenants: Donald Nosely, Albert Achurch, Fredk Hubbard, and John Siddons.*

There was no running water on site in 1919 but a note on the sale catalogue indicates that: *A right is reserved for the tenants to draw water from the pump on the allotments opposite as now enjoyed.*

The rental for each house in 1919 was £5 4s per year. (This seems a reasonable income for a purchaser, but the row did not reach the price demanded. Col Packe had to try selling again in 1932. At that point they were advertised[1] as *Packe's Row LOT 2, five Brick and Slated cottages, 16,17,18,19, 20, each containing four rooms and a pantry with common yard and out offices. Let to: Gould, Marshall, Margetts, Coleman and Riley. Gross annual rental £36. 8s. 0d and four similar cottages LOT 3: 12, 13, 14, 15 Packe's Row, now occupied by Nosely, Moore, Hubbard and Williamson. Gross annual rental £27 6s 0d.* But the sale again fell through. The five cottages were withdrawn at £310 and the other four were withdrawn at £230. They were however sold later the same year.

All nine cottages, together with the yard, outbuildings and appurtenances, were bought in 1932 by Frederick Checkley (of the Greyhound Hotel in Billesdon). He sold them again in 1945 to Herbert Arthur Thomas Whittle. Some of the tenants listed in 1945 had been there since 1932, while others were more recent arrivals. Arthur Whittle, their new landlord, died in 1961, the same year as their old landlord, Col Packe.

The History of the cottages:

Charles Packe speaks of owning the row in 1876[2] and in the 1878 Valuation the cottages are listed under his name, (each rented at £3 per year) but whether he or CWP had purchased them, and when, is still not clear. The *Victoria County History*

---

[1] DE 4674 394 Sale Document.

[2] DE 5047/144/1-41 letters from Chas Packe to his brother William 1876: *There are eight cottages which are to be sold by auction on Sept 5th ... and the row on the opposite side belongs to me.* Peep row is on the opposite side of the road to Post Office Row.

states that Peep Row in Main Street is *a range of ten dwellings said to have been built for framework knitters.* (One has been added later to the original nine.)

Peep Row cottages from an album of 1984.[1]

The anonymous author of the album says: *An examination of the cottages shows that they have been added to and altered possibly about the middle of the nineteenth century. The end two cottages* [on the right as you face them] *must have been added to an original older row of five cottages and two on the left* [next to the end one] *added on to fit between the row and the end cottage on the left.*[2]

The clue to the origin of the cottages lies in documents relating to Robert Haymes. In the *Schedule of Gt Glenn Estate and cottages Shewing who they were purchased from,*[3] we find included a row of nine houses which were *Formerly one house and shop purchased from Strickland and after converted by the Testor* [Robert Haymes] *into nine houses.* We learn from another Haymes document that the purchase of the house and shop from Strickland took place in 1785[4] but we are not told when the conversion into the row of cottages was made. The suggested date of 1830-1840 seems a reasonable estimate.[5]

Robert Haymes (born 1768, died 1855 aged 87) is described in the church monuments as *a friend to the poor, the fatherless and the widow.* It is pleasing to

[1] DE 3736 re Packe Row. There were 10 houses (one slightly bigger than the rest). No. 39 now extended, no. 29 was always slightly bigger than the rest, and nos. 23 and 27 were knocked into one dwelling. In the 1960s, no. 39 was owned by a Mrs Allan and the rest were owned by a Mr Whittle

[2] DE 3736 album of photos

[3] 11D 58/10 Haymes documents

[4] 11D 58/15.

[5] Victoria County History Leics vol V 1964 p 123 suggest date of 1840. Bennett's *Leics Architects 1851-1899* suggests a comparison with Hog Lane charity houses in Hallaton designed by Wm Holloway in 1842.

know that it was Haymes who was responsible for these cottages.[1] Everything about the man indicates a kindly landowner! He was, after all, one of the *Gentlemen already entered into to improve the condition of Frame Work Knitters* when he subscribed £10 in 1833.[2] In the 1837 Valuation he is listed as owning twenty eight dwellings.[3] Nine of his tenants live in this row of cottages and it is possible to discover something of the history of the cottages by looking at the census details. In 1841 the nine tenants all had some sort of FWK connection and most were in the 40-50 age-range. We can recall the situation of FWKs at this time and remember how poor these people were and in what conditions they had to live. We know they had to bring up their families in cottages like this, with no running water and inadequate heating. We note the small windows in the houses and wonder how they managed to get enough light to work by.

The names of the tenants of these nine houses appear in the 1841 census and can be tracked through later documents: William Dencher, Edward Foster, Laurence Grain, Samuel Burdett, John Roe, John Clarke, Robert Dickman, Wm Bird and Wm Carver. These are the tenants who were living in the row when CWP first arrived.

Wm Dencher was a FWK aged 43 in 1841 with a wife and 12 year old son, both FWKs. In 1851 he was alone in the house, a master glover, employing two men. By 1871, aged 71, he is back to being described as a FWK, so presumably still working.
Edward Foster, another FWK (aged 50) lived in the row in 1841 with his wife Alice and two daughters, Sarah aged 19 and Jane aged 17, but by 1861 Alice is widowed and living alone and there is no entry for her in 1871.
Laurence Grain a widower FWK (aged 37) has a son aged 11, also a FWK and a daughter aged 7 in 1841. In 1851 he appears with his daughter, Maria, a glove-stitcher aged 17.
Sam Burdett, also a FWK (aged 30) lived here in 1841 with three children, Elizabeth aged 9, William aged 6 and Joseph aged 3. In 1851 William aged 16, and Joseph aged 12, both followed their father as FWKs. Samuel worked as a labourer in 1854, earning three shillings a week, but this may simply have been a temporary

[1] The cottages were not built by CWP as is popularly thought and stated in various history books of Glen. The history of who built the row, and when, has required some prolonged detective work. It was suggested, wrongly, that they were built in about 1840 and financed by CWP who *fitted the dwellings with every necessary convenience which might render them a comfortable asylum for persons customarily considered to be superior of that class of persons for whose residence they are designed.* The reference is not given. The author goes on to say they were *Let out at rents so low as to make them a grateful charity to those who may be allowed to obtain them.* I cannot find the source of this quotation but it seems more applicable to Robert Haymes than to CWP!
[2] See Chapter 3 the 1840s.
[3] mainly cottages with low rents (RV of about £3).

job, to make ends meet.[1] In 1861 the older boys had left home but there were others to replace them! There were then three younger children at home. Elizabeth his daughter was 19 and working as a servant, Daniel at 13 was an agricultural labourer, and George, the youngest, was 4. (A very spread-out family!) In 1871 only George, aged 14, lived with his father, who was by then 62.
John Rowe is a widower, a FWK with a 15 year old daughter also a FWK.
John Clark, a FWK, lives with his wife Mary and daughter Ann, aged 14 in 1841. He and Mary are still there in 1851 but by 1861 Mary, aged 66, was widowed and lived here, with a lodger.
Robert Dickman was aged 71 in the 1841 census, with two sons. Thomas, the elder son was a FWK aged 32, and he later took over the tenancy. He is recorded in 1851 as an unmarried 41 year old living here with his mother, Sarah Dickman, a 73 year old widow. He does not appear here in the 1871 census and may have moved to another part of the village, to be nearer his younger brother in Oaks Road.
William Carver, aged 60 and Mary Carver have a son who is a widower FWK aged 20 in 1841 (with a son aged 4). By 1851 the son and grandson have left and William and Mary are here together, aged 71. In 1861 Mary is a widow aged 85 and she does not appear in 1871.

By 1861 there were various changes in tenancies. Laurence Grain, John Roe and Wm Bird were succeeded by John Webster, Wm Coleman and Wm Peberdy.

John Webster is a FWK aged 60, with a 74 year old lodger, Alice Musson.
William Coleman was recorded in 1851 as a FWK, with a 14 year old son George, also a FWK, and a younger son Samuel, aged 6. His wife Jane (Burdett), born in Oadby and some fourteen years younger than her husband, seems to be a second wife, with two daughters. Mary Burdett aged 12 and Sarah Burdett aged 11, are recorded as his *daughters in law* (meaning step daughters) in the census. Both work as seamstresses. In 1861 George, Mary and Sarah have all left home and the only one of their siblings still at home with his parents is Samuel, now 16. By 1871, William, aged 71 and still a FWK, was living here with his wife, Jane.
William Peberdy, the youngest person in the row in 1860 was described in the 1851 census as an ag lab aged 25, with his wife Ann. In 1861, when he was 35, they had one child, Alfred, aged one.

William Peberdy's wife, Ann, becomes a crucial link in tracing the later tenants, as she is the one resident to remain in the Row for the next thirty odd years. She appears as a widow aged 54 in 1881 with her unmarried son, Alfred, a railway worker, and a lodger, his friend Geoffrey. She remains there in 1891 and in 1901 and is named in the Valuation of 1909. As a 73 year old widow, it is Ann Peberdy, who enables us to link back to Robert Haymes' *Schedule of Properties* and forward

[1] DE 24/15 Highway Accounts 1854

to the sale of the cottages by ECP in 1919, by taking note of the names of her neighbours in the row over such a long period of time.

Ann Peberdy's landlord, Arthur Haymes, the last surviving son of Robert Haymes, died in 1872, aged 66. His will,[1] dated July 1869, requests: *that my remains be kept for seven days and then interred in the plainest possible way at Great Glen as near the remains of my ever lamented parents as may be and that six of the most honest industrious and generally deserving of my cottage tenants do carry my body to the grave and be paid ten shillings each for their trouble.* I wonder which, if any, of Ann's neighbours were deemed worthy enough to carry his coffin and to receive this generous payment.

After 1871 there was a great change in the tenancies of Peep Row. Before that date, Ann's neighbours had all been about thirty years older than herself and had lived for nearly 40 years in the same houses. Ann must have seen the deaths and departures of all of them in turn. The FWKs, Sam Burdett and his son George, Wm Dencher, William Coleman, John Webster and the widows, Alice Foster and Mary Carver, who had lived beyond the great age of 85, had all gone by1878.

By 1909 Ann Peberdy's was the only remaining name from the 1860 schedule.[2] New tenants, some not born in Glen and mostly not FWKs, had taken over the tenancies of the original FWKs who had lived here in 1860. Framework knitting as a cottage industry had changed. By 1874 the growth of the factory system meant that less of the work was done by home workers. They increasingly became *hosiery hands* in a factory. Peep Row, however, continued to have its share of FWKs. In 1871 there were new names, like that of Wm Neale, a young 21 year old FWK and William Achurch with his wife Mary who was born in Newton Harcourt and John Grain[3] a labourer aged 37 with a wife, Sarah, who worked at the cooperative store, and then later became *a FWK in fancy goods,* still working when she was 67. (Their daughter Mary Ann, is similarly employed in 1891.)

William Achurch was a tenant in 1881, when he was 60, with his wife Mary and a lodger, William Cobley.[4] Achurch is a frequently occurring name in Glen. His tenancy is taken by another Achurch. Ann Achurch appears in 1891 aged 48 with her children, John (16) an ag lab, Ann (12) Kate (9) and Albert, aged 3. We learn a little more about her from the 1901 census, where she is named as a widow, a charwoman aged 58, born in Staffordshire. By 1901 her eldest daughter had left home but Kate, a machinist (aged 19) and Albert, a butcher's assistant (aged 13) are

---

[1] 11D58 7 Arthur Haymes' will.

[2] It is interesting, but a bit puzzling, that her rent actually goes down from 1901 when she paid WJ Packe £3, the same as her neighbours, to £2 10s in 1910 when they pay double that amount. I wonder why this is. Could it be a long service bonus?

[3] John Grain is listed in the 1909 Valuation.

[4] Wm Cobley see Lot 10

still living with her. Kate's name appears as *occupier* in the 1909 Valuation. But it is Albert whose name appears as tenant in 1919, when Packe sold the house.

In 1881 more new tenants are listed: William Barnes (aged 48, born in Herts, with a wife Sarah, 65, born in Great Glen) stayed here for about thirty years. Thomas Grant aged 60, formerly a shepherd, with his wife Hannah, formerly a sock stitcher, and three children[1] was still here in 1901 aged 79, with Hannah aged 70. His son Thomas later lived in one of the neighbouring cottages and is named in the 1909 valuation.

A new tenant appears in the 1891 census: Henry Hubbard, a FWK aged 40, born in Countesthorpe, living here with his wife Mary (40) a charwoman born in Glen. They had three children born in Countesthorpe and one, young Frederick aged 3, born in Glen. By 1901 Henry was a widower, a bricklayer's labourer, with four children[2] in the hosiery trade and Reginald, a grandson 11 months old, born in Great Glen. Four grown men, a woman and baby in a two-bedroom cottage sounds like crowded living! Most of the households in Peep Row must have been very cramped, but by this date the FWKnitting would have been done in factories and so the machinery would not have taken up space in the cottage, as it had done in earlier years. In 1919 it is Henry Hubbard's son Frederick who is listed as tenant when the house was up for sale.

Frederick Coltman, who had been living in The Nook in 1891 with Mary his wife, a laundress, and three children[3] moved to Peep Row by 1901. He is described as a 58 year old builder's labourer, born in Billesdon, with Mary his wife and his daughter Annie 25, a hosiery hand and son Arthur 20, a baker's assistant.

By 1909 Daniel Nosely appeared. In 1901 he was a FWK aged 60, living in The Nook, with a wife called Betsy from Willoughby Waterless and three children (Samuel, aged 25, a hosiery hand, Susannah aged 20 and Lucy, 15, both laundresses) all born in Great Glen. Daniel Nosely is named as a tenant when ECP put the houses up for sale in 1919. These are names remembered by elderly residents of Great Glen, like Miss Aston: *I knew several of the people in Peep Row: Nosely, Achurch, Hubbard and Siddons.*[4]

---

[1] Robert a groom aged 17, Eliza a Fancy Hosiery Worker aged 14 and Tom aged 12, still at school.

[2] 1891 Henry Hubbard's children: Mary 24, William 21 a machinist, Albert 16 and Frederick 13, a hosiery winder.

[3] 1891 Coltman children: Anne aged 16 in hosiery, George aged 14, an ag lab and Arthur aged 10, all born in Great Glen.

[4] Miss Aston, interviewed in 2004

Peep Row 1984. The fine architectural details and brickwork were then more visible.

Peep Row in 2002:

The houses today are certainly very attractive dwellings, having been considerably modernised. Several of the cottages have been combined into one, most of the windows have been altered and the brickwork stuccoed but the original 'eyebrow' brick moulding has been kept as an attractive feature.

LOTS 35 and 36 High Street.

Lot 36, nearest the camera, has a door on the side, just to the right of the picture.

Postcard Haddon Series c.1900, courtesy of Mrs Parris.

The same view c.1900. The side door is hidden by the bushes on the right of the picture.

Photo courtesy Fraser Gilbert.

LOT 35 is advertised in the 1919 sale catalogue as a *terrace of three gabled cottages and gardens (coloured grey on map). Tenants: John Achurch, Ernest E Mason, Ernest W Bland. Rental £6 10s each per year. Terrace of three gabled cottages.* The one on the right was a two bed-roomed house and the two on the left had three bedrooms. When Harry Parris bought the two on the right he converted them into one house. *Harry Parris lived here for 50 years. When he came out of the Forces he wanted to buy a house for his first marriage. This is two knocked into one, as you can see*[1].

In 1910 Ann Clarke rented the two bed-roomed house (on the right) for £4 a year and Ezra Mason (a gardener with five children) and Ernest Bland both paid £6 10s a year for their three bed-roomed houses.

By 1919 Ann Clarke's two bedroomed house was tenanted by John Achurch and the rents were £6 10s per year for each of the three houses.

At the 1919 sale the cottages received *no bid* and in 1932 Packe again offered them for sale.

In 1932 they were then advertised as LOT 4. *Three Very Eligible Houses, Of Brick and Slate, Nos 33, 34, and 35, High Street each containing Living Room, Kitchen, Pantry and Three Bedrooms (except No 35, which has Two Bedrooms) also outpremises and Good Gardens. Gas laid on. Let to Achurch, Mason and Franks. Gross Annual income £20 16s 0d.* Stuart Norman's pencilled notes to the 1932 sale document[2]tell us that the houses were *withdrawn at £330.* They were sold soon afterwards *for £350,* to Mr Thomas Franks Gilbert, who died in 1941. In 1946 the three houses were sold for £510 to Mrs Ellen Snowden, who resold two of the houses to Harry Parris in 1951 and 1957. She offered him the chance to buy the third, as well, but he refused. It was sold separately in 1972, after her death.

These are substantially built, superior cottages with fine brick moulding and slated roofs, three bedrooms and good gardens.

---

[1] Mrs Parris, speaking outside her house, in 2003.

[2] DE 4674 394 The auction *by Lt/Col Packe DSO OBE and CWC Packe at The Greyhound Hotel Great Glen Fri June 17th 1932 at 7 pm*

LOT 36 *A pair of Capital Cottages (coloured yellow on plan)*

The door to the second house was round the corner on the right. The houses were built by Charles Packe in about 1874. A letter from the vicar to WJ Packe in 1898 refers to a piece of church land, on the corner of High St and Church Road *about opposite to those new cottages of yours that your brother built.* [1]

They are described in the 1919 sale catalogue as both having the same yearly rental, £9 15s, though in fact the houses were of a different size. In 1910 the estimated annual rental value was £9 15 shillings for the larger of the two houses, rented by Wm Pywell and £4 for the other, rented by Joseph Henson.

Joseph Henson's father had been in the village since before 1891, when he is recorded as a farmer, aged 66, born in Ashby de la Zouch, with children who were all born in Burton Overy. In 1901 he was a widower, aged 76, living with his sons, including another Joseph, aged 50, and a granddaughter. In 1919 this son, aged 69, was the tenant when the house was auctioned.

Emma Pywell, the other tenant in 1919, was a laundress, the widow of William Pywell. (In the 1871 census William Pywell, the 16 year old son of John Pywell, is described as an undergardener, born in GG and living in The Nook. William seems to have become a railway worker and lived in the Nook in 1881, married to Emma, who came from Bedford. By 1891 William (still a railway worker) and Emma (a laundress) were living in *Top End* (High Street) with three daughters, Ann (12), Gertrude (5) and Beatrice (2). In the 1901 census Emma was recorded as aged 43, wife to William Pywell aged 46, a railway worker. They then had two daughters living with them, Gertrude aged 15 and Beatrice aged 12. By 1919 Emma was a widow. She was the tenant of her house (*number 37 on the door*), paying £9 15s a year in rent. She also rented two fields, *coloured blue on the map,* for 1s 0d a year. The fields are described as *admirably suited for building plots.* In 1919 the rents of £9 15s per year were quite high for the period. At the auction the cottages received *no bid,* so perhaps the asking price seemed high, too.

---

[1] DE 5047 154 letter from Wm Oddie to Wm James Packe dated Feb 23rd 1898.

LOT 39 Bott Stone cottages

Three brick and slated cottages, High Street. The three cottages are joined together on the corner of High Street and the date of 1851 and the initials of CWP are proudly displayed in the brickwork of the end house. The tenants in 1919 are listed as Thomas Capell, with two of the cottages, and Isabella Peers in the third.

Bott Stone cottages, with the initials of CWP and the date 1851. The three cottages are now combined into two houses.

Bott Stone cottages, a similar view, seen from the ford, c 1900[1]

One of the three cottages was lived in by Thomas Capell, tenant in the 1878 Valuation, paying £3 15s a year rent, living next door to Wm Grain, his father in law. In the 1881 census, Thomas Capell, the Parish Clerk, aged 43, lives with his

[1] Photo courtesy Fraser Gilbert

wife, Eliza, in the house of Wm Grain his father in law, aged 79. There are many Capells and Grains in Glen. Another Thomas Capell (labelled *junior*, although he is aged 72!) appears nearby with his wife Mary and an unmarried 60 year old ag lab lodger called Wm Clarke, appear to be living in the two adjoining cottages in 1881.

The Capells outside Bott Stone cottages c. 1900.[1] *The wooden erections adjoining cottage No. 32 are claimed by the tenant.*[2]

Capell's house was reported as having a dangerous water supply in 1898, when the vicar, Arthur Oddie referred to the condemned well beside Capell's house.[3] The water does not seem to have damaged Thomas Capell, for he lived to be a hundred. Born in 1837, he became a glover. In 1881 (aged 44) he is named as Parish Clerk, living with his wife Elizabeth and her father, William Grain, who is head of the house. He still held the post of clerk in 1891, by which time he had his 84 year old mother, Mary, living with him. In 1910 they paid an annual rent of £3 18s for one cottage and £4 4s for the second. Isabella Peers paid £5 4s a year for the third.

Miss Aston remembers Capell: *he was Parish clerk, married and lived to be 100. I remember he lay in bed and we had a party for him outside. It would be some time after 1936-7.*[4] Walter Allen also remembers going to the street party for Capell's 100th birthday. It must have been a memorable occasion.

---

[1] Photo courtesy of Mrs Selway.
[2] DE 688/66 Sale document 1919.
[3] See Chapter 3 Floods and droughts
[4] Miss Edna Aston, 2004

HOUSES SOLD IN 1932.

The mill house, like Glen Hall and its lodge house, was not offered for sale in 1919. The hall and lodge continued to be let to Theodore Walker, who also rented the mill cottage for his gardener. They were put up for auction in 1932, after Walker died.

The Mill Houses

The sale document[1] advertises the present mill house as *5 and 6, Millerdale. Two Brick and Slated houses: With the range of outpremises, ATTRACTIVE ROCK GARDEN which has a wealth of Rough Stonework, intersected by running stream and pools...and PADDOCKS of PASTURE or BUILDING LAND adjoining, occupying a prominent position with an extensive frontage to London road and adjacent to beautifully timbered Grounds of Glen Hall. Attached to this property is a **Spacious area of grass land** with Timber Trees. **The Weir Waterfall** also the 'Duck's Bill,' a prominent site for development...a unique Property for conversion for Residential purposes or admirably adapted for Café and Tea Garden with room for Motor Park, Sites for Garage or Petrol Station or other development.*

The Houses are semi detached with black and white exterior decoration. No. 5 is of three storeys and contains Living Room, Scullery and Five Bedrooms (one suitable for another Sitting Room). No. 6 has Sitting Room, Living Room, Scullery, Larder,

[1] DE 4674/394 Property sale leaflet, with handwritten pencilled notes by Stuart H Norman, 1932.

Three Bedrooms and Boxroom. Now respectively let to Peberdy and Watts on fortnightly tenancies at a Gross Annual Rental of £15 12s 0d and...occupied by the Rev J F Anderson,[1] *who will give possession subject to six weeks notice.*

Stuart Norman notes that it was *Withdrawn at £530.*

THE MILL

Great Glen had a mill as far back as 1352, when it was valued at 1 mark per year. It was still here in 1563.[2] Ogilby's map marks it in 1675, as does John Prior's in 1777. In September 1830 it was leased for a year to Wm Bradley [3] and then in October 1836 the water mill was conveyed to CWP by the trustees of *the late Mr Bradley.* In the 1837 Valuation, Sir Henry Halford owned the mill, valued at £30 a year rental, with William Oswin as occupier. The 1841 census names Wm Horton[4] aged 35, as the miller. He appears in the 1851 census as a miller and baker, born in Mowsley, employing one man. By 1861 Alfred Freeman had taken over as miller and his family stayed at the mill for another generation. The census of 1861 shows him as aged 23, with his widowed aunt (whose name I cannot believe to be Salato Wasllolow, though that is what it looks like!). In 1862 Alfred and Joseph Freeman are listed as the millers, tenants of CWP. They continue as tenants in KPR's account book, with the mill house as *46a Mill, garden, orchard* etc. In the 1878 Valuation, Joseph Freeman continues as the miller and tenant of Charles Packe.

The lands around the mill have a complicated history. The Parish originally owned the mill land. At the time of the Enclosure Award some sort of swap was done by Sir Henry Halford's solicitors in an arrangement to group his holdings more conveniently and the old *Town Land* (15 acres or thereabouts) was exchanged for a rent of £29 a year, except for one patch of land (2 roods 3 poles) *occupied free by the miller, in consideration of his supplying the parish pit with water.*[5]

In Jan 1819 Wm Burton paid Sir Henry Halford £1,050 for the Mill pasture, (the field on which Glen Hall was built) and the Mill cottages and garden, described as *formerly held by Joseph Pywell and his son Wm, with the cottage formerly occupied by Sturgess.*[6] In May 1834 Wm Burton's son's mortgage for Glen Hall

---

[1] Son in law to Theodore Walker

[2] Nigel Moon: *Leics and Rutland Windmills.*

[3] DE803/24

[4] Not to be confused with the other Wm Horton, named in the 1841 census as a carpenter aged 58 with a son of 19, also a carpenter, one apprentice and two servants. In 1837 his house (The White House) was valued at £20 rental and he also owned land.

[5] White's Directory of 1846

[6] The deed is based on a covenant between Sir Henry Halford and Thomas Franks for a close of land in the name of Mill Pasture and also a cottage or tenement adjoining in the occupation of Mary King. It refers to earlier owners as Winstanley and Vann.

describes the mill pasture *and also that Capital Messuage* [Glen Hall] *now built on the mill pasture, now in the occupation of Wm Burton in and upon part of the said close of ground inclosed with all houses and outhouses edifices barns stables* etc., etc. The land is variously assessed as 17 acres or so, or 18 and a half acres, including *a small piece of land near the entrance gate taken in on the diversion of the Turnpike Road.* In March 1837, on Wm Burton's death, his heirs sold the mill pasture and Glen Hall to CWP, as agreed some two years previously. In 1840 CWP took out another mortgage for £4000 for *the watercorn mill with millstones utensils implements and appurtenances and malt office, closes and lands, water courses, all the wood and willow trees.* In it he is contracted *to protect and insure against fire, according to the last will and testament of Wm Burton deceased.*[1]

By 1845 CWP acquired the neighbouring lands of Top Mill Close and Mill Close and Mill Close Meadow, when he purchased the Stretton Hall estate. The 1848 conveyance refers to *the mill close in two parts formerly in the tenancy of Jos Pywell and two cottages occupied by Ino Harrison and then of Mary King or her undertenant.* It also gives the name of Sturges. In 1855 the Mill Pasture (16 acres 3 roods 27 perches) is described as having formerly belonged to Franks, Pywell and Halford.[2] In a mortgage of 1865 there is mention of the water mill and farmhouse with barns, stables, cattle sheds and other agricultural buildings. Thirteen acres of the land was farmed by Mrs Sarah Clements.[3] In 1881 the miller was Thomas Slater but by 1885 the mill ceased operating.

In 1911 the mill is described in the Leicestershire Footpath Association book of walks as *the picturesque cottages known as Glenn Mill.* The author recommends a small diversion to look at the lake at Glen Hall before continuing along the London Road to pass the mill house. *After feasting our fancy and imagination on this tranquil scene, return to the road and continue for 200 yards until the picturesque cottages are reached. The old water mill is gone, crowded out by the huge steam mill: the water wheel was removed some 25 years ago. The exterior of the houses have been renovated to represent old brick and timber framed houses as seen in Cheshire and other counties, and look very picturesque with their white walls and black timber frames. The head gardener to Mr Walker resides in one cottage and he keeps the garden gay and bright with flowers.*[4]

The Leicester Advertiser, Friday March 10th 1961, included a picture of the mill, described as the home of Mr and Mrs W T Gray, beside the caption informing the readers that the miller's cottage, mill and bakehouse *have been splendidly converted into one house.* The article reports that the Mill House is *mentioned in*

---

[1] DE803/20
[2] DE803/19
[3] DE803/24 Sarah Clements of North House farmed most of the land in the vicinity.
[4] 1911 LFA book of walks published in 1911. See page p. 259

Domesday Book and goes on to say that *Miller Wm Horton lived and worked here in 1846. The building was later condemned but repaired and saved by Mr Gray, a trained carpenter who did much of the work himself.*[1]

Dick Hull, who lived at Glen Hall lodge house in the 1950s and 60s, remembers the house: *Mr and Mrs Gray renovated it. A little bridge from the spinney led into it.*[2] *I called it the road sweepers house.* Sheila Ball also remembers the houses at this period: *At the mill there lived the road man and his daughter Ruth who went to live in The Nook.* [3] And Lilian Haines remembers another family: *The Kings lived at Millers Dale. Hilda King used to help us at the Hall.*[4]

The Mill House transformed. 2003

[1] DE 2148 114-5 Leicester Advertiser Friday March 10th 1961
[2] Dick Hull 2003
[3] Sheila Ball 2003
[4] Lilian Haines 2003

GAMEKEEPERS LODGE

The Entrance Lodge to Glenn Hall on the London Road.
Built probably at the same time as the hall, 1830.

When CWP leased the hall to Anna Raymond in 1848 it included *that cottage at the entrance from the Turnpike Road now occupied by Henry Langley.*[1] Henry Langley is described in the 1841 census as a manservant, aged about 35, with a wife Elizabeth and two children (William 11 and Jane 9), all born in Hoton. (Hoton is near Prestwold, part of the Packe estates. He probably worked for the Packes and came to Glen with CWP in about 1837 to live in the lodge house and work in the grounds.)

For some reason,[2] the Langleys moved from the lodge house into a different Packe house by 1851 where they appear in the census, near Turlington, the schoolmaster, in Main Street. By this time, Henry's son William had left home.[3] The daughter Jane Langley (aged 18) is a dressmaker and unmarried and a third child, young Henry (aged 6) is a schoolboy. They rented the cottage and garden on what is now

---

[1] DE803/26

[2] The move may have been because a new tenant of the hall brought his own servant for the lodge.

[3] By 1861 William had settled in Branksome in Dorset, with a wife and daughter. He became a gardener at Branksome Towers for CWP and stayed on to work there after Charles Packe sold the property. It is interesting to see so many references to Langley in street names etc in Branksome today. Wm Langley's son, another Henry, came to stay with his grandparents in Glen in 1861, where he appears in the census aged 8. Ten years later he stayed on at Branksome to work for the next owner of the Towers.

Main Street (the road to Little Stretton), where the doctor's surgery now stands. Henry Langley is recorded as tenant there in CWP's account book of 1862. He also rents Boggy Close (plot 42) and Mill Meadow by the hall and the mill. He is still there in Kitty Packe Reading's 1869 account book, with 8 acres of land.

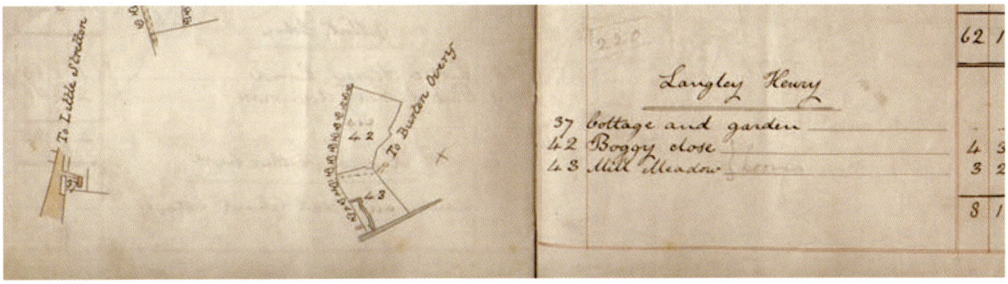

After the Langleys moved from the lodge house, the tenant in the Porters Lodge (when Capt Baillie was at the Hall) was Thomas Law, aged 52, with his wife Mary and daughter Peggy, aged ten (all born in Yorkshire). Ten years later they are no longer there and the Langleys are back in the Lodge House. By 1871 (Hoton-born) Henry Langley, a grazier aged 69 is recorded here with his Glen-born son, Henry, a wheelwright, aged 25, with a wife and two children. In the 1881 census (Glen-born) Henry has become head of the household and his father, Henry senior, aged 79, lives with him. (Glen-born) Henry, wheelwright and joiner, was on the Vestry committee in 1887, when Theodore Walker was at the hall but by 1891 he had moved out of the lodge house and lived in Church Road, near the Fox and Goose pub. The tenant of the Lodge house in 1891 was John Tilley, who was also there in 1901. Henry Langley, aged 56, lived with his wife Elizabeth, near the Fox and Goose in 1901. The Langleys do not appear in the 1910 Valuation.

A Langley gravestone in Glen churchyard.

In Affectionate Remembrance of Henry Langley who died Dec 3rd 1882 aged 83 years

The neighbouring one reads:
In Loving Memory of Henry Langley who died May 17th 1905 aged 65

Mr Stan Gibson talked to me about the Lodge House, where the Langleys lived: *My wife's mother's grandparents in the early 1800s lived in your house* [Gamekeepers Lodge]. *My wife's mother's parents were Langleys. Ginny Langley, her grandmother died only 5 years ago, aged 97. Ginnie Langley married Harry Smith, who was a stonemason and his initials are on the Langley graves in the churchyard. There are a lot of Langley gravestones and if you look at the corner you'll see 'H Smith' and he used to make all the grave stones.*[1]

By 1929 the lodge was occupied by the Symes family. The Sale Particulars of Glenn Hall advertise it as *protected by a substantial lodge. Now occupied by Mr Symes,*[2] *the chauffeur, on a service tenancy.*[3] LOT 1 includes the *substantial entrance Lodge, constructed of Leics white bricks* [actually a pale yellowish brick] *and slate with Verandah, comprising Sitting Room, Living Room, Scullery, Larder and two private bedrooms...a small enclosed yard with pigsty and Closet.*

Both the hall and the lodge were withdrawn from sale when Col Packe decided to move into the hall and to sell Stretton Hall instead. The Haines family who worked for him at Stretton Hall, came to live in the lodge house in 1930. Their son, Arthur Haines remained a great playmate of Margaret Packe, growing up together on the Stretton Hall estate. They were both about ten at the time of the move.

When Mrs Packe died, the Haines family helped the colonel look after his young daughter. As Margaret Packe said: *Arthur's mother practically brought me up. She was housekeeper to my father.*[4] Mr Haines had worked for Col. Packe at Stretton Hall. Like the Langleys before them, the family moved with their employer! He was gardener and general factotum and his wife was house-keeper at Glen Hall.

The Haines family.
Lilian (at the front of the picture) was born in the Lodge house.

---

[1] Mr Stan Gibson 2003

[2] His family is remembered by people living in the village today. The Hulls and the Gilbert boys mention the Symes boys playing by the lake and skating on the ice.

[3] DE 4674/263.

[4] Margaret Packe, 2002

My grandmother Mrs Bamford was here after I was born. She came to look after me so that my mother could go out to look after the colonel. Nobody else would have done what my mother did for him. She walked up the drive in all weathers to give him morning tea at 8 o'clock, give him his breakfast and go up again for lunch and up again for evening meal, always a three course meal. [Later] *I helped my mother and cleaned one or two evenings a week to help her. She had to clean and cook and everything else. I took over down here* [at the Lodge]. *I cooked my first roast dinner when I was nine.*

The Lodge House to Glen Hall.

That picture was early. We didn't have all that greenery on the roof.[1]

The Haines family lived in the two bedroomed house, without water, electricity or gas. Arthur Haines, revisiting the house in 1990 found it much changed. He remembered that there had been no sewage or water supply or electricity. They had some gas lamps but only candles in the kitchen. The front door led straight into the front room and there was a long corridor with coats hanging there. The kitchen had a sink, but no running water, and a copper and a fireplace, a gas cooker and a fold-down table.

The house was always subject to flooding. (Mr Gibson told me about the flooding in the house when the Langleys were here: *And when my wife's mother's grandparents lived in your house the water was up to the ceiling I've seen it when Arthur Hull lived there, after the Haines, with the water up to the window sill.*[2] Fraser Gilbert tells me that the house was *condemned for human habitation, because it flooded.*[3] Arthur Haines remembered neighbours helping when the house was flooded: *The kitchen larder had a sunken floor and was often flooded and all the neighbours used to come to help my father brush out the flood waters, which came in through the front door and had to be brushed out to the back.*

---

[1] Lilian Haines
[2] Stan Gibson
[3] Fraser Gilbert

Lilian, twelve years younger than Arthur, remembers how very cold it was stepping down into water in the larder.

There was no piped water supply in the house, no indoor bathroom or lavatory. Drinking water had to be transported in churns from the hall. Mrs Haines would come back from her work at the hall wheeling a churn full of water on each journey for cooking and drinking. *There was a water butt for other everyday use: The back yard had a huge, absolutely huge, water butt for rain water...just below the bedroom window...an absolute death trap. If anyone had fallen out of the bedroom window they would have drowned, it was so deep.*[1] *We had chickens in the yard and a coalhouse against the wall and a henhouse further along. There was a back gate and then to the right, the toilet. There was an outside loo [in the yard] which a man came to empty into the Halleluja cart.*[2] *He used to eat his sandwiches here with no thought of washing his hands.*

The house was, like so many other cottages in the village, quite cramped for a large family. When she visited one small room now used as a study, Lilian remembered how it was when she was young: *We ate in here. We had the fireplace and a table in front of the window and all six of the family plus all the friends and visitors, often twelve or more, had a meal. The table had leaves to make it big enough.* Margaret Packe had happy memories of being in this room with Mrs Haines. She remembered the cosiness of the cottage and the delight of having such luxuries as *fruit salad and cream for tea*! The Haines family provided her with the loving family needed by a motherless child.

The cottage had only two bedrooms and the family had four children: *Upstairs we had a double bed and mattress on the floor and the big bedroom had a double bed, a single bed and a mattress on the floor.*[3] But this did not inhibit the hospitality offered! Lilian remembers her mother's kindness during the war, when people from Leicester drove out to Glen for the night, in an attempt to escape from bombs which might be dropped on the city. Mrs Haines took any children from the cars on the drive indoors to make them more comfortable for the night: *People were afraid when Coventry was bombed, and came out from Leicester into the country and slept in cars. They were all along this drive to sleep overnight. Mother used to go out and bring any children in to sleep head to tail with us. My younger brother and I never knew who we'd wake up with, for several weeks until the panic was over.* Mrs Haines also helped with Col Packe's evacuees during the day: *During the war of course there were the evacuees. My mother looked after all the evacuees. There were ten of them and their teachers.*

---

[11] Lilian Haines.

[2] The 'halleluja cart' driven by Hiram Asher, was a well known feature in the village.

[3] Arthur Haines

Lilian now agrees that her family seemed *very comfortable in the Lodge* but says it was because *we didn't know any different.*[1] The Haineses moved out of the lodge and into the increased comfort of the cottage built for them close to Dell House, when Col Packe moved there, in 1953. The next people to live in the lodge were the Hull family, who moved in when the hall was sold to the Foxes.[2] Mr Fox, having moved into Glen Hall, had apparently persuaded Mr Hull to do some work for him and to take on the rental of the lodge house, which by them was somewhat run down. Mr Hull's son Dick tells the family version of the move: *Mr Fox took my dad down for a drink and said, 'I've got a proposition for you' and he must have given him one too many, because my father accepted the job, and the house with it! My dad could visualise how it could be but my mother couldn't stop crying because it was in such a state.*

The house was then modernised and given electricity and mains water. *We had a kitchen and a bathroom and the downstairs renovated and made habitable by Mr Fox. My father decorated everything. We had water hot and cold. Mr Fox must have fitted that after Haines left. My mum kept the house immaculate As soon as we had the floods my dad redecorated.*
There were only two bedrooms. Mr Fox offered to make the big one into two rooms but my parents said that would spoil the character. We had a three quarter bed and two single beds and two wardrobes. We three boys had that room and there was still room to move around and my parents had the other.

Post card courtesy Fraser Gilbert

We had back steps to the back door. No one used the front door. It was nice and open before the wall was built round the garden. My father was known for his garden. People stopped and took pictures as they went by.[3]

---

[1] Lilian Haines.
[2] Mr Fox *owned Bond St Fabrics.*
[3] Richard Hull interviewed 2002

When the Foxes left, the hall was sold again. By the time of the sale in 1981 the lodge, like the hall, had been left empty and neglected. The doors and windows were blocked up. *The local police checked it regularly to prevent vandalism. Squatters got in.*[1] The sale notice describes its condition, in estate agents' euphemistic language, as 'requiring improvement':*At the entrance to the hall is a small gate lodge which again requires modernisation and improvement and this could be made into a delightful separate cottage.* It was bought in its derelict state by John Tasker in 1981 for £18,000, repaired and done up and sold five years later for £78,000.

The Lodge house, modernised, *a delightful separate cottage.*

[1] Richard Hull interviewed 2002